*f*P

WHAT SHALL I DO

THE FREE PRESS

New York • London • Toronto
Sydney • Singapore

WITH THIS PEOPLE?

Jews and the

Fractious Politics

of Judaism

MILTON VIORST

THE FREE PRESS
A Division of Simon & Schuster Inc.
1230 Avenue of the Americas
New York, NY 10020

Copyright © 2002 by Milton Viorst

THE FREE PRESS and colophon are
trademarks of Simon & Schuster, Inc.

For information about special discounts for bulk purchases,
please contact Simon & Schuster Special Sales:
1-800-456-6798 or business@simonandschuster.com

Designed by Leslie Phillips
Manufactured in the United States of America

10 9 8 7 6 5 4 3 2 1

LIBRARY OF CONGRESS CATALOGING-IN-PUBLICATION DATA

Viorst, Milton.
What shall I do with this people? : Jews and the fractious
politics of Judaism / Milton Viorst.
p. cm.
Includes bibliographical references and index
1. Judaism—History. 2. Jews—History. 3. Judaism and politics—Israel.
4. Jews—Israel—Identity. 5. Ultra-Orthodox Jews—Israel.
6. Reform Judaism—Israel. 7. Orthodox Judaism—Israel. I. Title.

BM155.3 .V56 2002
296'.09—dc21   2002027116

ISBN 0-684-86289-1

TO MY GRANDPARENTS
who started me on the journey through Judaism

TO MY FAMILY
my parents, my sons and their wives,
especially my wife, Judy,
who have accompanied me

TO MY GRANDCHILDREN
Miranda, Brandeis, Olivia, Nathaniel,
who continue the journey

Moses cried out to the Lord saying,
What shall I do with this people?
Before long they will stone me.

EXODUS 17:4

Contents

WHAT SHALL I DO WITH THIS PEOPLE?

MY SYNAGOGUE, YOUR SYNAGOGUE

JEWS OFTEN TELL THE STORY of a certain Mendel of Lodz, a religious man, who, after some decades marooned on a tropical island, was rescued by a passing ship. When the captain came ashore, the grateful Mendel invited him to visit the extended miniature city that he had built as a hobby to while away his loneliness. "That's remarkable," the captain observed. "I see a town hall, a post office, a school, a police station, a hotel, a theater. I also see two synagogues. Tell me, sir, why do you have two synagogues?" Mendel of Lodz looked at the captain incredulously. "That," he explained, pointing to one of the structures, "is the synagogue I go to. And that," he added, disdainfully fingering the other, "is the synagogue I *don't* go to."

Old as this story may be, it contains—like all fables that endure—a significant element of truth. Mendel gave voice to a characteristic that God Himself first noted. In Exodus, He described it as "stiffnecked," and it seems to have remained a part of the Jewish nature. Over centuries, it has perpetuated needless conflict among Jews, when a bit of flexibility would have had better results.

The Jewish people are today deeply riven. Not only do they attend different synagogues, dissimilar in fundamental ways. Although living in their own state at last, they also hold violently hostile views, which they often claim to be divine commands, of how Jews should relate to one another and to their neighbors. In their mutual antagonism, they remain as vulnerable as Jews have ever been.

In the modern world, religious and political diversity are not surprising. What is alarming is that Jews have learned so little about how to accept diversity, preferring all too often to fight rather than to live and let live.

Mendel's stiff neck may be a source of amusement, even affection. But over history, this trait has had a recurring impact on the fate of the Jews, usually for the worse.

ᔕ   ᔕ   ᔕ

SYNAGOGUES OF MANY variations were a major element in my upbringing. I was reared within an eastern European immigrant community in an old industrial city in New Jersey. My grandparents on both sides had settled there at the turn of the twentieth century. On the High Holy days, my parents would instruct me to put on my new suit and make my way, successively, to the synagogue in which each set of grandparents prayed. There I would pay each of them the homage of an hour's visit.

The tiny shuls patronized by my father's and my mother's parents were both squeezed between stores in our city's shabby downtown. The two were within walking distance of where they had settled when they arrived from the Old Country, though both sets had since moved into better neighborhoods uptown.

All my grandparents were Orthodox and reasonably devout, but it never occurred to either side to worship at the other's shul. My father's family was from Bialystok, and his parents prayed with other Bialystokers; my mother's was from Lithuania, and prayed with other Litvaks. In the Bialystoker shul, the women sat with the children in the rear; in the Litvak shul, they occupied a balcony. I seem to remember the women chattering continuously while the men, wrapped in tallith, solemnly recited prayers in center stage.

The ritual language of both synagogues of course was Hebrew, but all the other discourse was in Yiddish. Being of the generation that yearned for cultural integration, I never fully learned either, to my subsequent regret. In later years, my work would lead me to synagogues throughout the world where I would attend services, but never was I more than a visitor to observant Judaism.

My grandparents all died a half-century or more ago. Like the culture they brought with them from Europe, neither shul lasted much longer than they did. I was no doubt shaped by the tradition they and their worship embodied, but in ways that I shall never fully understand or appreciate.

My own parents, when they worshiped at all, attended a high-ceilinged sanctuary with glass chandeliers called a temple, not a shul. The Bialystoker-Litvak distinction had faded for them. With their upwardly mobile friends, they preferred the Conservative rites, which were less stringent than the Orthodox. The center of my preadolescent life was the Conservative temple.

The women in the Conservative temple sat beside the men. Except for Yom Kippur, which lasted all day, the services were more succinct. The rabbi spoke in English. A cantor, with years of musical training, led the congregation in song, often accompanied by a pipe organ tucked into the wall. Later I learned that the pipe organ was once a symbol that distinguished "modern" Judaism from Orthodoxy. My own preference was clear. I was at home in the Conservative temple, far more than at my grandparents' services downtown.

My Jewish education, such as it was, took place in the school attached to the temple, where, two afternoons a week, I learned a smattering of Hebrew, ritual and Bible history. To prepare me for Bar Mitzvah, the cantor drilled me in my Torah portion, while the rabbi had jurisdiction over my speech. Bar Mitzvah, at the age of thirteen, was, I regret to say, the culmination of my formal Jewish education.

It was snowing, I recall, on the morning of my Bar Mitzvah and the service began late. But everyone I cared about arrived. My friends were there, classmates from both public and religious school. My parents and grandparents were also there, of course, along with my many aunts, uncles and cousins. A few of them regularly went to the temple. Others attended different synagogues, including the Reform temple, home of the city's oldest and most aristocratic Jewish families.

Some followed a trend already of long standing among Jews and rarely went to a synagogue at all.

Along with the formal, I acquired an informal Jewish education. Like Mendel, I learned there was a synagogue that I attended and others that I did not. I became aware of different customs: Orthodox Jews sometimes ate raisins and nuts after the service; Reform Jews prayed without head coverings and conducted confirmations in which girls participated. It did not take a sociologist to teach me that synagogues revealed class differences and that, in my grandparents' time, they represented Old Country rivalries. My mother's younger brothers teased me for having my Litvak genes mixed with those of my father, the Bialystoker, but even within the family such humor soon grew stale.

But for all that, the gulf between Jews never seemed profound. Each Jewish family in our city chose—or inherited—an attachment to Orthodox, Conservative or Reform Judaism, but the choice did not bespeak a rift between them. My grandmothers lit candles every Friday night and my mother did not, but we all took for granted that we were Jews. Theology did not figure much in the denomination to which we became attached, and religious practice certainly was not a measure of who was Jewish.

In the course of doing the research for this book, I came across an observation by Ahad Ha'am, the pen name of the Ukrainian-born Asher Ginzberg, which trenchantly summed up what I felt. Though trained in the Talmud, Ahad Ha'am took a rather non-Orthodox position to define a Jew:

> Why are we Jews? How strange the very question! Ask the fire why it burns! Ask the tree why it grows! . . . So, too, the Jew may be asked why he is a Jew. It is not within our capacity not to be what we are. It is within us; it is one of our laws of nature. It has an existence and a constancy of its own, like a mother's love for her children, like a man's love of his homeland! It rises and bubbles forth from the depth of our souls, it is part of our hearts! . . . It would be easier to uproot a star from the heavens than to uproot from our

hearts that certain mysterious something, beyond the grasp
of reason, that makes us Jews . . .

My friends and I, as boys, regularly debated the question implied in
Ahad Ha'am's statement, and for all I know young Jews still do. It was,
as we phrased it, whether the Jews were a nation, a religion or a tribe,
and we would go around endlessly without any resolution.

While working on this book, I came upon some impressive research
related to this question by Zvi Zohar and Avi Sagi, professors at Bar
Ilan, Israel's only Orthodox university. They found that, through most
of history, Jewish law based identity not on religious practice but on
kinship. They concluded that the Jewish people—unlike Christians
and Muslims, whose communities were always defined by belief—
were traditionally treated in their own codes as a tribe. Orthodoxy,
they said, shifted to a religious definition only a few centuries ago in
response to the rise of Reform and Conservative Judaism.

I liked their findings, since that was how my friends and I thought
of ourselves when we were growing up. We did not judge the degree
of one's Jewishness by the synagogue he or she attended. We never in-
quired into the lowest common denominator of religious practice that
signified being a Jew. We all knew, without asking, who was Jewish.
We accepted without challenge that all Jews, whatever synagogue
they attended, prayed—or did not pray—to the same God, and were
part of the wider Jewish family.

Historians might explain that our outlook was the product not of
particular *Jewish* values but of the religious tolerance that defined
modern American society, even when the cultures from which it derived were rigidly sectarian. Most Jews who arrived in America were
anxious to integrate into the society and willingly absorbed American
values. These values, historians say, were crucial in averting the communal conflicts that characterized Jewish life elsewhere.

I would hypothesize that this live-and-let-live attitude was a gift
from the society in which I was raised. The people who were different
from us in our city were not other Jews. They were Anglo-Saxons or
Irish or Italian or Poles. Some were our friends, but they knew we
were Jewish and we knew they were not. The differences did not sub-

ject us to anti-Semitism; on the contrary, I remember few instances of anti-Semitism in my life. But the differences mattered, nonetheless. In growing up, the question on which young Jews focused was making our way within this polyglot culture, establishing ourselves in a non-Jewish world. And in this aspiration, we were all Jews together.

ə   ə   ə

DURING MY JEWISH BOYHOOD, I rarely encountered the super-devout, those we call Ultra-Orthodox today, whose appearance was so different from ours. Occasionally, two or three bearded men in black coats and hats, wearing side curls, knocked on our door to ask for a donation for some distant yeshiva, where others who looked like them studied the Torah and the Talmud.

Such men had to have come from another city, probably New York, since I knew of none like them in our own. I had no more idea how they got to be the way they were than I did how we got to be the way we were. I confess that, as a child, their somber demeanor frightened me a little, but my mother assured me they were Jews like us. She responded sympathetically to their cause, and when they came soliciting at our door she routinely gave them some change.

We called them Hasidim, a term that in retrospect may not have been accurate. I have since learned that, though most Ultra-Orthodox may belong to Hasidic sects, many do not. As their dress announced, however, all Ultra-Orthodox lived apart. That distinguished them from my grandparents, whom they regarded as fallen-away Jews for making a transition to the modern world.

Israelis call all Ultra-Orthodox Jews by the term Haredim. It is derived from a verse in Isaiah, "Hear the word of the Lord, you who tremble (Haredim) at His word." Ultra-Orthodox Jews accept the designation for themselves. They understand it to mean those not only who tremble but to whom God pays heed.

Many years later, I frequently encountered Haredim during extended visits to Israel, where I worked as a journalist. My initial disposition, surely bred of my upbringing, was affectionate. At Mea Shearim, Jerusalem's Haredi quarter, for example, I was invariably exalted by a feeling of being on a wonderful voyage to the world from which my ancestors came. I recall the pleasure of buying a tallith in a tiny Mea Shearim shop and presenting it to my first son for his Bar Mitzvah.

I was even pleased when, at the Western Wall, a friendly Haredi with a scrawny beard grabbed my arm and proposed that I *macht a bracha*. I agreed, and he led me in a prayer that came back to me from my youth. He then proceeded to shake me down for a donation to whatever. Though, as an experienced traveler, I had anticipated as much, I was, I confess, a little disturbed that the solicitation had frayed our tribal bond.

Only later, as a regular observer of the intensifying conflicts between Jews, did I acquire less favorable opinions of the Ultra-Orthodox. My quarrel was not with their values or practices, any more than it had been when I was a boy in New Jersey. My quarrel was in their contention that theirs was the only legitimate Judaism and their insistence that all Jews acknowledge this legitimacy.

My work, in those days, took me not just to Israel but to the Arab world, where I often encountered super-devout Muslims. They evoked in me no historical memories. But they were, I found, much like Ultra-Orthodox Jews. The term *fundamentalist* can apply to both. They both divided human society not by nationality, a secular standard, but according to faith. They rejected the temptations of modernity, believed all truth lay in ancient texts and yearned for a putative golden age of the distant past. They were both male-dominated, imposed restrictive dress codes and enforced strong sexual taboos. They also tended to be religiously and politically authoritarian.

For two centuries, Europe's Ultra-Orthodox Jews rejected the religious practices on which other Jews, under the influence of the Enlightenment, had embarked. Most of the Jews, like my grandparents, who came to America in the great wave of migration at the turn of the twentieth century had already adopted less rigid forms of observance. The Ultra-Orthodox, persuaded by their rabbis that the New World was a godless place, tended to stay at home.

Even as the clouds of Nazism gathered in the 1930s, most of the Ultra-Orthodox community chose to leave its fate in God's hands rather than flee. By the war's end, the community had been shredded and its very survival appeared in doubt. Of the remnants, a few migrated reluctantly to America, but most went to Israel, where they proceeded over huge odds to rebuild their traditional culture. Mea Shearim provides evidence of their success. But in the new arena, hardly had Ultra-Orthodoxy rediscovered its old rivals of lesser piety than it resumed its campaign to discredit them.

When I began routinely journeying to Israel in the 1960s, Israelis were likely to cite animosities between Ashkenazim, European Jews, and Sephardim, Jews who came from the Arab world, as the country's most divisive social issue. But soon afterward came the Six-Day War, and as a by-product of the huge victory that Israel won, the society's foundation shifted. Many Ultra-Orthodox believers declared that God had sent a message to have all of Jews submit to God's rules, which they interpreted as being synonymous with their own. This assertion of power widened the rift with secularized Jews, creating a breach of unprecedented breadth.

My personal exposure to it took place on a Friday evening when, looking for a restaurant to have my dinner, I inadvertently drove past a street barrier into Mea Shearim. I had been forewarned about disturbing the Haredim on the Sabbath and, sure enough, I was pelted with stones by a black-hatted mob shouting in Yiddish, "Shabbos, Shabbos." Though I was more than ready to apologize, no one was interested in listening. Even as I made a U-turn to beat a retreat, Haredim kicked at the doors of the car.

Some who have made a similar mistake fared worse. Jewish newspapers told a few years ago of an Israeli judge who was spat upon and beaten on the Sabbath when he stopped at a traffic light at the edge of an Ultra-Orthodox quarter. The papers also quoted a leading Haredi rabbi who proclaimed the right to kill Sabbath violators in Mea Shearim. Though he later retracted the threat, it seemed like a foretaste of frightening intolerance, a reassertion of the stiff-necked trait in Jewish religious life.

❧   ❧   ❧

AFTER MY EXPERIENCE, I found accounts of skirmishes in the Jews' religious wars appearing almost daily in the Israeli or the foreign press.

I filed one that told of female soldiers in Israel's army who questioned an Orthodox education officer about a traditional blessing in which men express thanks to God for not making them women. A Reform woman said her rabbi had rewritten the blessing to thank God for making men and women as they are. "Reform and Conservative Jews are not Jews to me," the officer snarled: "The Reform and Conservative movements caused the assimilation of eight million Jews, and this is worse than the Holocaust, in which only six million Jews were lost." The army, the article said, promptly relieved him of his duties.

The *New York Times,* about this time, carried the story of "an ugly confrontation, [in which] 100 strictly Orthodox yeshiva students surrounded a group of American Reform rabbis who went to pray at the Western Wall, booing loudly and hurling insults past officers from the border police." The students were especially upset, the *Times* noted, at the women rabbis who challenged Orthodox male prerogatives by wearing *kippot* on their heads and *tallithot* around their shoulders, while cradling Torah scrolls in their arms. "What was most chilling to the Americans," the report said, "was that the youths, their faces contorted in anger under their black hats, screamed that the rabbis should 'go back to Germany' to be exterminated."

In attacking Reform worshipers, the demonstrators were exercising what they regarded as Orthodoxy's proprietary rights over Judaism and particularly the Western Wall, its most sacred shrine. During centuries of Turkish rule, visits by Jews to the Wall had been limited, and during the two decades of Jordanian occupation of the Old City, Jews were barred from the Wall altogether. After it was liberated in the Six-Day War, however, the government placed the Wall under Orthodox authority, denying equality of access to other Jews.

From 1967 on, not only Reform and Conservative Jews but even Orthodox women have been subject to abuse at the Wall. Women were required to pray apart from the men, as my grandmothers were in their shuls in New Jersey. They were also barred from conducting their own services. Israel's supreme court, after a lawsuit was brought by modern Orthodox women, reaffirmed the segregation of genders but authorized separate services in which women were to be allowed to wear the tallith and read from the Torah.

An Orthodox Knesset member denounced the court's ruling, compromise though it was, as a "stab in the back" of Judaism. The deputy minister of religious affairs, also Orthodox, lamented that it would "nullify the state of Israel as a Jewish state." To mollify the rabbis, the Justice Ministry petitioned for a reversal, but the Orthodox parties, insisting on more, submitted a bill to classify the Wall as an Orthodox synagogue, and to make any woman who usurped men's prerogatives in praying there liable to seven years in prison. A secular Knesset member said the bill recalled Iran during the frenzy of the Khomeini revolution.

Turning violence upside down, Orthodoxy condemned the victims of the assault at the Wall for sowing Jewish disunity. "It is unfortunate and, sadly, all too telling," said one Orthodox group, "that some members of the Reform clergy seem to create confrontation not only in the Jewish State's courts and legislature but at what Jewish tradition considers the holiest spot in the world." The reference to the leaders as "clergy" rather than "rabbis," it was noted, signaled a deliberate rejection of Reform's legitimacy.

ﬡ　ﬡ　ﬡ

RELIGIOUS DISPUTES, however, were by no means limited to ritual matters. After the Six-Day War, the most contentious issue became territory. Orthodoxy had held historically that Jewish sovereignty in the Holy Land could be restored only by the Messiah. After the victory, many rabbis decided that the West Bank and the Gaza Strip, respectively ruled by Jordan and Egypt, belonged to the Jews alone.

In fact, Orthodoxy itself was divided on this question, at least at first. The Haredim, who condemned Zionism for its secular nature, were largely indifferent to territory. But religious Zionism, a movement that for nearly a century had preached the priority of the Jews' return to their homeland, saw the victory as an opportunity. Religious Zionism's position, long at the margins of Jewish mysticism, held that Zionism, however secular, was God's way of preparing the land for the Messiah's arrival. To its rabbis, the victory was a message from God to seize the land for all time.

"Under heavenly command, we have just returned home in the elevations of holiness and our holy city. We shall never move out of here," declared Rabbi Zvi Yehuda Kook, who spearheaded the religious Zionist movement. "We are living in the middle of redemption. The entire Israeli army is holy. The Kingdom of Israel is being rebuilt. It symbolizes the rule of the[Jewish] people on its land."

Kook and his followers reshaped Halacha, religious law, to serve their political ideology. Not only did they insist the law required permanent Jewish rule in the territories but they proclaimed its supremacy over secular law. Many Jews rejected these dubious claims, but in the postwar euphoria Rabbi Kook's beliefs became hugely popular, creating a movement that became Israel's most dynamic political force.

Religious Zionism was not alone, it must be added, in urging Jewish hegemony over all Palestine. Since the 1920s, Zionism had contained a minority wing known as Revisionism, progenitor of the present-day Likud Party, which promoted the kind of territorial nationalism that pervaded Europe in the nineteenth and early twentieth centuries. Religious Zionism's role was to sanctify this nationalism, imparting huge energy to it by characterizing it as God's command.

Religious Zionism after 1967 sparked the Jewish settlement movement in the occupied territories. It built communities across the land and brought in thousands of Jews to live in them. In doing so, it often acted in violation of Israel's civil law, justifying its acts by claiming a divine calling. Every stake driven into the soil, it maintained, served God's will. Over the opposition of the international community and much of the Jewish world, its ardor has been key to perpetuating Israeli rule over the populations of the conquered land.

Most of the followers of religious Zionism, it should be noted, did not come from the Ultra-Orthodox community. Haredim, for the most part, continued to regard the rule of holy law as more important than the acquisition of territory. They were indoor people, and though supportive of the occupation, they preferred studying the Torah in their yeshivot to trampling over the hills of the ancient Israelites. Proponents of religious Zionism were basically recruited from the body of Jews described as modern Orthodox.

Modern Orthodox, unlike Haredim, wore contemporary dress. As a sign of identity, most crowned themselves with a knitted *kippa* secured by a hairpin. Their women were not subject to Ultra-Orthodox constraints in dealing with the outside world. Their settlements were well designed and solidly built, their homes spacious and comfortable. Their worldview, far from nostalgic, was very present-day.

Religious Zionists did not share the Haredi disdain for the secular state; even in overriding its laws, they esteemed it as an agent of Jewish power. Only at some unspecified future time did they imagine attaining messianic redemption, in which rabbis would secure God's realm under the Torah's authority. Meanwhile, they focused on retaining the holy soil, reshaping Halacha with the single objective of barring territorial withdrawal.

In the years just after the Six-Day War, few Israelis understood religious Zionism's dynamism. Most accepted the U.N. resolution that called for Arab-Israeli negotiations based on the exchange of land for peace. They recognized that settlements were an unnecessary burden on any such talks and were even prohibited by international law. But as long as the Arabs refused to talk peace, they regarded the relentless creep of religious Zionism's settlements as essentially innocuous.

In 1977, Egyptian President Anwar al-Sadat shattered the stagnation in Arab-Israeli relations with a peacemaking mission to Jerusalem. In a speech to the Knesset, he promised Israel full peace in return for its withdrawal from Egypt's Sinai. Not the least of the advantages Israelis saw in the proposal was the security of no longer having the Arab world's strongest power as a sworn enemy.

The religious Zionists opposed Sadat's offer as an effort to separate Israel from a sacred possession. But the Likud government, notwithstanding its nationalist ideology, was sensitive to the strategic advantages. In 1979, Israel signed a formal peace treaty with Egypt. Under the terms, it agreed to withdraw from the Sinai in steps, the last of which contained a small settlement town called Yamit.

On the eve of the scheduled evacuation, hundreds of zealots— Haredim and secular Revisionists as well as religious Zionists—took over Yamit. Chanting prayers and reading the Torah, they vowed to resist to the death efforts by the Israeli army to evict them. They finally capitulated, in return for money and amnesty, but not before issuing solemn warnings to the government that they would die before surrendering even a stone of the West Bank. Events would corroborate that they were not bluffing.

ॼ ॼ ॼ

IN 1992, YITZHAK RABIN, a hero of Israel's War of Independence and commander of the army in the Six-Day War, was elected prime minister, promising a concerted effort to extend the peace treaty with Egypt to an agreement with the Palestinians. A year later, he signed the Oslo Accords with Yasser Arafat, chairman of the Palestine Liberation Organization. Though based on the land-for-peace principle, its outcome was left unspecified, in recognition of the deep differences between Israel's political parties on Palestinian statehood, borders, settlements, refugees and Jerusalem. Talks to implement the agreement began at once, aimed at turning over some West Bank and Gaza territory to Palestinian rule.

Religious Zionism, in accordance with its principles, opposed any withdrawal. For years, its militants, claiming Halachic guidance, had resorted to vigilantism, a word they preferred to "terror," to intimidate the Arabs. The Arabs retaliated in kind. While each side blamed the other for the violence, the cycle grew more destructive. The Oslo Accords only aggravated the settlers' wrath, shifting their target from the Arabs to the traitors they perceived in their own society.

Rabin's proposal to evacuate a small settler enclave in Hebron, considered especially vulnerable to Arab attack, provoked a defining crisis. Hebron, where Abraham is said to be buried and David made his first capital, is sacred to Judaism. Jews have almost always lived there; sixty-seven died there in an Arab attack in 1929. Rabin's plan to remove the settlers signaled to religious Zionism the defeat of its holy mission, and its forces mobilized to fight.

Led by a former chief rabbi of Israel, religious Zionism issued a Halachic ruling. Not only did God command the settlers to resist evacuation, it said, but He instructed Israeli soldiers to disobey any orders to withdraw. The ruling pitted Halachic judgments against democratic legitimacy. Rabin, fearing civil war, backed off, and the Hebron settlement remains on its site to this day.

Having humiliated the state, religious Zionism intensified its campaign. Some rabbis circulated charges through its network of yeshivot that Rabin, in proposing to surrender Jewish territory, was a religious outlaw. Orthodox circles debated whether, under religious law, he was guilty of capital crimes. In New York, hundreds of Orthodox rabbis signed a statement declaring that Rabin deserved to die.

On November 4, 1995, Yigal Amir, an Orthodox student, killed Rabin with two pistol shots in the back.

The son of Orthodox parents born in Yemen, Amir had attended a Haredi elementary school and then a Haredi yeshiva before embracing religious Zionism during his military service. He later attended Bar Ilan, the Orthodox university, where he studied at its institute of Halachic education. Amir was an excellent student who also found time for street demonstrations and solidarity visits to West Bank settlements, all aimed at defeating the Oslo Accords. Competent rabbis, he declared, had persuaded him that it was his Halachic duty to commit the murder. Though police investigated charges of incitement, they found no proof that the Orthodox establishment was an accomplice. Many secular Israelis disagreed.

After his arrest, Amir told investigators, "According to Jewish law, the minute a Jew gives over his land and people to the enemy, he must be killed. . . . I do not have a problem with it." Amir, who was sentenced to life imprisonment, never expressed remorse. In killing Rabin, Amir was convinced he was doing God's work.

🔯　🔯　🔯

RABIN'S ASSASSINATION became the germ of this book. During the decades I worked as a journalist in Israel, I had been puzzled by the level of zealotry I observed. I became increasingly bewildered at how rabbis could, quite serenely, attribute expressions of extremism to God's will. I wondered whether the Halachic pronouncements of these rabbis were really Jewish law, or their personal politics. Their justification of stoning was bad enough. Killing Rabin was beyond anything I could imagine as emerging from Judaism's bosom.

The fanaticism that produced this murder was far from the religion on which I—and, I think, the vast majority of Jews—had been raised.

It certainly did not correspond with the ethics I had been taught were intrinsic to Judaism. Though I never claimed to be observant, I strongly believed I was being faithful to my religious heritage in respecting decent differences in outlook between people and for valuing a compassion for Jews and non-Jews alike.

Had I been misguided about the nature of Judaism? Could Rabin's murder have come out of some authentic corner of its heritage? Even if Rabin was misguided, how did it happen that the Orthodox establishment, while denying an *intent* to kill, nonetheless imparted to this young man, Amir, the attitude and beliefs from which killing emerged? In search of answers to these questions, I embarked on a study of the history and texts of the Jews. This book is the product.

As a schoolboy, I had been introduced to Jewish history. But conventional Jewish education does not dwell much on history, not even on the history of the faith. Later, as a university student, I specialized in history—other peoples' history—and went on to spend much of my professional life seeking to fuse history with the craft of journalism. But the absence of Jewish history in my education, I realized, had left me with a gap in self-understanding, as well as in understanding of the culture to which I belonged. After Rabin's murder, I decided it was time to close this gap.

My goal was not to write another book of Jewish history. The literature is already filled with distinguished works. My objective was to find within history some understanding of why the Jews of our own day often behave impossibly about matters crucial to the well-being, if not the survival, of the Jewish community.

Let me sketch an overview of the product of this study. My sense is that Judaism still lives within the crisis triggered by its involvement in the Enlightenment in Europe more than two centuries ago. Crises are not unusual within religions and not easily resolved. Each of the three great monotheisms—Judaism, Christianity, Islam—has encountered them, repeatedly. In each case, the outcome has shaped the societies at which they are the core.

Let me elaborate. Christianity, growing within the bosom of the Roman Empire, took centuries to define the nature of Jesus and build the church that governed the faith. Islam spent almost as long deciding whether it would remain the austere desert faith established by the Prophet or become more worldly under the influence of Persia and ancient Greece. Judaism faced a defining crisis in the first century C.E., when its state and its Temple were destroyed by Rome, scattering its believers across the globe. The cataclysm divided Jewish history into two periods: homeland and exile. To deal with exile, a rabbinic elite rose from the ruins and created the law that remained unchallenged for some seventeen centuries.

But while Judaism was stable, the world around it was not. By the twelfth century, the Renaissance, having undermined the Dark Ages' God-centered universe with a culture that placed man at the center, had imposed a fresh crisis on Christianity. The secularism that emerged from the turmoil produced the dynamism of today's Western civilization. Islam, in contrast, remained mired in traditionalism. As for Judaism, which had kept secularism at bay until the eighteenth century, its historic unity was shattered by the Enlightenment, when a majority of Jews embraced Western beliefs while a minority held tenaciously to the ancient ways.

A century ago, Enlightenment Jews founded the Zionist movement as a remedy to Europe's anti-Semitism; rabbinic Judaism declared Zionism a heresy. The secular state that Zionism created opened the third era of Jewish history. But, as Rabin's murder makes clear, the conflict between Judaism's two wings is far from over.

The three periods I have cited account for the structure of this book.

- If we classify Abraham as monotheistic but pre-Judaic, the first period extended from Moses and the covenant at Sinai about 2000 B.C.E. until the Roman wars of the first century C.E. In this turbulent era, the Israelites reshaped themselves from a collection of nomadic tribes into a coherent Jewish nation.
- The second consisted of exile, or Diaspora, in which the Jews lived for two millennia in uncomfortable, often baneful, dependency on foreign hosts. Under the leadership of their rabbis, they preserved their identity by fidelity to the law and by adapting their practices to the fancy of their rulers.

- The third began only in the last century, when a growing segment of the Jews returned to the homeland and, upon the ashes of the Holocaust, founded a sovereign state. From it, tensions between Orthodoxy and various forms of Enlightenment Judaism have created unprecedented instability within the community, both inside Israel and worldwide.

Is it valid to treat the Jews of Moses' time, after the passage of four thousand years, as the same people as the Jews of Rabin's? Conceding genetic changes after centuries of intermarriage, are the Jews of these two distant eras linked in any way? Are there enduring cultural characteristics that shed light on the Jews of Israel and the Diaspora today? I believe the answer to these questions is, basically, yes.

Jews—quite justly—are wary of efforts such as I have undertaken to describe them collectively. Anti-Semites have long abused this practice. They have burdened Jews with the crucifixion hex, the Fagin syndrome and countless other characterizations to impose suffering. But this aversion is not license to deny that there is a heritage that can genuinely be called Jewish. Some of it, I would contend, can even be traced back to the time of Moses.

This heritage is not synonymous with predestination. Though most Orthodox Jews believe God arranges all, I myself doubt it. Central as He has been in our culture, I suspect that God, having created us, turned us loose to make our own fate. That is not to say the responses of Jews are totally improvised. Jewish history reveals recurring patterns, a kind of cultural predisposition. The solutions Jews have devised to their problems over 4,000 years contain much consistency—and many warnings.

To cite one: Well before my own quest, eminent scholars pointed to parallels between Jewish zealotry in the first century, which led to the demise of Temple and state, and Jewish zealotry in our own. Many Jews see a scary portent in the parallel. There may be other warnings. In making the transition to the third stage of their history, Jews have revealed an immoderation not unlike what they demonstrated in the tumultuous Judean era.

Have we digested the right lessons of the Holocaust? A half-century ago the image of the Jews was of a passive people. In Europe, millions imbued with a sense of their weakness perished at the hands of evil with barely a struggle. We remember with tears the photos of yeshiva students digging their graves in the shadow of Hitler's guards, reciting the *Shema*. We promise ourselves "never again."

Jews are now perceived as tough, self-willed and aggressive, and there is much to be said for the new image. But I question the value of what we have learned when yeshiva students now curse and spit at other Jews before Judaism's holiest shrine, when a zealot kills the elected leader of the Jewish state, claiming divine authority. Should Jews celebrate these changes, or is it that we have reverted to being as stiff-necked as God found us when we defied Him in Sinai?

In exile, under foreign rule, disputes between Jews generally simmered on a low flame. Violence was rare. Religion brought comfort, not conflict. It is no coincidence that Rabin's murder comes as Jews, detaching themselves from exile, retake charge of their destiny. Our history suggests that, sovereign over ourselves, we turn our political differences into bitter religious wars.

Rabin's killing is the product of unresolved religious conflict, dating back centuries. It emerges from the faith's grievous failure to solve the challenge imposed by modern times. In exile, the dispute was conducted by shrill invective but almost never brutally. In sovereign Israel, civil strife spills blood. It reached its climax in a murder that has no precedent in Jewish history.

Can this murder be looked upon as an unfortunate growing pain, which time and further maturity will relieve? Or is it the expression of a religious extremism that, removed from the constraints imposed by exile, will continue to exact great cost? Jews would surely be wise to contemplate the warning that Rabin's murder contains. History may be telling us that the Jews' descent into violence casts doubt on the ability of the state, and perhaps of the community itself, to survive.

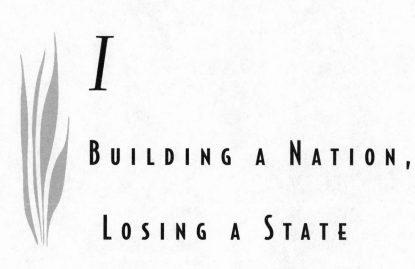

I

BUILDING A NATION, LOSING A STATE

MOSES VERSUS GOD

GOD FIRST DESCRIBED the Israelites as *stiff-necked* in Exodus, the biblical account of their flight from centuries of slavery in Egypt. He rendered the judgment when they were still in Sinai, midway between the pyramids and the promised land, and Moses, their leader, concurred in it.

Stiff-necked is a metaphor derived from the practice, common to tillers of the soil since biblical times, of harnessing oxen for work in the fields. To secure the yoke properly, at the joint between the head and shoulders, the tiller had somehow to persuade the beasts to relax their necks and lower their heads.

In Sinai, at the seminal moment of Judaism's history, God had just used His powers to emancipate the Israelites from Pharaoh. But they not only withheld their gratitude; they also could not be persuaded to relax, lower their heads and submit dutifully to His authority. On the contrary, God found the Israelites to be persistent malcontents, rebels and finally apostates. So, in His irritation, He denounced them for their attitude. The Jews have been described as stiff-necked ever since.

One might reasonably hold that only by happenstance does a description applied collectively to the Israelites in Exodus serve also as a commentary on the Jews today. Scholars have never confirmed, apart from the biblical account, that the Egyptian sojourn took place at all, but they hypothesize that the flight may have taken place about 1250 B.C.E. The date means that Jews have been considered stiff-necked for some 3,250 years, surely an endurance record for a trait of character.

One might also question whether God really applied the description. Religious tradition holds that the Torah is His personal creation, dictated to Moses word for word. Secular scholars, naturally, are skeptical of this belief. Most regard the Bible as an account written by mortals of events they did not themselves witness, in a context much changed by time. Whether a reader favors God's authorship or man's depends, of course, on personal convictions. But even if God Himself did not choose the metaphor, He is immutably linked to it. The link gives it ongoing credibility, and surely accounts for its durability.

But whatever God's role, it does not necessarily imply a divine presence in the transmission of the trait. The Jews have been a rather closely knit people since Moses' era, perhaps even from Abraham's, a far longer span than any other people that has played on history's stage. Some authorities do not preclude that a character trait can be transmitted, more or less intact, from one generation to the next, even for thousands of years.

Sigmund Freud, the father of psychoanalysis, argues in behalf of such a notion. Freud is convinced that, through conscious and unconscious communication, the generations routinely pass on aspects of their heritage. In *Moses and Monotheism*, he goes back to Abraham to postulate the source of the Jews' reactions to God in Sinai. "We must . . . adopt the hypothesis," Freud wrote, "that the psychical precipitates of the primeval period became inherited property which, in each fresh generation, called not for acquisition but only for awakening."

What Freud meant in that murky assertion was that each generation does not build anew an attitude toward life. Whether human or animal, parents transmit to their children, by cultural as well as genetic means, instincts that predetermine values and behavior. The instincts may remain latent until a circumstance arises that demands a response. But the response, he says, is foreordained.

In *Totem and Taboo*, Freud quotes approvingly from Goethe's Faust: "What thou has inherited from thy fathers, acquire it to make it thine." He goes so far as to say that the demanding strictures absorbed long ago into standard Jewish practice may result from the "rapture of moral asceticism" produced by the guilt feelings of Jews for the stiff-necked treatment they dealt to God in Sinai.

Rabbi Jonathan Sacks, chief rabbi of Great Britain, adopts a mystical approach but makes an observation very close to Freud's:

> On Pesach, *we* are slaves in Egypt; *we* experience the Exodus. On Tisha b'Av *we* endure the grief and suffering of all Jews throughout history, from the generation condemned to die in the wilderness through those who saw the Temple destroyed, to the Spanish exiles and those who awaited death in Auschwitz. Jewish consciousness is constructed in terms of *memory*, not *history*. History is what happened to *others*. Memory is what happened to *us*.

Sacks contends that Jewish memory fixes a permanent kinship between previous generations of Jews and our own.

Raphael Patai combines Freud's notion of "inherited property" and Sacks's reference to "memory" into the category "folk memory." Patai, an anthropologist born in Budapest in 1910, received in 1936 the first Ph.D. awarded by the Hebrew University in Jerusalem. In *The Jewish Mind*, he contends that every people stores an image of its own history, a tribal memory, in a reservoir of data that establishes its collective character.

For Jews, the chief source of memory is the Bible, most notably its first five books, the Torah, which means "guidance." The preeminence of one man in its pages leads to its also being called the Five Books of Moses. The Torah's major concern is the experience of the Jews, under Moses' leadership, in the desert of Sinai, which is the point of departure of Judaism as we know it. Mosaic law, the guide to Judaic practice, is the Torah's major product. Folk memory, Patai says, is its by-product, exercising a powerful impact on Jewish character.

Patai contends that the Jews' sense of personal identification with the lessons learned at Sinai is the foundation of their tribal outlook. It is, he says, what sets them permanently apart from the Gentile world.

The Bible, especially the Torah, provided a unique assist to the Jews' memory. It gave them, alone among contemporaries, a written reference to refresh the mind. While Gentile peoples were creating mythology and folklore, Patai writes, the Jews were studying the Bible. Moses himself, in the Torah's last chapter, urges his people to remember their experiences. "Regard the days of old," Moses says. "Consider the years of ages past."

The British historian Paul Johnson, contemplating the Bible's impact on the Jews, holds that it derives largely from its literary merit.

> The biblical historians achieved a degree of perception and portraiture that even the best Greek and Roman historians could never manage. There is nothing in Thucydides to equal the masterly presentation of King David. . . . But the stress on the actors never obscures the steady progression of the human-divine drama. . . . Most of the books of the Bible have a historical framework, all related to the wider framework, which might be entitled "A history of God in his relations to man."

It is hardly surprising that, in the Bible, history is secondary to divinity. The Bible's lessons are solemn. They impart to the Jews a deep-rooted religious orientation. Still, the Bible is more than God. The history it contains is the thread that winds its way through Jewish memory, the opening experience in the shaping of the collective Jewish mind.

Patai makes the valid point that the Jews have never been very interested in their secular history. The explanation is surely that during their centuries of exile, they did not make their history; it was made for them, or done to them. After the biblical era, Jews had neither kings nor great warriors as heroes. They had only pain to put in their memory bank, inflicted on them in the Crusades, the Inquisition, the pogroms, the Holocaust. The Bible, however, was their very own possession, the egg from which they grew, their real history. It was, in Patai's words, the charter of Jewish life. It served them as a source of ethics and of law. The Bible also provided them with a sense of themselves as permanently linked to God.

Maimonides, the great Jewish philosopher of the twelfth century, told Jews that the study of history was a "useless waste of time." It was an unusually shallow position for him, but rabbinic Judaism still holds this view, on the grounds that history contributes nothing to the understanding of God's will. Yet ignoring secular history does not nullify its impact. The past is as much prologue for the Jews as for other peoples. To dismiss it is to lose an instrument of self-knowledge, markers to a common destination.

Examples of history's ongoing power are abundant. The organization of Jewish life during the exile—around self-governing communities called *kehillot* in Hebrew, but more conventionally known as ghettos—still influences the character of Jewish communal life. The deference accorded in the *kehillot* to rabbis as political leaders shapes the way traditional Jews think about politics today.

On another level, it is fair to say that Jews, unwisely, have shown a lack of interest in Christianity's rise during the era of the Second Temple. Similarly, they have overlooked dealings between the Jewish tribes in Arabia and the Prophet Muhammad during Islam's seminal years in the seventh century. To treat as useless artifacts events that, even today, help shape relations with the two other monotheisms surely represents missed opportunities.

Patai says that "inner" history defines the Jews. He argues that on Passover, Jews commemorate not the end of their enslavement or their escape from Egypt but the miracles that God performed in their behalf. Hanukkah, in his understanding, memorializes not liberation from the Greeks but the rededication of the Temple. Jews, he contends, have paid heavily for the scant attention they have given their connections with the outside world.

My own experience, based on participation in countless Passover seders, Hanukkah festivals, Bar Mitzvahs, and *brits* (circumcisions), is that Jewish celebrations can be at the same time sacred and profane.

The Bible itself, whatever Orthodoxy claims, is both. God's presence imparts its holiness. But Moses is clearly a grouch, David is adulterous, Jacob is a cheat and many of Israel's kings are politically corrupt. If God's Bible is the foundation of folk memory, He has seen to it that the lowly have passed with the lofty, the profane with the sacred, into the national memory.

The greatest impact upon the Jewish psyche came, no doubt, from the covenant with God that Moses negotiated in the Israelites' behalf at Sinai. No two Jews can agree on its precise meaning. Many interpret it literally, many others symbolically. But every Jew acknowledges its inherent holiness and its centrality to Judaism, even today.

Juxtaposed with the story of the holy covenant, however, is the Israelites' thoroughly profane embrace of the golden calf. This is the act that, having provoked God's wrath, led Him to proclaim them a stiff-necked people. Moses concurred, but even he, God's favorite, periodically irritated God and provoked His displeasure.

The Book of Exodus, it might be parenthetically noted, does not use the term *Jew*. It calls the people by a name God imparted to Jacob, Abraham's grandson, after the mysterious wrestling match narrated in Genesis. Bestowed as an honor, "Israel" translates, curiously, as "God-fighter," a term that seems to foreshadow the turbulent relationship between God and the Jews that lay ahead.

God's perception of His people as stiff-necked is in this tradition. The story of the golden calf can, quite reasonably, be considered a parallel to the Christian conception of original sin. The Jews, whom God had described as a holy people, proceeded to forge an idol, imposing on their holiness a permanent burden. In God's mind, it seemed for a time to put the covenant itself in doubt. God finally resolved His dilemma in the Jews' favor, but the burden remains. Even in this, the opening chapter of their book of memory, the central experience of the Jews combines the sacred with the profane.

🔊   🔊   🔊

EXODUS IS THE BOOK that deals with Judaism's birth. Great moments preceded it in Genesis: Abraham's agreement to sacrifice Isaac, Jacob's wrestling with God, Noah's deliverance from the flood. But Judaism took shape in Exodus, beginning with Moses' emergence as a prophet and going on to the liberation from bondage in Egypt, the covenant with God at Sinai and the scandal of the golden calf.

But beneath this narrative lies the tension on a most palpable level between God and His people, with Moses serving as the intermediary. This subtext reveals how much the Jews' journey to self-identity has been fraught with internal quarrels. These quarrels, as our daily newspaper reminds us, characterize relations among Jews, and relations between the Jews and God, to this day.

Exodus opens with God's ruminations on bringing the Israelites out of Egypt. He encounters Moses, an Israelite who had only recently escaped from Egypt after killing an abusive overseer while shepherding a flock of sheep. Moses was living in the desert with a tribe called Midianites when God, from within the flames of a burning bush, proclaimed, "Moses, Moses." In Genesis, He had similarly addressed Abraham at the altar, prior to conveying His command to spare the boy Isaac. As Abraham had once answered, Moses responded, "Here I am."

Though God declared His identity, and kept the bush from being reduced to ashes to prove it, Moses responded warily. He was clearly frightened. God declared He had decided to rescue those He called "My people" and send them to a land flowing with milk and honey. Moses, He said, must go to Pharaoh and announce this plan. He instructed Moses to invoke His authority by declaring, "Thus says Yahweh," the name God most often used.

Moses was unconvinced and, in a touching display of humility, declared, "Who am I that I should go to Pharaoh?" God sought to reassure him, saying, "I will be there with you." Referring to the Israelites, Moses asked, "What shall I say to them? . . . They will not trust me, and will not hearken to my voice." God responded with another dazzling display of power, transforming Moses' staff into a snake, then changing it back into a staff.

But Moses, still resistant, said to God, "No man of words am I . . . for heavy of mouth and heavy of tongue am I." He pleaded with God to find someone else, and God responded impatiently, "I Myself will be there with your mouth . . . and will instruct you as to what you shall do." Only after God assured Moses that his accusers in Egypt were dead did he accept the mission for which he had been selected.

So Moses packed up his Midianite wife, Tsippora, along with his sons, and mounted them on a donkey for the trip back home. At God's instructions, Aaron, his older brother, came out from Egypt to meet him on the road. Moses conveyed to Aaron his apprehensions about seeking to win over both the Israelites and Pharaoh. Together the two finished the journey to face their destiny.

Given his modesty about his gifts, Moses assigned Aaron the responsibility for relaying God's plan to the Israelites at a mass gathering in Egypt. The Israelites, after hearing Aaron out, accepted the offer. "The people trusted, they hearkened," Exodus says. Later, at a perilous moment in their flight, some of them would—to Moses' dismay—recall the exhilaration of the moment quite differently.

The two brothers then set off for their encounter with Pharaoh. Notwithstanding their invocation of divine power, however, Pharaoh dismissed their pleas with contempt and ordered his overseers to punish the Israelites by augmenting their workload. When the Israelites complained about their added duties, Moses dutifully appealed to God. "For what reason," he asked, "have You dealt so ill with this people? . . . You have not rescued Your people." So well did he argue that God apologized and promised, "Now you will see what I will do to Pharaoh, for with a strong hand he will set them free."

Moses' advocacy had by now changed him from God's reluctant agent into a middleman, even into the people's representative. The role, which he would play until the Israelites looked upon the promised land, would place him in constant confrontation with God.

God, faithful to His promise, proceeded to inflict on Egypt the ten plagues that are familiar to those who hear them reviewed each year at the Passover seder. It is not a pretty review. The first plague turned the Nile to blood, the second rained frogs over the land, the third spread lice, the fourth brought flies, the fifth killed Egypt's livestock, the sixth inflicted boils, the seventh battered the land with hail, the eighth spread locusts, the ninth plunged the country into three days of darkness.

On the eve of the tenth plague, with the Egyptians already reeling,

God issued instructions for Israel's escape. He commanded Moses to have each family slaughter and roast a lamb and eat it with matzo (unleavened bread), "your hips girded, your sandals on your feet, your sticks in your hand." He also ordered the Israelites to paint the blood of the lambs on the doorposts of their houses. The Israelites obeyed and prepared for flight. Taking note of the blood-painted sign, God proceeded to "pass over" the Israelite houses to pour out His anger on Egyptians alone. The tenth plague was the most appalling, killing all of Egypt's firstborn, humans and animals alike.

The next morning Moses rallied his people. They were, according to Exodus, six hundred thousand strong, plus their sheep and oxen. God led the way "by day in a column of cloud, by night in a column of fire." Guided by these columns, the Israelites trudged across the desert toward the sea.

But as soon as they learned that Pharaoh's charioteers were in pursuit, the Israelites were stricken by a faintness of heart. Summoning Moses, they revised their recollections of the night they hearkened to God's plan. "We spoke to you in Egypt," they said reproachfully. "Let us alone that we may serve Egypt. Indeed, better for us to be serving Egypt than dying in the wilderness."

Though incensed, Moses was not insensitive to their fears. "Yahweh," he promised, "will make war for you. Be still!" Indeed, Yahweh redeemed Moses' pledge. The story is well known. God split the sea to allow the Jews to cross on dry land, then closed the waters over the racing charioteers, drowning them all. Looking upon Egypt's dead, Exodus says, "The people held Yahweh in awe, they trusted in Yahweh and in Moses, His servant." Then they burst into song.

After only three days of rejoicing, however, they faltered again. When they complained of thirst, Moses told God, who provided them with water. But they later complained to Moses again, saying, "Would that we had died by the hand of Yahweh in the land of Egypt, when we sat by the fleshpots, when we ate bread till we were satisfied. For you have brought us into this wilderness to bring death to this whole assembly by starvation."

Moses went straight to God, Who once more answered the call. "I have hearkened to the grumblings of the children of Israel," God said, and delivered to them coveys of quail. Still, the Israelites persevered in their faultfinding, and Moses cried out to God in despair, "What shall I do with this people? A little more and they will stone me."

Finally, God sent down the all-purpose food the Bible calls *manna*. Despite their repeated violations of the Sabbath in gathering it, He provided it for them during the entire duration of their stay in the desert. Still, the Israelites were not satisfied. Once God, to slake the Israelites' thirst, instructed Moses to strike a rock with his staff, sending forth water. Moses, with some irony, named the place Massa, "challenging," and Merivah, "quarreling." The names would come back to Moses later as reminders of how vexing his people could be.

The Israelites were also unwilling to acknowledge God's exertions in providing for their security. He empowered Joshua, Moses' young deputy, to defend their camp from attacks by hostile Amalekites, promising "to wipe [them] out . . . from under the heavens." Joshua did; despite his victory the people remained sullen.

After three months in the desert, the Israelites reached Mount Sinai, where Moses had them pitch camp. God had foreshadowed His plan for them long before, having promised Abraham in the Book of Genesis that the Israelites were to be His people. Once in Sinai, He laid His irritations aside, clearly conveying the message that, though quick to anger, He would not forsake His people or abandon His plan.

Scholars of religion say the tribe that Moses led through Sinai was at best a desert cult, already monotheistic but otherwise not far different from its pagan neighbors. Its faith, too primitive to be called Judaism, had hardly changed from the days of Abraham. In Sinai the Israelites were transformed into a society of laws, probably history's first such. At Sinai, the scholars say, Judaism acquired a structure, institutions, ritual and a set of values based on a code that bound its believers. The practices it adopted emphasized the rules of daily life over any spiritual bond with the divine. The form Judaism took under Moses strongly resembled what it is today.

The events at Sinai were seminal to all who have ever called themselves Jews. Religious skeptics, of course, do not believe the account in Exodus; some wonder whether the journey ever took place at all.

Yet there is a consensus that *something* happened at Sinai, which became the foundation of all of Judaism's subsequent development.

According to Exodus, God, perched on Mount Sinai, delivered His seismic offer to Moses, poised in the camp below. "Tell the children of Israel," He said, "If you will hearken, yes, hearken to My voice and keep My covenant, you shall be to Me a special treasure from among all peoples . . ., you shall be to Me a kingdom of priests, a holy nation."

God's message, scholars point out, contained a dual promise: Jews would be a kingdom of priests *and* a holy nation. Were the two parts synonymous or not? What did it mean to be a kingdom of priests? What did it mean to be a holy nation? Religious Jews, aware that neither promise was kept, still debate God's intent.

Summoning Israel's elders, Moses conveyed God's proposal and, says Exodus, "All the people answered together. They said: All that Yahweh has spoken we will do." Moses hurried back to the mountain with the message, but God was clearly dubious. In Egypt, the Israelites had accepted His proposals with enthusiasm, yet had proven rebellious throughout the entire desert journey. Exodus makes clear that God did not fully trust them.

Nonetheless, God invited Moses to proceed. In one of literature's most dramatic narrations, Exodus tells readers that while the Israelites hovered nervously around the tents, Moses prepared for his meeting with God on the mountain.

> There were thunder sounds, and lightning, a heavy cloud on the mountain, and an exceedingly strong *shofar* sound. And all of the people that were in the camp trembled. Moses brought the people out toward God from the camp and they stationed themselves beneath the mountain. Now Mount Sinai smoked all over, since Yahweh had come down upon it in fire; its smoke went up like the smoke of a furnace, and all of the mountain trembled exceedingly. Now the *shofar* sound was growing exceedingly stronger. . . . Yahweh called Moses to the top of the mountain and Moses went up . . .

Moses later returned to the camp with God's conditions, conveyed verbally, for the covenant. They later became the Ten Commandments.

The first commandment—"I am Yahweh your God Who brought you out of the Land of Egypt"—is not a commandment at all. It is a statement of authority, effectively legitimizing the terms that follow. The second was a warning that went straight to the issue of Israel's stiff-necked character.

> You are not to make yourself a carved image or any figure that is in the heavens above, that is on the earth beneath it, that is in the waters beneath the earth; you are not to bow down to them, you are not to serve them, for I, Yahweh your God, am a jealous God.

Scholars regard this as history's first clear statement of monotheism, and the first explicit enjoinder against idol worship. The words tell us that, though Israel had vowed since Abraham's time to worship only one God, it had often strayed. The commandment admonished the Israelites sternly to stay in line. The commandment was so important to God that He had Moses repeat it to his followers twice, then convey it a third time. Finally, for a fourth time, He has Moses tell the people, "You are not to bow down to their gods, you are not to serve them, you are not to do according to what they do, but are to tear, yes, tear them down, and are to smash, yes, smash their standing stones. You are to serve Yahweh your God."

Moses' repeated admonitions serve as clear evidence of the depths of God's concern and, at least for a moment, the admonitions worked. After Moses relayed God's message, the Israelites replied in one voice, "All the words that Yahweh has spoken, we will do."

Exodus tells us that Moses, after writing down God's instructions, sacrificed a bull and used the blood, the symbol of life, to seal the deal. But he, like God, had doubts about the people. Moses insisted on still another affirmation from them, and when satisfied that it had not been given lightly, he headed once more to the mountain with the inscribed vows in his hand. This time, feeling the need of witnesses in meeting God, he was joined by Aaron and several elders of Israel. God, however, dismissed the delegation, instructing Moses to make the journey alone, making clear that, of all the Israelites, He had confidence only in Moses. Amid the heavy clouds covering the mountain,

God ordered Moses to climb to the summit to receive the Ten Commandments permanently inscribed on tablets of stone.

In his absence, the Israelites waited apprehensively. Exodus says Moses was gone for "forty days and forty nights," surely long enough, in the supercharged atmosphere of thunder and lightning, to generate fears that something was amiss. Finally, the people summoned Aaron and said, "We do not know what has become of him." Breaking the vow they had only recently taken, they told Aaron, "Make us a god who will go before us."

Scholars say the alacrity with which the Israelites violated their pledge demonstrates the fragility of their commitment to monotheism. The scholars cite the expression "*make* us a god" as evidence that they had not yet absorbed the *idea* of Yahweh or the principle of a distant, invisible God. Under stress they were more comfortable with the idols their neighbors worshiped. In a pinch, the scholars say, the Israelites found relief in falling back on near-pagan practices.

Aaron, amply depicted as the weaker brother, gave in without even an argument. "Break off the gold rings that are in the ears of your wives, your sons and your daughters," he said, "and bring them to me." Having collected these items, he took a graving tool and, in the fire, shaped the mass into a calf. The mob then mocked Yahweh's earlier declaration that "I am your God," as if their vows of loyalty were without meaning. Pointing to the golden calf, they cried out, "This is your God, O Israel, who brought you up from the land of Egypt."

While his people frolicked with the idol, Moses was still at the summit. When God learned what was happening below, He declared to Moses:

> *Your* people, whom *you* brought up from the land of Egypt, has wrought ruin. They have been quick to turn aside from the way that I commanded them, they have made themselves a molten calf, they have bowed to it, they have slaughtered offerings to it. . . . I see this people—and it is a *stiff-necked* people. So now, let Me be, that My anger may flare against them and I may destroy them—but you I will make into a great nation.

The passage bewilders scholars, in that God, after denouncing the Israelites as stiff-necked, offers to make Moses into "a great nation." Moses, who certainly shared God's anger, must have been sorely tempted by the prospect. Was He testing Moses? God's intent is not clear. The words suggest He was in the market for another partner, and, at the least, it implies that He and Moses should together turn away from the people of Israel.

But Moses, faithful to his tribe, would have none of it. Rather impudently, he poses a question, asking God whether He had gone to the trouble to rescue the Jews from bondage so that Egypt could have the pleasure of saying, "With Evil intent He brought them out to kill them in the mountains, to destroy them from the face of the soil?" Even more audaciously, he advises God:

> Turn away from Your flaming anger, be sorry for the evil intended against Your people. Recall Abraham, Isaac and Jacob Your servants, to whom You swore . . . : I will make your seed many as the stars of the heavens, and all this land which I have promised I will give to your seed, that they may inherit it for the ages.

Moses' daring succeeded, perhaps better than he anticipated. "Yahweh," Exodus says, "let Himself be sorry concerning the evil that He spoke of doing to His people." This may be the only story in the Bible—or in any other religious source—that culminates with God's apology.

Moses finally came down from the mountain, holding in his arms what he had been promised, "the tablets [that] were God's making, and the writing [that] was God's writing, engraved upon the tablets." But what he found was a heady festival of drinking and dancing among Israelites celebrating the golden calf. Moses seized the idol, threw it in the fire, ground it up, spread the powder over water and forced the Israelites to drink it. So angry was he that he also "threw the tablets from his hands and smashed them beneath the mountain."

Moses then confronted his brother, who tried to weasel out of his complicity, but Moses showed him no sympathy. He accused Aaron of a "great sin" that brought guilt upon the people. He then turned to his own tribes, the Levites, who had refrained from joining in the revelry. Use your swords, he ordered them, to "kill every man his brother, every man his neighbor, every man his relative." That day, Exodus says, three thousand Israelites fell to Levite swords.

It is noteworthy that this punishment was ordered by Moses, not God, Who had still not shown His hand. Moses, as the people's advocate, clearly sought to forestall even greater wrath, and returned to God to plead for forgiveness. To make his case, he played what was, even for Moses, unusually tough poker. He bet that by placing on the line his own good name, God would defer to him. If He refused forgiveness, he told God, he wanted to be "erased from the records that You have written." Like much in Exodus, the precise meaning of the offer is obscure. But God, acknowledging that Moses was personally free of the sin of the calf, gave in. God and Moses had gone head to head, and it was God Who blinked.

The episode did not end there. God imposed a costly plague on the Israelites. He agreed to their continuing the journey to the promised land. But, penalizing them symbolically, He informed Moses that He would not be their guide, as He had been leading them in flight from Egypt. "I will not go up in your midst," God said, "for a stiff-necked people are you."

Though reaffirmed by God, the holy covenant was thus off to a bad start. Both God and the Israelites, the parties to the bargain, embarked on the relationship with a grudge. In fact, the Bible itself makes clear that the Israelites continued to turn to idols, particularly in hard times, for several centuries more. Biblical verses depict a people that was still primitive, relating only with great difficulty to an incorporeal god.

God Himself, the Bible tells us, was constantly tormented by this failing. In a touching lament in Psalm 95, God recalls His command to Moses early in Sinai to strike a rock—Merivah and Massa—to produce water for a thirsty people, and calls on a new generation to rise to a higher ethic.

Do not be stubborn as at Merivah,
As on the day of Massa, in the wilderness
When your fathers put Me to the test,
Tried Me, though they had seen My deeds.
Forty years I was provoked by that generation;
I thought, "They are a senseless people;
They would not know My ways."
Concerning them I swore in anger,
They shall never come to my resting place!

What mattered most, however, was that God overcame His disappointment. He did not abandon the covenant and did not replace the Israelites with another people. Much as their misdeeds infuriated Him, much as their grumbling exasperated Him, He paid heed to Moses and directed them to the promised land. Though He punished them, He also forgave them. A reader might conclude from Exodus that, while God wanted His people holy, He understood they would also be profane, and He accepted them in both parts.

God even forgave Aaron for his weakness. He not only spared Aaron's life; He also named him the Israelites' high priest, an honor Aaron would pass to his descendants. And Aaron repaid God's confidence by performing the duties of the post with honor.

*   *   *

TRADITIONAL RABBINIC sources recognize that the tragedy of the golden calf left a wound in the folk memory of the Jewish people. Judaism has made much less of this wound than Christianity has made of the concept of original sin. Yet the golden calf remains a source of guilt, a burden on the Jewish spirit.

Rabbinic sages have found it difficult to explain how the Israelites could have sought out an idol so soon after Sinai, and how Aaron could so readily have accommodated them. Some sages have hypothesized that the Israelites were infiltrated by foreigners; others say they panicked after miscalculating the date on which Moses was to return from the mountain. The Talmud makes a comparison between the Israelites at Sinai and a "shameless bride." More often, the rabbis have maintained an embarrassed silence.

The Jews' embarrassment passed into Christian theology, where it was cited as evidence of inherent Jewish sinfulness. Jesus' followers regarded the golden calf as the germ of Jewish evil. Augustine linked it with the worship of the devil, a notion that medieval Christianity adopted. The church long claimed the calf proved the Jews were not God's chosen people, that the covenant was never consummated. Not surprisingly, these arguments served as a buttress of anti-Semitism.

The Jews had no real defense against these attacks. Louis Ginzberg, among the greatest of Talmudic scholars, writes that the conventional rabbinic view holds that "the worship of the golden calf had more disastrous consequences for Israel than any other of their sins."

Ginzberg's classic, *The Legends of the Jews*, draws upon the midrash, the diverse body of popular and rabbinic literature composed over centuries, to understand the attitudes of ordinary believers. He writes of a widespread conviction among traditional Jews that God, having created the Torah as a weapon to defeat the Angel of Death, changed His mind after the apostasy of the golden calf. The legend holds, Ginzberg writes, that God:

> had resolved to give life everlasting to the nation that would accept the Torah, hence Israel upon accepting [the covenant] gained supremacy over the Angel of Death. But they lost their power when they worshipped the golden calf. As a punishment for this, their sin, they were doomed to study the Torah in suffering and bondage, in exile and unrest, amid cares of life and burdens, until, in the Messianic time and in the future world, God will compensate them for all their suffering. But until that time there is no sorrow that falls to Israel's lot that is not in part a punishment for the worship of the golden calf.

Rabbi Abraham Isaac Kook, a religious scholar whom we will later encounter in the context of territorial Judaism, leaned more to the mysticism of the Kabbalah to find the meaning of the golden calf. He found it an extremely costly sin for the Jews. But as a founder of the religious wing of Zionism, he was convinced that, in resettling the Holy Land, the Jews had entered a messianic era, which would set matters right. Kook wrote:

> Had it not been for the sin of the golden calf, the [Canaan-ite] nations that dwelled in the Land of Israel would have made peace . . . , for the name of the Lord would have aroused in them sublime awe. No matter of war would have been conducted. . . . This sin alone caused peace to be delayed thousands of years. But now all the factors in the world are joined together to bring the light of the Lord into the world, and the sin of the golden calf will be erased entirely.

The Messiah did not arrive for Rabbi Kook, and the sin of the golden calf has not been erased from Jewish memory. But the golden calf is only a part of the substance of Exodus. The covenant remains its dominant lesson. Yet surely the protagonists themselves, with their complex personalities, have had an impact on Jewish character, influencing the course the Jews have taken.

God is multifaceted, jealous by nature but also compassionate, irascible, forgiving and even modest enough to admit mistakes. Moses is petulant, but clearly a man of huge wisdom and rectitude. As for the body of Israelites, much as they aspire to attain God's expectations of them as a holy nation, they remain irremediably stiff-necked. Such dramatis personae make a volatile mix.

These personalities produced in Exodus two great events, the proclamation of allegiance to God in the awe-inspiring covenant and its reverse side, the apostasy of the golden calf. The juxtaposition foreshadows the sparks Jews have generated among themselves throughout history. It also created a bifurcation in the folk memory of the Jews and perhaps in their collective soul. The aim of Mosaic law was to provide the structure for a holy nation, while the Jews' disposition to the profane placed the promise of holiness out of reach.

It is not too much to visualize Jewish history as essentially the interaction of the protagonists of Exodus, maneuvering within the framework of the two poles of the covenant and the golden calf. Exodus is, more than anything, the story of a tumultuous relationship among God, the Israelites and the law. Its principal message may well be that the volatility among the three will define Judaism forever.

Chapter Two

MAKING AND LOSING A STATE

THE JEWS, LIKE MANY prehistoric peoples, had their beginning as nomads, constantly in search of food and shelter. The Bible tells us that the covenant they reached with God at Sinai changed them from a gaggle of tribes linked by a common ancestry into a community defined by a sacred purpose. It also transformed them from wanderers into a people settled on a land of their own.

But God's offer at Sinai was conditional. The gift that was promised them across the Jordan offered milk and honey, necessities for a prosperous sedentary life, but it seemed clearly contingent on fulfillment of the divine mission of being a "holy nation." Exactly what God meant by holiness was not apparent, and Jews have since argued its meaning. But the standard was clearly more arduous than was asked of other peoples, and the Israelites never found its realization easy.

Once they reached the promised land, the Israelites reorganized their tribal system of government into a primitive state, presumably a step toward meeting the divine challenge. Yet they had not absorbed the lesson of God's wrath delivered to them at Sinai. The state they created looked much like systems under which their pagan neighbors lived.

41

The Bible makes clear that the Israelites, over the centuries, showed no particular aptitude for statehood. They often fought, with other tribes or with one another. They were sometimes corrupt. Their rulers ignored the voice of the people. The temples they built as houses for God were often profane. The Israelites in their own state made little progress toward achieving the ideal God had demanded of them.

The drama of Israel's statehood was played out in cycles of triumph and despair. If we accept the Bible as its chronicle, the Israelites who wrote of it must be commended for honesty. While portraying the state as no worse than its neighbors, they depicted it as no better either. It endured, we might surmise, only because its citizens, for all their quarrels, shared an allegiance to a single God. Indeed, with all its ups and downs, the state lasted far longer than most, but when it came to an end after a dozen centuries, a Jewish state would not rise again for two thousand years.

The fall of the state in the first century C.E. caused the Jews to resume their life as wanderers. But this journey was not across an arid landscape, under God's eye. Its site was a harsh and frequently inhospitable Gentile world, in which they implored God to provide them succor and send the Messiah to redeem them.

Bequeathing monotheism and the Bible to the world was no small achievement for this people. But the Israelites left behind no great philosophy or art, as the Greeks had done, and no pervasive system of law like that of the Romans. If we take the Bible as historical evidence, it is also fair to ask why, unlike Greece and Rome, the state rarely provided its citizens with social stability and external peace.

The Bible makes clear that the stiff-necked attitude the Jews displayed at Sinai remained with them in the promised land. Though the term itself vanished from the text, Jews are presented as rebellious, contrarian, uncompromising. God had chosen the term to describe their dealings with Him. But it also applied to how they responded to great empires and to one another, even when their actions placed the community at risk.

Such a nature is not always a fault. If being stiff-necked invited much suffering, to be sure, it also preserved the Jews' identity within a hostile world. As exiles, the Jews consistently refused to bow their necks to the suffering that Christian intolerance imposed on them. Had they abandoned their God, they might have avoided massacres, expulsions, burnings at the stake. But from within their collective memory came the summons of the covenant at Sinai, and in persevering in their fidelity to God, the Jews as a people survived.

Can anyone doubt that the Jews' stiff-necked commitment to their own values saved them from vanishing into the mass of their neighbors? Some part did disappear, of course; conversion to Christianity and Islam took its toll. But unlike, for instance, the Sumerians and Nabataeans, their neighbors in the ancient world, the Jews were not reduced to archaeological remnants, a paragraph in the dusty chronicles of time.

Still, the posture that expressed an inner strength in some circumstances took the form of mindless obstinacy in others. The characteristic common to both the positive and the negative implications of "stiff-necked" is inflexibility, and an undiscerning dedication to it often serves a people poorly. To determine when to adopt it and when to refrain requires prudent judgment. One lesson of Jewish history is that when a stiff-necked nature manifests itself in defiance of reality, its consequence can be catastrophic.

The current chapter is about one such disaster—a disaster of such magnitude that it blighted nearly two thousand years of Jewish life. It began with a refusal to recognize that Rome was the superpower of the age and culminated in two unsuccessful wars that the Jews, being a tiny nation with limited resources, should never have waged. These wars resulted in the annihilation of the state, the destruction of the holy Temple and the scattering of the Jewish people to the ends of the earth.

The Jews' decision was more than a strategic mistake. So great was its folly that religious and secular scholars alike have searched for explanations within the attitudes and outlook of the time.

Had the religion of the Jews persuaded them that God, who once forgave them for forging a golden calf in Sinai, would reward them for turning the same stiff neck toward Rome? Was their collective psyche imbued with the conviction that, as His chosen people, they

could rely on Him to deliver them from the consequences of any action, no matter how ill considered?

Whatever the explanation, the Jews lost their homeland and spent
centuries dreaming of return. In our own era, they have regained their
state, but it is still tiny and with limited resources, and its inherent
fragility raises the question whether their stiff-necked nature does not
again place their national life in peril.

⅁   ⅁   ⅁

LOOKING BACK, HISTORIANS calculate that the Israelites, about 1050
B.C.E., recognized that the loose confederation they had set up, in
which each tribe ran its affairs with indifference to the others, placed
their survival in jeopardy. The powerful Philistines threatened to destroy them. If the Israelites were to defend themselves against such an
enemy, they would have to replace tribal autonomy with strong, centralized rule.

At the time, Samuel, a prophet and judge, was Israel's dominant
force. He was too old to assume authority himself, however, and his
sons, the Bible says, had forfeited their eligibility for leadership by
taking bribes and subverting justice. So the elders approached Samuel
and said, "Appoint a king to govern us like all other nations." Samuel
hesitated, and prayed to God, Who answered:

> Heed the demand of the people, for it is not you they have
> rejected, it is Me. Like everything else they have done since
> I brought them out of Egypt to this day—forsaking Me and
> worshiping other gods—so they are doing to you. But warn
> them solemnly, and tell them about the practices of any king
> who will rule over them.

Samuel passed on God's warning. Using his own words to describe
what a Jewish monarch would be, Samuel said:

> He will take your sons and appoint them as his charioteers
> and horsemen. . . . They will have to plow his fields, reap his
> harvest, and make his weapons and equipment. He will take
> your daughters as perfumers, cooks and bakers. He will

seize your choice fields, vineyards and olive groves, and give them to his courtiers. He will take your male and female slaves, your choice young men, and your asses, and put them to work for him. He will take a tenth part of your flocks, and you shall become his slaves. The day will come when you cry out because of the king whom you yourselves have chosen; and the Lord will not answer you.

Yet the Israelites persisted, so God, after surveying the available candidates, selected Saul, whom He presented as tall and handsome, in all an "excellent young man." Saul's psychological flaws would soon become apparent, but Israel required above all a warrior. "The sword of Saul," the Bible says, "never withdrew empty." Saul's task was to deliver Israel from the Philistines and to organize a monarchical state.

The Bible notes that from the start, a cloud hung over this state. Given to brooding, Saul was obsessed by David, a young shepherd boy who had entered history as the slayer of the Philistine giant Goliath. "Ruddy-cheeked, bright-eyed and handsome," David had risen quickly as a military commander, inflicting on the enemy a succession of defeats. Saul grieved when Israelite women showed him their favor, chanting, "Saul has slain his thousands, David his tens of thousands."

Saul's melancholy, the Bible says, cost him God's confidence. "The spirit of the Lord departed from him, and an evil spirit from the Lord began to terrify him." After a brief reign, Saul, with his three sons, fell in battle, and he was replaced by his young rival. David, crowned king at the age of thirty, founded a dynasty, extended the state's frontiers in all directions and captured the mountain stronghold of Jerusalem. Under his rule, the Israelite kingdom became a regional military power. David moved its capital from the provincial town of Hebron to Jerusalem, a city which in time became synonymous with Israel itself.

In Psalm 132, the Lord registers his pleasure with David and particularly with his choice of the capital at "Zion," a synonym for Jerusalem. In recognition of David's service, God vowed:

One of your issue I will set upon your throne.
If your sons keep My covenant

And My decrees that I teach them,
Then their sons also, to the end of time,
Shall sit upon your throne.
For the Lord has chosen Zion;
He has desired it for His seat.
This is My resting place for all time;
Here I will dwell because I desire it . . .
I will clothe David's enemies in disgrace,
While on him his crown shall sparkle.

God kept His promise, and for centuries David's dynasty was immutably linked to the Israelite throne. But few of his lineage—the exception being Solomon, his son—kept to the terms of God's covenant, and the Israelite people, says the Bible, were never particularly well served. Soon the dynasty fell on hard times and surrendered Israel's independence. In the succeeding centuries the state, more often than not, existed in subordination to a foreign suzerain. Yet, even though their powers were severely circumscribed, David's descendants continued to reign.

From biblical accounts, it is clear the monarchy reached its pinnacle early, then gave way to declining integrity and vigor. Solomon made Israel the foremost state in the eastern Mediterranean, with borders stretching from Mesopotamia to Egypt. Jerusalem, once a frontier town, became a metropolis, the destination of great caravans from exotic places. Inside the thick city walls, Solomon built a grand palace, where he presided over a court that other monarchs envied.

Nor did Solomon, for all his worldliness, overlook God. He erected a magnificent Temple, conceived as God's habitation on earth. Sheltering the Ark brought by Moses from Sinai, it sanctified the city itself. A priestly cult presided over animal sacrifice, rituals that, whatever the resemblance to those of the pagans, defined Judaism for as long as the monarchy lasted. Jews prayed facing the Temple; pilgrims journeyed there to pay God homage.

But the Israelite tribes, poorly governed, gravitated into rival blocs, identified regionally as Judah and Israel. Under Solomon, the Bible says, "Judah and Israel dwelt securely, every man under his vine and under his fig tree, from Dan to Beer-Sheeba." This was ancient Israel's golden age. After Solomon died in 928 B.C.E., the tensions between the two blocs increased, producing a weakness that the monarchy never overcame.

Solomon's successors proved incapable of preserving the stability of the Israelite state. They presided over an arena of squabbling contenders and authoritarian excesses, with a restless army, an oppressive bureaucracy of tax collectors and boundaries that fluctuated from one war to the next. The monarchy, distinguished from its pagan neighbors by its allegiance to God, was nonetheless consumed by ambitions, schemes, jealousies and scandals.

In time, the state split into two independent, competing kingdoms. Israel, the land of the northern tribes, ran westward from Transjordan to the sea. It seemed to have strategic advantages over Judah, to its south, which was landlocked. But Judah embraced Jerusalem, and the dynasty's roots were there, giving it political preeminence. From its name the term *Jew* entered into history.

While often at war with each other, the two monarchies were also undermined by incursions from the outside and by Gentile uprisings within. Then, in 722 B.C.E. Israel, the northern kingdom, was crushed by Assyria. Its population, scattered, would pass into history as Israel's "ten lost tribes." Judah endured for roughly a century more, before it succumbed to Babylonia, which had become the region's preeminent power.

The Bible says that during Babylonia's siege of Jerusalem, Jeremiah the Prophet fought bitterly with Zedekiah, Judah's king, over whether to surrender to the powerful enemy. Both purported to speak for the Jews, but Jeremiah's fidelity was to God, Zedekiah's to the kingdom.

"Thus said the God of Israel," Jeremiah declared, claiming, as religious leaders do, divine authority, "If you surrender to the officers of the king of Babylonia, your life will be spared and this city will not be burned down. . . . But if you do not surrender, this city will be delivered into the hands of the Chaldeans [Babylon's dominant tribe], who will burn it down; and you will not escape from them."

Resounding with common sense, Jeremiah's argument in reality urged giving the Jews' faith priority over Judah's sovereignty. If Jews were free to worship God, he reasoned, the kingdom's fall was of little importance. The king's reply was that prayer was of less importance than sovereignty, which alone could safeguard worship. Theirs was the first clash on record between religious and secular values, a dispute that endures to this day.

As king, Zedekiah had the authority to settle the argument. He arrested Jeremiah and threw him into a muddy pit. His forces, commanded to confront the enemy, held out bravely until reduced to starvation. The Book of Kings tells us that the Babylonians, after breaching the city's defenses, torched "the king's palace, all the houses . . . [and] tore down the walls of Jerusalem on every side." Of more historical significance, they also "burned the House of the Lord," Solomon's great handiwork, the Israelites' homage to God.

The Book of Kings thus records the destruction of the Jews' First Temple. A milestone of Jewish history, it is still lamented by a fast on the ninth day of the month of Av. The Babylonians, following the practice of the times, proceeded to carry off much of Judah's population. It was the first of the great waves of Jewish exile.

Jeremiah was mistaken in fearing for the faith because, both in exile and at home, Babylonia respected the Jews' right to worship. But the king's personal interests fared less well. Placed in chains himself, Zedekiah was forced to witness his sons' execution. Their deaths brought the line of David, after five hundred years, to an end. Other ambitious men would now compete for the throne. The state survived, but Israel, no longer sovereign, became a Babylonian vassal.

Not surprisingly, the Jews were hardly happy with the arrangement. A few years after the defeat, extremists among them assassinated a Jewish governor appointed by the victors, but the murder did not advance their cause. On the contrary, the Babylonians executed hundreds of Jews in reprisal, and added more to the community in bondage. This was not the last time that extremists would lead the Jews to calamity. Only when a larger military power appeared would Israel escape from Babylonia's yoke—to become a vassal of Persia.

A HALF-CENTURY AFTER Babylonia's conquest, Persia supplanted it as the region's strongest power. Persia occupied Judah, and in 538 B.C.E. its king, Cyrus II, issued an edict permitting the Jews in Babylonia to return home. Even more startling, he authorized them to rebuild the Temple in Jerusalem. Notwithstanding Judah's vassalage to Persia, the gesture enshrined Cyrus forever in the Jews' pantheon of righteous Gentiles.

The Second Temple, though probably less grand, duly rose to replace the First as the hub of Jewish life. For nearly six hundred years, it served as the Jews' religious and social center. In vassalage, it was also the symbol of lost independence, the focus of the dream of restored sovereignty.

Though Persia ruled benignly, the stability it brought to Judah was short-lived. By the fourth century B.C.E., the seductive culture called Hellenism began to spread its ideas eastward from the rising power of Greece. In 332, the Greek armies of Alexander the Great conquered the region. Judaism, for the first time, appeared threatened not so much by foreign military and political power as by foreign values.

The Jews, preponderant among a heterogeneous population within Palestine, had long been considered impervious to the temptations of foreign values. The Jews' obstinate dedication to their own customs, oriented to religious law and practice, made them an oddity in the region. Since biblical times, relations with Samaritans, Nabataeans, Phoenicians and other neighboring peoples had never been easy. Tacitus remarked that the Jews alone looked on their neighbors as enemy tribes; other Gentile writers stressed the Jews' sense of themselves as religiously superior. As their neighbors gravitated toward Hellenism, most Jews saw Hellenism as the golden calf. The more tightly the region embraced it, the more the Jews seemed out of step in rejecting it.

But Hellenism's appeal was seductive. The great Hebrew poet Judah Ha-Levi would warn: "Do not let Greek wisdom, which has no fruit but flowers, beguile you." The Greek language was increasingly adopted by Israel's rich, and Greek concepts—pagan gods, personal freedom, secular literature, rational thought—provided a major challenge to Judaism's austere worldview.

It was the poor and working-class majority of the Jews that Hellenism most offended. Their attitude separated them from the worldly and sophisticated upper strata, producing deep class resentment. At the very moment that Greece and Rome, two powerful new empires, were rising, the Jews were being riven by Greco-Roman cultural values, gravely compromising their ability to deal with the danger.

The death of Alexander the Great in 323 B.C.E. brought the crisis to a boil. Alexander's eastern empire fractured between two hostile dynasties, the Ptolemies of Egypt and the Seleucids of Syria. Each aspired to incorporate Judah into its own realm.

The Ptolemies were the first to annex Judea—the Greek name, which passed into history, for Judah—and they treated it carefully. Sensitive to the Jews' reputation as troublemakers, the Ptolemies granted them substantial religious and political autonomy. The local government was allowed to follow Mosaic law, and a high priest seated in the Temple served as the Jews' chief communal authority.

Ben Sira, a Jewish conservative often quoted in the Talmud, encouraged his fellow Jews not to disturb the Ptolemies' arrangement. Obviously close to Jewish priestly circles, he wrote a book of maxims that urged acceptance of the status quo. Ben Sira counseled:

> Fear God with all thy heart
> And revere His priests.
> With all thy strength love Him that made thee,
> And forsake not his ministers.
> Glorify God and honor the priests,
> And provide their portion as has been commanded.

But events overtook this advice. In 198 B.C.E., the Seleucids seized Judea from the Ptolemies and embarked on a Hellenizing program among the Jews. They made the gymnasium, hallmark of Greek civilization, the focus of Jerusalem life, and used their powers to name the Temple's high priest and his assistants from the ranks of Hellenized Jews. Jewish accounts note with bitterness that neophyte priests often slipped away from their duties at the Temple to attend the gymnasium's sporting events.

In time, the Seleucids went further, plundering the Temple treasury to support their armies. When Jerusalem's Jews took to the streets to protest, the Seleucids canceled Judea's remaining autonomy, installing administrators from Greece over the province. In 167, they performed the ultimate offense of forbidding Jews to practice their faith, decreeing the death sentence for circumcision and Sabbath worship. Finally, they rededicated the Jewish Temple to Zeus, requiring all Jews to participate in their pagan rites.

Having been pushed to their limit, the Jews stiffened their necks and rebelled. Their uprising against the Seleucids was the first of three that marked Judea's bloody history. It was such a dazzling success that it clearly distorted the Jews' strategic judgment. The two that followed were grievous failures that would shatter Jewish life and deprive Jews of their homeland for two thousand years.

The rebellion against the Seleucids took place under the banner of the Hasmonaeans, a priestly family also known as the Maccabees. Salo W. Baron, an eminent Jewish scholar, calls it the world's first war of religion, but it clearly contained elements that can also be called nationalism.

Mattathias, the Maccabees' patriarch, led the Jews to a series of victories until his death. His successor, his son Judah, crowned Mattathias's effort by capturing Jerusalem, symbol of both the nation and the faith. Judah ordered the Temple's purification and rededication, an act celebrated at Hanukkah, a festival that is both sacred and profane, as much nationalist as religious.

Judah Maccabee, more than four hundred years after the defeat by the Babylonians, restored Jewish independence, but the war dragged on. After Judah was killed in battle, command passed in turn to his brothers, Jonathan and Simon, and in 142 B.C.E. they brought about the Seleucids' surrender. Jonathan was named high priest and king. The triumphant Hasmonaeans, spurning popular nostalgia for the family of David, thus made themselves Judea's ruling dynasty, which they remained for a century.

Conventional Jewish history has immortalized the Maccabees and exalted their triumph. Their exploits were recorded in a book of the Bible, named for them. Jews are taught that overcoming huge odds, Judea vanquished a mighty empire, restoring the faith. "Miracle" is often pronounced in Hanukkah celebrations, though careful historians tend to be more sober.

The late Israeli historian Yehoshafat Harkabi, a retired general in the Israeli army, contends that the Hasmonaeans, effectively mobilizing popular reaction to Seleucid abuses, actually brought superior force to the battlefield. The Seleucids were stretched thin by military commitments at other borders, and fought among themselves over rival claims to the throne. He says they also had to look over their shoulders at Rome, the rising power that served its own ambitions by supporting the Jewish rebels.

Jews are mistaken, Harkabi writes, in attributing the Maccabean victory to God's munificence, when the explanation was more mundane. The belief, he says, seriously skewed Judea's judgment on the two wars it had yet to fight against Rome. He says it similarly distorted the perception of Jews after the Six-Day War of 1967, convincing many that it was a miracle wrought by God.

The independent state that the Hasmonaeans established after their victory was ostensibly successful. It annexed much land, extending its western frontier to the sea, thus making Judea a regional power once again. Pursuing a policy of Judaization, rare in Jewish history, it converted many of the Gentiles, some by force, who were living within or near its borders.

But in combining the offices of king and high priest, the Hasmonaeans created a monarchy without constraints. They devised a Temple-based theocracy that, ironically, promoted Hellenist values, which remained foreign to most Jews. They also tyrannized their subjects and exhausted them in dynastic wars, squandering their popular mandate. Their excesses, like those of a succession of David's heirs, sealed their ultimate doom.

Looking back geopolitically, historians say the Hasmonaeans preserved Judea's sovereignty as long as they did thanks largely to a peculiar vacuum among its enemies. Tacitus, the first-century Roman historian, summed it up this way: "At that time, inasmuch as the Hellenistic rulers were weak, the Parthians [Iranians] had not yet developed into a power and Rome was still distant, the Jews succeeded in setting up for themselves a royal dynasty." Tacitus meant that Judea was living on borrowed time, and it would not be long before the sand in the hourglass ran out.

In 63 B.C.E., taking advantage of the recurring struggles between Hasmonaean pretenders, Rome marched in and captured the country. It was not a painless conquest for Rome: the Jews inflicted heavy losses in defending Jerusalem. Over the ensuing decades, moreover, the Jews spilled blood in repeated insurrections. During the turmoil that followed Julius Caesar's assassination in 44 B.C.E., for example, the Jews held the country for seven years before Rome, in heavy fighting, regained control. Though a warning to Rome, the war once again reduced Judea to vassalage.

Rome's rule at that time was not oppressive. Rome conventionally relied on strong local governments to administer imperial policies, promoting no social or religious agenda. It selected a Jew named Herod, regarded as friendly, to serve as its representative, with the title of king. Herod claimed descent from David and asked the Jews to accept his dynastic legitimacy.

Though he could be iron-handed, Herod averted military occupation by raising local contingents, which included Jews, to enforce Roman rule. He rebuilt the Jews' war-ruined cities and, in a special show of his Jewish credentials, he renovated the Temple, reviving Jerusalem's religious life. Some scholars say Herod was the Jews' best ruler since Solomon.

But when Herod died in 4 B.C.E., Rome, for whatever reason, shifted its course radically. Faithful to its tradition, it remained tolerant of Jewish worship. But it fanned Jewish resentment by moving the capital from Jerusalem to Caesarea, a pagan city on the coast. Emulating the Seleucids, moreover, it placed the country under direct administration, dispatching governors from Rome to rule.

As the Christian Gospels make clear, these were years of uncommon religious fervor. Baron, the Jewish historian, has written that with Rome's power rising and Hellenism in decline, the times offered a "multicolored picture of groups of men striving for new religious formulations to solve some of the age-old riddles of existence." Many Jews, it seems, adopted an almost fundamentalist form of observance, characterized by severe austerity. Amid the turbulence, Jews yearned for "supernatural intervention," Baron writes, to rescue them from their travails. Claimants to messianic leadership—Jesus of Nazareth among them—came and went.

According to the Gospels, the Jewish religious establishment, dominated by the Temple priesthood, took the messianism in the air as a threat to its powers. In reviewing the period, the Talmud—less a chronicle than a reflection of rabbinic values—tells of a prominent priest who disparages the Messiah, saying, "If you hold a sapling in your hand and someone says to you that the Messiah is there, plant the sapling first." The verse is meant to convey the priesthood's fear of religious upstarts.

The Romans, too, sensed trouble in the rebellious mood. Only during the brief reign of Emperor Caligula, who placed a statue of himself in the Temple as a symbol of his divinity, had they actively denied religious freedom to the Jews. But if not religion, some other malaise was roiling civic order. Rome repressed the Jews' periodic rioting by force, but conditions slipped increasingly out of their control.

Some historians hold that the disorders deluded Jews into thinking the occupation was near collapse, when in fact it was getting tougher. Extremists among the Jews, committed to doing the Lord's work, organized a secret sect that they called the Zealots. Christian sources say the Zealots began to harass Romans as early as 5 C.E. Their strategy was to assassinate Romans along with Jewish collaborators, in preparation for a full-scale revolt.

Among the Zealots was a vanguard called *sicarii*, whose name was derived from the dagger its members were known for carrying beneath their robes. In our own time, the word has reappeared among Jewish terrorists in the occupied West Bank. Harkabi finds in the Talmud a story of two Jewish brothers who vowed to kill any Roman who came through their town, which he regards as a reference to *sicarii*. Baron says that these extremists believed they were preparing the way for the Messiah, whom they expected to appear, sword in hand, to lead the Jews to freedom.

The Zealots' campaign for liberation was based on their belief that Jewish allegiance, belonging only to God, could be imparted to no mortal, and surely not the Roman emperor. It distinguished them from the Jewish upper classes and their minions, the priests, who benefited from Rome's favors and who saw war with Rome as a threat to their privileges. Within the demands of the Zealots for independence, historians say, again appeared a measurable dose of class conflict.

For different reasons, sages belonging to a rising rabbinic body also opposed the Zealots. Their views recapitulated Jeremiah's in his famous debate with Zedekiah at the time of Babylonia's attack on the First Temple. The rabbis had no quarrel with Rome, as long as Jews were free to worship. They scoffed at the Zealots' efforts to wrap their nationalism in the Torah. The rabbis opposed war with Rome because their interest was not in independence but in prayer.

Yet the Zealots, through energy and ardor, captured wide popular favor, and they carried the day. In 66 C.E., the Jews rose up in what has come to be known as the Great Revolt. Rome called it the Jewish War, the grandest in scale that any subject people ever waged against its empire. This was the second of the three rebellions of the Judean period, and it culminated in catastrophe for the Jews.

Catching the Romans undermanned and unprepared, the Jewish forces, like the Maccabees two centuries before, won early victories. In capturing Jerusalem, they wiped out the Roman garrison and destroyed the symbols of Roman paganism.

But the Jews erred badly in thinking they could repeat the Maccabean "miracle." Rome's borders, unlike the Seleucids', were secure. Judea, moreover, was a crucial link—both north to south and east to west—in its imperial communications. Judea's ports, the eastern terminus of its Mediterranean seaway, were too important to abandon. In contrast to the besieged fragment of the Greeks' fading empire that the Maccabeans challenged, the Jews were taking on Rome in its prime. Their odds were much less favorable.

But, no less important, the Jews themselves were deeply divided. The working classes seemed to fight valiantly, but neither the rich, the priests nor the rabbis gave the war their full support. Harkabi sees the outcome of the Great Revolt as a product of the "causeless hatred"—a Talmudic term—that characterized the Jews' attitude toward one another. Recapitulations in the Talmud seem to confirm as much.

The Talmud says one famous rabbi, burdened by foreboding, fasted for forty years in a failed effort to stave off the disaster. It also tells of a Zealot leader, proposing to recant his views in the face of imminent catastrophe, who declared, "What shall I do? If I say anything to them [his fellow extremists], they will kill me."

During the Great Revolt, Harkabi says, the Jews lacked central leadership, had no clear strategy and mobilized only a fraction of their potential manpower. Their deficiencies forced them to concentrate their soldiers in forts, which the Romans systematically subdued. Though it took four years to quell the revolt, the outcome was never in doubt. Jewish resistance did not delay Rome's victory as much as the death of its emperor, whose successor took time out from the fighting in Judea to stabilize his rule at home.

Jerusalem was the last Jewish stronghold. Inside its walls, supporters of the Zealots engaged their opponents in what can only be described as a Jewish civil war, in which each side bloodied the other badly. When Rome's legions arrived to begin the siege in 70 C.E., the Jews, already weakened, failed dismally to organize a common defense. Roman soldiers, after a brief investment, penetrated the defenses against scant resistance.

The Romans, once they had breached the walls, put the Second Temple to the torch. They then leveled the rest of the city, and whatever Jews they did not execute they transported as slaves to the amphitheaters of Rome or the mines of Sinai. In Rome, a triumphal arch celebrating the victory still stands. The Jews' loss of the Second Temple, like the loss of the First six and a half centuries before, is a milestone remembered by fasting on the ninth of Av.

The Zealots, however, were still not ready to concede defeat. A diehard band of *sicarii* barricaded themselves with their women and children in the mountain fortress of Masada, built by Herod on the shore of the Dead Sea. Surrounded by Romans, they held out for three years. Heroic as their efforts were, their resistance had no military purpose. Finally, the band chose collective suicide over capitulation.

Josephus Flavius, history's chief source on the era, paraphrases in *The Jewish War* the valedictory at Masada of Eleazar, the *sicarii* leader:

My loyal followers, long ago we resolved to serve neither the
Romans nor anyone else but God, Who alone is the true and
righteous Lord of men. Now the time has come to prove our
determination by our deeds. At such a time we must not disgrace ourselves. Hitherto, we have never submitted to slavery. . . . We must not choose slavery now, and with it
penalties that will mean the end of everything if we fall alive
into the hands of the Romans. For we were the first of all to
revolt, and shall be the last to break off the struggle. It is
God who has given us this privilege, that we can die nobly
and as free men.

The Romans, to commemorate Masada's fall, struck coins on
which a woman representing Judea sits mournfully under a palm tree.
Around its edges, the inscription reads *Judaea devicta*, Judea subdued.

🔯   🔯   🔯

ONCE THEIR RESISTANCE ended, Rome set out to teach the vanquished
a lesson. For some five hundred years, Jews throughout the region had
voluntarily paid a tax to maintain the Temple in Jerusalem. The
money served as a bond between the homeland and the early Diaspora. The victors, in deliberate mockery, decreed the tax to go henceforth to support a temple in Rome, where Jupiter, the symbol of
paganism, reigned.

But more important, the fall of the Temple shattered the priesthood
and brought to power the new class of rabbis that had been waiting in
the wings. As long as Rome tolerated Jewish prayer, the rabbis had rejected resistance to its rule. Yet with Jerusalem in ruins, one of them
mourned, "Since the destruction of the Temple, there has been no day
without some curse, the dew has not fallen to the good of the crops,
and the taste of the fruit was gone."

The defeat, however, did not stamp out Jewish zealotry, and whis-
pers of insurrection soon circulated among the people once more.
The Talmud says that a rabbi, alarmed at the threat of new fighting,
lamented that "good counsel and clear-thinking ceased." Disorder in
the streets resumed, and Rome sent soldiers to supersede the local

contingents that Herod had organized. In 116, a new Jewish revolt broke out that Rome suppressed by destroying towns and executing militants. It was a small uprising, but the Roman commander feted his victory immodestly, erecting an idol to himself among the Temple's ruins. To Jews, his gesture was still another pagan insult to God.

Tempers cooled temporarily when Hadrian became Rome's emperor in 117 and dismissed the offending commander. Hadrian seemed not only to be without hostility toward the Jews; he appeared to admire them and was willing to improve the conditions of life in Judea. He delighted them—or, according to some, deceived them—by hinting that he would soon authorize the reconstruction of the Temple.

Historians regard Hadrian as perhaps Rome's wisest emperor and point out that the Jews, alone of his subjects, made trouble for him. But the Jews, by their standards, found ample grounds. Hadrian, as a Hellenist, held no religion above any other and so rejected the Jews' belief that their covenant with God was unique. A lover of art and athletics, he banned circumcision on the grounds that it constituted physical disfigurement. Though his aims may have been benign, the Jews took them as an assault.

When Hadrian announced a plan to replace the ruins that still covered Jerusalem with a new city, the Jews were not pleased but offended. It was to be a pagan city, named for him. In the new Jerusalem, Jews were to be equal to the Gentile residents. Reasonable as that status was to Hadrian, the Jews could not abide it. Their feeling about Jerusalem—then, as now—was proprietary, and Hadrian's decree dashed hopes that the city would again be a holy Jewish site. Zealots quietly dusted off their old plans for war.

In *Memoirs of Hadrian*, Marguerite Yourcenar, a French novelist celebrated for the precision of her historical accounts, depicts Hadrian's pain at the Jewish reaction to his policies. She attributes to Hadrian, ruminating on how his vision for Jerusalem had alienated the Jews, these thoughts:

> Nothing in all that was beyond repair, but the hatred, the
> mutual contempt, and the rancor were so. In principle, Ju-
> daism has a place among the religions of the empire; in

practice, Israel has refused for centuries to be one people among many others, with one god among the gods . . .

No people but Israel has the arrogance to confine truth wholly within the narrow limits of a single conception of the divine, thereby insulting the manifold nature of the Deity, who contains all; no other god has inspired its worshipers with disdain and hatred for those who pray at different altars.

I was only more anxious to make Jerusalem a city like the others, where several races and several beliefs could live in peace; but I was wrong to forget that in any combat between fanaticism and common sense, the latter has rarely the upper hand.

Yourcenar's words represent the understanding of most historians of the Jewish attitude. What has bewildered historians is why the chief Jewish fanatic was Rabbi Akiva, the foremost rabbinic sage. Most rabbis looked upon the looming war with foreboding. Akiva greeted it with enthusiasm. To him is attributed the initiative that sparked the third and most devastating Jewish rebellion.

Though contemporary sources recount little of Akiva's politics, the evidence leaves no doubt that, if not a Zealot, he was a committed nationalist. He also proclaimed wide authority for himself to interpret the Torah, while blurring the line between Mosaic law and his own political convictions. As we shall see later in this book, many present-day rabbis similarly wrap their political convictions in Jewish law. In Akiva's case, it produced one disastrous blunder after another.

A prolific writer, Akiva disseminated a belief in the impending arrival of the Messiah, who he promised would drive the heathens out of the Holy Land, restore the kingdom and reign over the Jewish people in justice. Akiva often traveled to Rome and to the leading communities of the Diaspora to expound his messianic vision, to raise funds and to rally support for the impending revolt.

The Talmud, which esteems Akiva for his theological erudition, acknowledges limits to his political understanding. Akiva spoke the verse, "There shall step forth a star out of Jacob and a scepter shall rise out of Israel and shall smite" the enemy. The statement reveals

Akiva's conception of the Messiah as a military leader. On meeting the warrior Bar-Kokhba, Akiva declared, "This is the king and the Messiah."

Save for skills as a fighter and an imperious personality, Simon Bar-Kokhba is largely unknown to Jews. At birth his family name was Bar Koseva, but those who regarded him as the Messiah gave the syllables a twist, which changed the meaning to "Son of a Star." Bar-Kokhba and his followers, unlike the inept insurgents of 66 c.e., planned astutely for rebellion, hiding weapons from Roman view and shaping recruits into a disciplined force. Even the Romans, when the fighting began, credited Bar-Kokhba with being a formidable foe.

The rebellion opened in 132 and, as they had in earlier wars, the rebels took the Romans by surprise. Support from outside Judea was slight, but Bar-Kokhba's army, fighting as guerrillas, inflicted serious damage on their enemy. The Jews quickly established their authority over all Judea, including Jerusalem, and with buoyant expectations struck coins with Hebrew inscriptions celebrating Israel's redemption.

The celebrations, however, were premature. Having fought initially against local contingents, the Jews were soon outnumbered by expeditionary armies dispatched by Rome, from Syria, Britain and the Danube. Using siege tactics they had mastered long before, the Romans retook Judea's walled cities one by one. After three years, the rebels were pushed back to Betar, a fortress in the hills near Jerusalem. When Bar-Kokhba was killed there, the Jewish forces capitulated. The victors took their vengeance by torturing and executing Rabbi Akiva, along with nine other rabbinic sages, known to Jewish history as the Ten Martyrs. The fall of Betar, like so many tragedies of this history, is commemorated on the ninth day of Av, elevating Bar-Kokhba's defeat to the level of the destruction of the First and Second Temples.*

Rome called Bar-Kokhba's uprising the War of Betar. Its chronicler was Dio Cassius, a Roman whose credibility as a historian has held up

---

* Rabbinic sages have ruled that Hadrian's decree to build a pagan temple in Jerusalem and the Jews' expulsion from Spain in 1492 also occurred on that date. They thus established Tishah-b'Av as a catchall day of Jewish mourning.

over the centuries. Summarizing the war, Dio Cassius wrote: "Fifty of the Jews' strongest fortresses were destroyed and nine hundred and eighty-five of their most important settlements razed. Five hundred and eighty thousand Jews were slaughtered in battles and skirmishes and countless numbers died of starvation, fire and the sword. Nearly the entire land of Judea lay waste. . . . Very few were saved."

Scholars point out that Dio Cassius's figures came from army field reports, a documentary source for historians to our own day. Even discounting the exaggerations that routinely characterize them, these scholars say, the figures reveal a Jewish catastrophe of huge proportions.

Harkabi goes beyond Dio Cassius. Military experience, he writes, discloses that deaths due to disease, particularly in besieged cities, generally exceed battlefield casualties. He concludes that Dio Cassius's estimates are low. Harkabi also cites records showing that so many Jewish survivors were sold into slavery that, in the slave markets of the Roman Empire, the price of captives dropped to a pittance. One witness, Harkabi notes, left to posterity the observation that in Hebron after the war, a Jew could be bought for the price of a horse's daily ration.

Harkabi calculates the Jewish population worldwide on the eve of the Bar-Kokhba rebellion at 1.3 million; he estimates that only half of that number survived the war. In Judea alone, he says, the death rate may have reached 90 percent. He cautions that these figures cannot be read in isolation, considering the huge losses suffered in the Great Revolt only two generations before. Until the Holocaust, he maintains, the history of the Jewish people was marked by no greater calamity than the Bar-Kokhba rebellion.

Dio Cassius conveys the war's ferocity further in his account of Rome's casualties. "Of the Romans, too, many fell," he wrote. "So many that Hadrian, in his dispatch to the Senate, refrained from using the customary introductory phrase: 'I trust you and your children are well; I and my troops are well.'" The omission, scholars note, represented a tacit confession of major Roman losses.

When Judea capitulated, Roman authorities, perceiving themselves as too lenient in the past, vowed that Judea would never rise again.

Razed cities were left in ruin. Arable land was confiscated and olive orchards uprooted. Synagogues were closed, and Jews were barred from study and prayer. Jerusalem was ruled off-limits. Even the use of Hebrew was barred. In these conditions, the Jewish emigration from the Holy Land soared, as the birth rate fell. In all history, Israel's existence as a nation never stood in greater doubt.

Calling these measures genocide, as some have done, would be an overstatement. Rome took no action against the Jews of the Diaspora, or even of Galilee. It did not revoke the Jews' citizenship in the empire. Though Hadrian made an effort to annihilate the Torah, his real target was Judea, the vassal state. The name *Judea* itself was banned, replaced officially by *Syria Palaestina*. After the Bar-Kokhba revolt, the Jewish state passed into blessed memory.

Henceforth, the Diaspora—Babylon, Alexandria, Damascus and dozens of other cities, including Rome itself—would define the Jewish people. Many Jews, it should be noted, would thrive in exile. But there would be no more uprisings. Jewish sovereignty would become a quiet dream, unrealized for nearly two thousand years.

In time, the Romans restored the religious autonomy of the Jews of Palestine. Some Jews journeyed from exile to make pilgrimages to the homeland, but few remained permanently. The hub of prayer became the wall that survived as the Temple's only remnant. Mourning their lost past, Jews everywhere called it the Wailing Wall.

Without the Temple, the new rabbinic class would seamlessly replace the priesthood as the chief authority among the Jews. Blaming the defeat on the Jews' failure to celebrate God, the rabbis counseled repentance and turned their minds to preserving the faith. They taught Jewish children—or, at least, Jewish boys—to read the Torah, making its study synonymous with Judaism. Gathered in synagogues, the Jews adjusted to landlessness by becoming more pious than before.

᠊᠊᠊   ᠊᠊᠊   ᠊᠊᠊

RABBINIC SCHOLARS in the ensuing centuries have not looked back kindly at the Bar-Kokhba revolt. They have depicted Bar-Kokhba himself as vainglorious and rash, a false Messiah. They made a pun of the name fabricated for him, shifting its meaning from "Son of a Star" to

"Son of a Lie." They have interpreted the uprising as a collective sin, so much a source of shame that they buried its records, depriving later generations of the sources to evaluate the episode for themselves.

Harkabi argues that the catastrophe broke Judaism's spirit at a crucial moment in its rivalry with ascending Christianity. He cites from rabbinic literature the observation of puzzled Gentiles: "What is their God doing to them that so many are forever being killed for Him?"

In time, the lessons that rabbinic leaders drew from Bar-Kokhba's defeat came to be expressed in oaths, tacit or explicit, that they elicited of the Jews in exile. These oaths constituted a renunciation of the stiff-necked disposition that had so consistently driven Jewish history. In exile, the Jews replaced it with calculated passivity. The oaths specifically vowed abstention from any collective effort to return to the Holy Land, along with a concomitant loyalty to the states in which the Jews might find refuge.

The oaths—to which we shall return—signaled a huge shift in attitude on the part of the Jews. They justified "ghettoization," voluntary concentration in communities in isolation from the Gentile world. The oaths became the foundation of the practice of generation after generation of nonresistance to the assaults of hatred routinely directed at them.

After the Bar-Kokhba uprising, Jews kept a low profile in world affairs. The tragedy of the revolt, Harkabi says, pressed Jewry to the margins of history. Henceforth, the society of Jews would be acted upon by others, while never acting itself.

Harkabi, to be fair, may be laying on the Bar-Kokhba revolt an excessive burden. He writes as a contemporary Israeli patriot, exultant that the Jews, in reestablishing a sovereign state, have at last escaped the shadows of the catastrophe. But he also fears that the Jews might one day be imprudent enough to repeat it. Harkabi is particularly alarmed at Israel's present-day habit of resurrecting not just the Bar-Kokhba revolt but the mass suicide at Masada, transforming them into a mythology of national glory. He calls the phenomenon the "Bar-Kokhba syndrome," enticing Jews into foolish, perhaps deadly, misadventures.

Harkabi's apprehension is a reminder that, from King David to Bar-

Kokhba, the Jews, bedazzled by nationalism, repeatedly surrendered their good judgment, with agonizing consequences. He grieves over the devastation that stiff-necked responses to danger repeatedly brought upon the Jewish people. Harkabi's work is suffused with foreboding that the Jews of our time, in responding unwisely again, may risk losing all that they have regained as a nation.

Chapter Three

DEPOSING THE PRIESTS

HISTORICAL NARRATIVE characterize the destruction of the Second Temple as an unmitigated tragedy for the Jews. Indeed, defeat in the war against Rome from 66 to 70 C.E. brought to an abrupt end a thousand-year era of Temple-centered Judaism linked tightly to the state. Jews are taught to mourn the Temple more than the state, and on the ninth of Av, the anniversary of the defeat, the lights in synagogues around the world go dim to commemorate its loss. Yet the facts surrounding the loss raise the question of whether the end of the Temple was a tragedy at all.

Beneath the history of the Jews' defeat lies a subplot, turning on the long-simmering conflict between priestly Judaism, with its emphasis on Temple-based animal sacrifice, and rabbinic Judaism, with its focus on religious law. At stake, however, was more than ideology. The priests were aristocracy, members of the ruling circle; the rabbis were linked to the common people. The war's subplot was a revolution in Judaism, in which the rabbis triumphed. The historians of the era, curiously, have largely overlooked it.

One explanation for the oversight is that the bloody war with Rome pushed conflict between priests and rabbis into the shadows. Another is that the Jews' tumultuous rivalry with Christianity wound up taking precedence among those who wrote the history of the times. Josephus, usually thorough and detached, occasionally alludes to the subplot but fails to examine it seriously.

The dispute between priests and rabbis, with its hints of personal ambition and class conflict, has always been a bit embarrassing to Jews. Later sages were no more willing than the early ones to confront it. The priesthood did not survive to tell its own story, and the Talmud, composed in a later age by rabbis, makes no pretense to objectivity. The void in subsequent discussion suggests that Jewish historians have deliberately shied away from the controversy.

Rome's victory in the war provided the framework for the outcome of the subplot. Rome may have favored the rabbis, who were more malleable than the priests; it does not, however, seem to have weighed into the contest. The role of the Jewish community's social leadership is also unclear. What is known is that Rome's destruction of the state left the priests without a structure of political support, and Rome's leveling of the Temple left them without a base. The rabbis in this conflict were the last ones standing.

Unlike Rome's legions, the rabbis conducted no triumphal parades. Any rejoicing by their supporters, at a time of painful military defeat, would surely have been unseemly. To this day, Jews take no real note of the transfer of power from one set of religious leaders to another. Yet the rabbis' victory was revolutionary, in fixing the destiny of the Jews more than did the destruction of the Temple. The victors emerged as the dominant class within Jewish society and set the course that Judaism would take right up until our own time.

🖫   🖫   🖫

LONG BEFORE THERE were rabbis to define Judaism, there were priests. Under the guidance of priests, the Israelite tribes for centuries performed rites based on animal sacrifice, much like those of their pagan neighbors. But priestly powers went well beyond ritual. Scattered through the Bible are countless items suggesting that priests played a crucial role in ruling the community.

The Book of Joshua tells us: "When the people set out from their encampment to cross the Jordan, the priests bearing the Ark of the Covenant were at the head." In Deuteronomy, God says, "Before you join battle, the priest shall come forward and address the troops. He shall say to them, 'Hear O Israel! . . . It is the Lord your God Who marches with you to bring you victory.'" When God promised in Exodus to recognize Israel as a "kingdom of priests," He might well have intended a people *ruled* by priests.

In Leviticus, God commanded Moses to tell the people, "When you enter the land that I am giving to you and you reap its harvest, you shall bring the first sheaf of harvest to the priest." Thus God provided for a permanent source of income for the priests. When the Israelites, having crossed the Jordan, were no longer nomads, one of their first activities was to build temples as permanent sanctuaries where the priests performed their sacrificial rites.

Within these sanctuaries, the priesthood evolved over time into an aristocracy distant from the common people. It preserved its bloodline by having its children marry only the children of other priests. It kept genealogical lists to certify its members' lineage. Whatever the popular resentment toward them, the prestige imparted by God insured the priests a high social rank and a comfortable life sustained by public largesse.

The priesthood's duty was to ward off what the Bible calls "bloodguilt." In Leviticus, God commands sternly, "Any man of the house of Israel who slays an ox or a sheep or a goat in the camp or who slays it outside the camp who does not bring it . . . as an offering to Yahweh before the dwelling of Yahweh, bloodguilt is to be reckoned to that man . . . and that man is to be cut off from amid his kinspeople." The command clearly legitimizes only those sacrifices performed under priestly authority. It served as the basis of priestly power for a thousand years.

The first high priest—*kohen* in Hebrew, a word of Canaanite origin—was Aaron, Moses' elder brother. Though incriminated in the scandal of the golden calf, he was forgiven by God and, once in the Holy Land, apparently fulfilled his duties estimably for forty years. The dynasty of high priests is, by tradition, descended personally from Aaron.

Just below the high priests, the Levites, Aaron's tribe and Moses', became members of the priestly class as a reward for their fidelity during the golden calf affair. It was presumably in recognition of the common responsibility to support them that they were the only tribe not allocated its own land when Israel reached Canaan. Initially, the Levites seem to have functioned as gatekeepers and musicians. Later, the monarchy expanded their duties to the supervision of Temple finances and maintenance, as well as personal service as retainers. Since they had no independent sources of support, the kings were able to transform the Levites into minions, dependent on royal favor. Inevitably, they became identified with monarchical abuses, and with the kings they grew distant from the people.

In Jeremiah, God Himself calls the priests "godless," adding: "Even in My house I find their wickedness." Zephaniah, a minor prophet, declares the "priests profane what is holy, they give perverse rulings." Deuteronomy, in noting that the priests have "foes and enemies," seems to confirm that they were at the vortex of popular discontent.

From the days of King Saul, the priests meddled in dynastic politics. Persuaded they were plotting against him, Saul commanded his guards, "Turn about and kill the priests of the Lord, for they are in league with David." The Book of Samuel says that when the guards refused, Saul ordered a courtier to "go and strike down the priests." The courtier, the Bible says, dutifully killed eighty-five men wearing priestly vestments.

Whether or not the priests conspired on his behalf, David understood the importance of a faithful priesthood. His own identification with the faith, he reasoned, could only enhance the power of his office. After becoming king, David named himself a priest, and in Psalm 110, God accepts the dual role:

> Sit at My right hand
>> While I make your enemies your footstool,
> The Lord will stretch forth from Zion
>> Your mighty scepter;
> Hold sway over your enemies!
> Your people come forward on your day of battle.

In majestic holiness, from the womb,
   From the dawn yours was the dew of youth.
The Lord has sworn and will not relent.
   You are a priest forever, a rightful king.

David governed in God's name, citing holy law, imparting to the monarchy a theocratic aura. His royal dress consisted of both crown and priestly garments. With a high priest at his side, he routinely ascended to the temple's altar to lead the holy ritual himself. As long as it lasted, the monarchy relied on priests to assure its legitimacy.

Solomon, by erecting the grandest temple in the realm, went further than his father in bringing the faith under monarchical control. Pilgrimages to Solomon's Temple served as homage to king as well as to priests. Hecataeus, a Greek historian of the fourth century B.C.E., described the Jews as being dominated by their priests, but it remained for the Hasmonaeans, two centuries later, to combine king and high priest into a single office.

Throughout these centuries, the priests' one consuming duty to the community was to preside at the altars of the Temple while sacrifices were conducted. They burned incense, inspected the animals to verify that they were without blemish and invoked God's blessing during the rites of incineration.

Jews of every station brought animals to the altars, offering them as atonement for sins, thanks for blessings, celebration for successes. Depending on the purpose, they might present cattle, sheep, goats or poultry. The rules of slaughter were strict, the ritual of burning elaborate. When the ceremonies were over, the priests and the donors divided up the remains and ate them.

By about 600 B.C.E., the provincial temples had vanished, and synagogues did not yet exist. Though some Jews apparently engaged in prayer, neither Torah nor tradition required it of them. The symbol of the faith was the Temple, and Jews whose homes were too distant to carry sacrifices to it signaled their symbolic presence at its rituals by turning toward Jerusalem in homage.

The priests made the Temple in Jerusalem not just a site for worshiping God through sacrifices but a platform for exalting monarchical virtues. They served the king further by interpreting divine will, expounding upon the mysteries of existence, even curing diseases at the royal court. The kings, in return, guaranteed the priests' income and kept their privileges secure.

Only as lesser duties did the priests also teach the Torah and preside as judges in legal disputes. Priestly interest in the Torah and the law, however, was largely limited to Temple practices. A Talmudic sage conveyed what was probably a common view in saying, "The uncleanliness of the knife was to them worse than the shedding of blood." Priests were not much involved with popular education. On the contrary, they clearly tried to limit learning to their own circle, resisting efforts to widen the Torah community.

The Prophet Isaiah, in the eighth century B.C.E., was early in conveying the sense that something was amiss with the priesthood's role. Notwithstanding the Torah, Isaiah attributes to God disdain for animal sacrifice, and he has God call for a system sensitive to the demands of social justice, which clearly was not a priestly priority.

> I am sated with burnt offerings of rams,
> And the suet of fatlings and blood of bulls,
> And I have no delight in lambs and he-goats . . .
> Who asked that of you? . . .
> Put your evil doings away from My sight,
> Cease to do evil, learn to do good,
> Devote yourself to justice, aid the wronged.
> Uphold the rights of the orphan,
> Defend the cause of the widow.

The Prophet Amos, more or less Isaiah's contemporary, delivered a similar signal of distress over priestly practices. His words carried an ominous ring for priests.

> I loathe, I spurn your festivals,
> I take no delight in your solemn assemblies,
> Even though you offer me burnt offerings, or your cereal
>   offerings,

I will not accept them;
I will pay no heed
To your gifts of fatlings.
Spare me the sound of your hymns,
And let me not hear the music of your lutes.
But let justice well up like water,
Righteousness like a mighty stream.

The prophets no doubt echoed common concerns, and such complaints might have served as a warning to the priests. But under royal patronage, they were confident of their position. Though animosity toward the priests grew, many centuries would pass before anything came of the recriminations.

ᔧ ᔧ ᔧ

THE GLORY DAYS of King David and King Solomon gave way to a succession of weak and corrupt monarchs who involved the priesthood in their escapades. During the Second Temple era, matters grew worse as priests, emulating the wealthy class, succumbed to the temptations of Hellenism, alienating the common people further. In the Temple's final years, when Rome made rules that the priests dutifully executed, the temperature of popular disaffection approached a boil.

By then, a new rabbinic class was bidding to supplant the priesthood. The rabbis, surely influenced by the teachings of the prophets, openly disdained animal sacrifice. Though their writings do not acknowledge an intent to defy the many Torah laws on animal sacrifice, they made abolishment of the practice their objective.

The term *rabbi,* literally "my master," never appears in the Bible. Rabbis seem to have emerged in the Second Temple era, rather late in Jewish history, from scribes, copyists of sacred works who went on to fill the need for Bible teachers. The term was applied only much later to interpreters of the Torah, and still later to the leaders who are familiar today, ministering to their congregations. As a class, rabbis seem to have initially been Temple employees, and some may even have started their careers as priests.

Early rabbinic literature refers often to the sacred mission "to make a fence around the Torah." The expression subtly attributes to the priesthood a subversive intent, implying that, while priests engaged frivolously in animal slaughter, rabbis were fixed upon a solemn duty to have the Jewish people live according to the real meaning of God's law.

As late as the Hasmonaeans' uprising against the Greeks in 167 B.C.E., the priesthood still appeared impregnable. In fusing the office of king with that of high priest, the Hasmonaeans even promoted a religious renaissance, recalled by historians as the apogee of priestly fortunes. But not long after the Hasmonaean victory, the priestly class, along with the dynasty itself, began slipping into decline.

In fact, the religious renaissance that the Hasmonaeans promoted proved to be more fertile for rabbis than for priests. The priesthood was aloof; it was the rabbis who identified most easily with the observant masses. Many rabbis, self-taught sons of farmers and artisans, lived among the common people. Hillel, soon to be their oracle, urged them to defy priestly efforts to limit education and open their doors to whomever wanted to study. His telling slogan, contrasting them with priests, was, "Do not separate yourself from the community."

But even in supporting the resurgence of piety, it is unlikely the rabbis called for the Temple's abandonment, much less its destruction. Hillel's chief concern seemed to be ritual reform, aimed not at undermining the Temple but at strengthening it by dignifying and popularizing its ceremonies. Fellow rabbis called for liberalizing Temple rules to encourage more pilgrimages. Still, the rabbis' growing influence distanced them from the priesthood, if not from the Temple itself.

The grand objective of the rabbis was to transform the core of Judaism to personal obedience to religious law. Recognizing that by itself the Torah did not contain enough law to govern all of Jewish life, they embarked on a campaign that was to define them until our own time. Led by their intellectual luminaries, called sages, they argued for going beyond the literal Torah, and they arrogated to themselves a wide freedom to proclaim law in response to the conditions presented by the rise of Rome. Their goal was to elaborate an Oral Law, a mirror of the Torah, that would take account of a changing world. Written and Oral Torah together, they reasoned, would serve as the foundation of Jewish religious life.

The rabbis of the Second Temple era even organized what might be called a political party, called the Pharisees, to promote their theological aims. Their politics resembled the views of Jeremiah the Prophet in an earlier time, in being more committed to piety than monarchy. Disdainful of the priesthood's collaboration with the Romans, they were also unsympathetic to the Zealots' shrill nationalism. With few exceptions, the rabbis considered it foolish, as long as the Romans allowed the Jews to pray, to challenge Rome's military might. Even though the Zealots carried the masses into rebellion, many historians believe the Pharisees represented a majority of Jews.

The chief political adversary of the Pharisees were called Sadducees, the party of the priesthood and the urban rich. Though a mixed group, they were generally more worldly, and they rejected the rabbinic commitment to the Oral Law as a force to promote Jewish unity. Their chief political concern was the preservation of the powers and privileges that Rome extended to them. If piety and learning linked the Pharisees, what united Sadducees was a commitment to wealth and status.

Historians are not clear about why many Sadducees, who had initially rejected the nationalism of the Zealots, ultimately gravitated to the support of the ill-fated rebellion. Practical men, they could hardly have entertained delusions of victory. On the eve of the uprising, they dominated Jewish politics by controlling the Sanhedrin, the Jewish community's chief political body. It was the Sadducees who, puzzlingly, declared the war on Rome by suspending the daily sacrifice offered on the emperor's behalf.

The New Testament, which contains more information on the period than Jewish sources, communicates Christian hostility to both Jewish parties. The Pharisees, in their quiet piety, may have been more like the followers of Jesus than were the Sadducees, but the New Testament treats the two, both foes of Christianity, with equal scorn. John the Baptist calls Pharisees and Sadducees alike a "vipers' brood." Jesus seems to side with the Pharisees in his disdain for the Temple, vowing, "There shall not be left here one stone upon another that shall not be thrown down." But, in the Book of Matthew, Jesus singles out the Pharisees to say, "Outside, you look like honest men but inside you are brimming with hypocrisy and iniquity."

The Talmud, which invariably favors the rabbis in their dispute with the priests, gives an indication of the class differences involved and describes the antagonism between them, which sometimes became violent. "Woe is me because of their staves," it quotes a Pharisee saying about Sadducees, "Woe is me because of their fists. For they are high priests, their sons treasurers, their sons-in-law trustees, and their slaves beat the people with staves."

Another well-known Talmudic tale records the exchange that passed between a gibing priest, who was a Sadducee, and two gentle and courteous sages, Shemaiah and Avtaylon, both of them of course Pharisees.

> It once happened that as a certain high priest came out of the Temple all the people followed him, but when they saw Shemaiah and Avtaylon, they left him and followed Shemaiah and Avtaylon. Eventually, Shemaiah and Avtaylon took leave of the high priest. They [the sages] said to him, "May the descendant of Aaron go in peace." And the priest replied, "May the descendants of Gentiles go in peace." And they answered, "May the descendants of the Gentiles, who do the deeds of Aaron, go in peace, and let not the descendant of Aaron, who fails to do the deeds of Aaron, go in peace."

The nuances of this story may be translated as follows: The priest by definition is a descendant of Aaron; the sages are commoners. The sages' greeting to the priest as Aaron's descendant is respectful, while the high priest's sneer at the sages as Gentiles is a patent insult. The sages' reply—that descent, even from Aaron, is hardly a virtue in the absence of the good deeds—expresses the importance the rabbis attribute to conduct. The sages' willingness to be called Gentiles if it links them to Aaron's deeds reflects the esteem that Moses' brother ultimately acquired, surmounting even the poor judgment he showed at the time of the golden calf.

In *Antiquities of the Jews*, Josephus Flavius, the celebrated chronicler, himself a Jew, presents another popular view. He contrasts the slick, sophisticated Sadducees, influenced by Hellenism, with the simple, sincere Pharisees, whose only concern is the law. Josephus leaves no doubt where his sympathies lay:

> Our people do not favor those persons who have mastered the speech of many nations, or who adorn their style with smoothness of diction. . . . But they give credit for wisdom to those alone who have an exact knowledge of the law and who are capable of interpreting the meaning of the holy scriptures.

Taken together, these statements constitute evidence of the tensions that existed within Judaism on the eve of the Second Temple's destruction. Historians have tended to see the rise of Christianity as the chief source of these tensions, and no doubt it was a factor. But Judaism, it is clear, was also grappling uncomfortably with a drift away from Temple Judaism toward a rabbinic Judaism based heavily on Oral Law. The Temple was gradually losing its preeminence as the synagogue spread its influence, one step at a time, throughout the Jewish world. Historians acknowledge that the origins of the synagogue, as an imstitution, are unclear. The Talmud claims biblical evidence of synagogues as far back as Moses' time. But they are more likely, historians say, to have begun among the exiles in Babylonia determined to preserve their connection to Judaism after the First Temple was razed in the sixth century B.C.E. When the exiles returned home from Babylonia, they apparently brought the synagogue with them.

The synagogue's major innovation was the invitation it extended to worshipers, as community members, to participate actively in religious observance. At the Temple, worshipers were largely bystanders to the fiery spectacles performed by the priests. The synagogue, in contrast, was collective, even democratic. Only after centuries did rabbis emerge as their powerful leaders.

The synagogue invented the Sabbath service, bringing worshipers together on a regular schedule. It formalized the selection of communal prayers and fixed the hours of their recitation. It established the centrality of the *Shema*, "Hear O Israel, the Lord is God, the Lord is one," uniting worshipers around the root statement of Jewish monotheism.

It is a measure of the institution's appeal that Christianity, from its earliest days, adopted the synagogue as its model for effective worship. Subsequently, Islam adopted it as well. None of the three monotheisms has ever departed from this pattern.

Rabbinic sages, in the age of Temple dominance, sought proof of divine sanction for the synagogue. They found it in God's statement in Exodus, "In every place where I cause My name to be remembered, I will come to you and bless you." They found further support in Ezekiel, where God says, "Although I have scattered them among the nations, yet I have been to them as a little sanctuary in the countries where they are come." Scattered among the nations, the exiles would remain Jews by praying together within the "little sanctuary," which the sages held was promised by God.

In its earliest days, the synagogue flourished far more widely in exile, where it served as a substitute for the Temple, than at home. Archaeologists have found in Alexandria, for example, remains of a major synagogue that may date from the Hellenic era or earlier. By the first century, Alexandria, the grandest city in the Diaspora, was said to have not just one great synagogue, built by the Jewish craft guilds there, but smaller synagogues in almost every residential quarter.

Such evidence confirms that by the first century, the synagogue was spreading both at home and abroad. Philo, a Hellenist Jew, wrote of many synagogues in Rome after he visited in a delegation to the emperor. In the New Testament, Jesus preaches at a Galilee synagogue, and Paul writes of synagogues in Damascus, Asia Minor and Cyprus. As for Jerusalem, the Talmud numbers them at four hundred, most serving small congregations but one on the Temple Mount, perhaps adjacent to the Temple itself.

The early synagogues, to avoid an appearance of rivalry, emphasized their links to the Temple, and were conventionally built facing in the Temple's direction. Jerusalemites, says a chronicler, often attended the morning sacrifice at the Temple, and in the afternoon went to one of the synagogues to pray.

It was not long, however, before the two institutions became open rivals. By the first century, large numbers of Jews had been won over by the appeal of communal worship, if not of rabbinic laws, and it seems apparent that the priesthood saw its traditional role in jeopardy. The angry disputes between Pharisees and Sadducees point not just to an ebb in Temple authority, but to a priestly elite no longer confident about its future.

By the eve of the Temple's destruction, the rabbis were busy building a body of Oral Law. A ceremony of ordination had been established that empowered rabbis to serve as judges. But those selected as sages were not necessarily ordained, and some had no formal religious training at all. It was the esteem of their colleagues that singled them out as lawmakers. The Talmud suggests that the absence of formal credentials did not humble them. It cites a sage who declared, "How stupid are some people, who rise in the presence of the Torah but do not rise in the presence of a great scholar."

No doubt, most sages possessed vast knowledge of the Torah and an ability to apply it persuasively within the context of everyday life. Such men, for the most part, worked inside yeshivot, Torah academies established by synagogue leaders to hammer out the new law. These yeshivot also became political centers for the forces that aimed to supplant the waning priestly elite.

Hillel and Shammai, rival sages whose lives straddled the era from B.C.E. to C.E., ran the Holy Land's two most celebrated yeshivot. Their squabbles are legendary. The Talmud suggests, quite improbably, that before them, Jews rarely engaged in religious disputes. But it makes clear which of them prevailed, saying of Hillel that "he drew his fellow men near to the Torah." It says no such thing about Shammai.

More significant than the quarrels, however, was the success of the yeshivot in establishing a tradition of scholarship directed at building a Judaism guided by Oral Law. Together, Hillel and Shammai left a

legacy of high standards of learning. Both, moreover, contributed enduring principles to the Oral Law and to the codification of Halacha,
the body of Mosaic jurisprudence. Not only did the tradition of legal
scholarship identified with them survive the Second Temple's destruction; the legacy that their heirs preserved would outlast Rome itself.

🕭   🕭   🕭

NEITHER HILLEL NOR SHAMMAI lived to witness the Temple's destruction, much less face its consequences. It is to Hillel's disciple, Rabbi
Yohanan ben Zakkai, that history gives credit for rescuing the law
from the rubble.

Rabbi Yohanan, in the years before the revolt, was a committed
Pharisee, involved in many disputes with the Sadducees. Some were
over doctrine, but others were over the priestly caste's use of power to
further its own financial interests. He took particular offense at the
priests' success in persuading the Roman administration to grant
them a waiver on certain taxes. The Talmud suggests a grain of wish-
ful thinking in a statement it attributes to him: "Oh Temple, Oh Temple . . . I know that you will be destroyed."

Rabbi Yohanan had sought to head off the looming rebellion against
Rome, preaching tirelessly in favor of accommodation. "Do not hasten to tear down the altars of Gentiles," he warned the Zealots, "lest
you be forced to rebuild them with your own hands." Apparently
caught inside Jerusalem during the civil conflict that was waged
among the Jews, he was barred by the Zealots from leaving the city.
Legend holds that, forced to resort to subterfuge, he directed his
pupils in 68 C.E. to smuggle him out of Jerusalem in a coffin.

Talmudic tradition says Rabbi Yohanan made his way to Rome's
commander, Vespasian, and prophesied to him that he would be im-
minently elevated to emperor. Yohanan's intention in flattering Vespasian was to obtain his permission to build a yeshiva at Yavneh, a
coastal town already known as the seat of scholars. He planned,
Yohanan said, "to teach his pupils . . . and to perform the commandments and teach Torah." Vespasian did indeed receive the imperial
crown, and in return granted the consent Yohanan sought.

With Yavneh's existing rabbinical community as his foundation,

Rabbi Yohanan assembled the greatest sages from among the survivors of the Jews' defeat to create a new center for the promotion of Torah law. In the gloomy days after the Temple's ruin, he also reconstituted the Sanhedrin, though without priestly representation, as an anchor for the dismayed remnants of the Jewish population.

To suggest that Rabbi Yohanan rejoiced in the Temple's demise might be overstatement. The Talmud tells us, in fact, that when he saw the Temple burning, "he stood and rent his garments, took off his *tefillin* and sat weeping, as did his pupils with him." The Temple, after all, had been integral to the Jews' sense of themselves for too long for any Jew, even a committed foe of the priesthood, to greet its destruction with indifference.

Dutifully, Yohanan embraced the conventional rabbinic view that the Temple's end was the product of the people's sins. The Jews' daily prayer book (*siddur*) still has worshipers confess, "Because of our sins we were exiled from our country and banished far from our land." But no sense of remorse could block his hope for a priest-free world, and he admonished Jews to abandon Temple ways, particularly animal sacrifice, as a link to God.

A Talmudic story says that Rabbi Yohanan was walking one day among the Temple ruins with a young acolyte who lamented, "Woe unto us that the place where the iniquities of Israel were atoned for is laid waste." And the Rabbi replied, "My son, be not grieved. We have another atonement as effective as this. It is acts of loving-kindness. It is said [in the Book of Hosea], 'For I [God] desire mercy and not [animal] sacrifice.'"

Yohanan clearly understood the opportunity presented to him and the other sages at Yavneh to transform the character of Judaism. Like the prophets of an earlier era, he argued that in God's eyes the practice of kindness and charity was superior to burning animals on an altar. His yeshiva produced so many permanent changes in the law that it was known as the "Yavneh vineyard." It also contributed to compiling and editing the books of the Bible, and presided over the Greek translation of what has since become the Old Testament. But, most important, the Yavneh sages took a major step in making the Torah the unifying element in the increasingly fragmented life of the

Jews, laying the groundwork of a system of rabbinic authority that would guide Jewish life in the exile that loomed ahead.

The labors of Ben Zakkai and his fellow sages at Yavneh ended abruptly with Bar-Kokhba's foolhardy revolt in 132 C.E. It is ironic that the fervid support given the revolt by Rabbi Akiva, considered Yavneh's outstanding scholar, was central to the academy's demise. After its victory, Rome banned Torah study entirely. The irrepressible Akiva proclaimed that compliance with the order was more dangerous to the Jews than disobedience, and, along with other sages, he was executed by the Romans for his defiance.

But if the Yavneh school died, many scholars survived. They scattered throughout the region, improvising yeshivot in which to fulfill the mission of building a body of Jewish law. "Ten times," the Talmud relates, "the [Yavneh] Sanhedrin was driven from place to place" in the decades after the revolt. It was the Yavneh tradition that preserved Judaism at a moment of unequaled crisis.

๑   ๑   ๑

RABBINIC JUDAISM THUS EMERGED the big winner from the Jews' two rebellions against Rome. Never again would an animal be slaughtered for burning in the Temple. The priestly class that lived upon the practice was shattered, never to rise again. The Sadducee party, its roots cut, promptly vanished into oblivion. Once the Temple fell, the doctrines of rabbinic Judaism had no rival. The rabbis were discreet about it, engaging in no celebrations, but the record makes clear they were exultant over the scope of their triumph.

"If children say to you, 'Come, let us build the Temple,' pay them no heed," wrote a prominent rabbi in the second century. "But if elders say, 'Come, let us destroy the Temple, listen to them for . . . the destruction by the elders is [tantamount to] building."

The Mishna, the earliest work of Jewish jurisprudence, is candid in declaring, "The study of Torah is greater than building the Temple." One of the great Mishna sages openly gloats in saying, "On the day the Temple was destroyed, an iron wall was removed from between Israel and their father in Heaven."

It is fair to speculate whether the Temple and the priesthood were doomed to extinction even without the Romans. The evidence of internal decay suggests the possibility. Was there any prospect of reform? Animal sacrifice, however anachronistic, was so intrinsic to the priesthood's nature that voluntary abolishment seems unlikely. Yet there is no telling how long, on its own, the institution might have survived. What is amazing is that a practice intrinsic to the Jews since the time of Moses vanished so abruptly, and virtually without a trace. Henceforth, Judaism would be identified not by priests and burnt carcasses but by rabbis, synagogues and Oral Law.

The subplot of the war against Rome from 66 to 70 C.E. was the unplanned revolution that transformed Judaism. The rabbis clearly had not wanted the uprising. Much as they dreamed of freeing Judaism from the priesthood's clutches, and even from Rome's, they never conspired to rebel. The priests, on the other hand, apparently helped bring on their own demise by backing the pro-war elements among the Sadducees, their political party. In the end, Rome's triumph was the catalyst, and the rabbis may themselves have been surprised at how overwhelmingly they had won.

Rabbis can make a persuasive case that the Jewish people, rather than any rabbinic class, were the chief beneficiaries of the outcome. Judaism, it is fair to say, would not have endured as a faith based on animal sacrifice. More important than the overturning of one ruling elite by another, the revolution shifted the foundation of Judaism to the law. The change was surely positive for the Jews.

Could it be said that the rabbis had anticipated the need for law, for a set of common values, as the only imaginable bond for a people that would soon be scattered throughout the world? At the least, their vision can be called providential. The law has served the Jews, in the absence of a homeland, as the anchor that preserved them as an identifiable community.

The rabbinic overturning of the priestly order is the only successful revolution in Jewish history. Christianity in the first century and Islam in the seventh were, in different ways, rebellions that came from within Judaism's bosom. But the rebels in both cases chose to take a separate course, leaving Judaism weakened but not significantly changed.

In the eighth century, the Karaites, promoting a Torah-based fundamentalism, conducted an uprising against the rabbinic commitment to Oral Law; they failed. Nearly a millennium passed before the next challenge, the Jewish world's brief intoxication with a messianic pretender named Shabbatai Zevi; the episode ended ignominously when he was unveiled as a fraud.

In the eighteenth century, Hasidism in eastern Europe attacked rabbinic Judaism, arguing that its dedication to the law had become an exercise in hair-splitting, an obsession that deprived the faith of all spirituality. After fierce fighting, the two sides forged a fragile truce that, until today, has kept their conflict in remission.

A century later, the Reform movement, emerging from western Europe's Enlightenment, rose up with the aim, first, of superseding rabbinic Judaism with a more modern set of principles and, failing that, of breaking the ancient rabbinic monopoly on defining the faith. This challenge is surely the most serious that rabbinic Judaism has faced since the destruction of the Temple, and compromising its issues has, thus far, proven unattainable. The final outcome is still in doubt.

In contrast, rabbinic Judaism's victory over the priesthood in 70 C.E. was unmitigated. It met the classic definition of a successful revolution, in replacing the leadership and values of one ruling class with those of another. The Judaism that triumphed—now known as Orthodoxy—shared the priesthood's attachment to the Torah but otherwise differed from it fundamentally. The masses of the era seemed grateful for the change. Almost overnight, rabbinic Judaism became the Jewish norm.

To the rabbis' credit, they sought to convey an illusion of continuity, pretending they had won no victory at all. In their Halachic deliberations, rabbis still conduct solemn discussions over the rules of sacrifice, as if the Temple's demise were temporary. They render homage to the Western Wall, the Temple's only remnant, known until recently as the Wailing Wall. In designating it Judaism's holiest shrine, they suggest with feigned modesty that their synagogues are hardly important at all.

Orthodox rabbis, in their prayers, lament the priesthood's disappearance. The synagogue service on Yom Kippur, Judaism's holiest day, cries out for the Temple's reestablishment and the reinstitution of animal slaughter. On the Sabbath, the call, though briefer, carries the same message. At the Sabbath Torah service, following an order written in the Mishna, the first of seven Jews honored to recite a blessing is a *kohen*, a descendant of high priests. He is followed by a Levite, a member of the tribe that supported Moses in Sinai. The preeminence accorded to these worshipers at the *bima* is a throwback to a vanished era. It is a gesture of nostalgia, a trifle disingenuous, if not hypocritical. Rabbinic Judaism surely has no intention—much less, desire—to reverse the victory it won two thousand years ago.

To suggest, as some Jews do, that such gestures keep memory alive until the Temple is again at Judaism's center defies historical reality. For all the talk, Halacha explicitly commands Jews to *do* nothing to hasten the return to the Temple Mount. Rabbinic Judaism holds that, without the Messiah's arrival to issue the command, no Jew has the authority to build a Third Temple. Rabbinic deference to the Temple's memory is, at best, an act of theological charity, conveyed without risk to the religious status quo.

II

ADJUSTING TO

EXILE

Chapter Four

THE HALACHA CONTRACT

FOR NEARLY TWO THOUSAND years, rabbinic Judaism has held that Jews must obey God's dictates as expressed in the canon of religious law, known as the Halacha. A vast and complex work, Halacha is the product of many sources, but the legitimacy of all of them is, at least in theory, traced ultimately to the Torah, the first five books of the Bible.

Rabbis traditionally regard the Torah, unlike wisdom generally, as the exclusive possession of the Jews. The word *Torah*, which means "guidance," is absent from the Bible, and appeared only in Talmudic times. More than half its text consists of laws for Jews to observe. The Torah's legal precepts take precedence over Prophets, the Bible's second section, whose emphasis is more on divine mandates in the realm of ethics and morality.

The Book of Exodus relates in detail God's imparting the law to Moses, particularly the Ten Commandments, the summary of His commands. Rabbinic tradition maintains that God dictated the entire Torah to Moses word for word, imbuing it with a pedigree of unparalleled holiness. Given this foundation, Orthodoxy regards Halacha, the Torah's direct product, as the essence of Judaism itself.

Very early in their history, however, the Israelites recognized problems with the Torah. Many of its precepts were simply statements of principle, frequently obscure and sometimes contradictory. Great gaps, moreover, existed in the laws of everyday life. Equally exasperating, many popular customs, which the Israelites treated as law, were not rooted in the Torah at all. From this they concluded that the Torah, however holy, could not, as a source of law, stand on its own.

The rabbinic solution was to complement the Torah with what was called Oral Law. The solution surely contradicted God's instructions: "All this word which I command you to do, you shall not add or diminish thereto." Rabbis decided, nonetheless, that Oral Law was necessary, and that its authority would be equal to that of the written word. This dualism became intrinsic to rabbinic doctrine. For several thousand years, Jews have said they are ruled by two Torahs, equally divine, one written, the other oral.

Given the dynamism of human life, however, a law code, even though divine, cannot be static. If the Torah is permanent, society is fluid. One Talmudic text states that God taught Moses the *principles* of Halacha, acknowledging that, as law, not even the Torah was adequate for all time. Oral law provided the mechanism for change. Though God's law was immutable, said a great Torah scholar, it was subject to a constant "process of renewal."

The sage Hillel recognized the role of Oral Law in an early expression of the Golden Rule. Challenged by a Gentile proselyte to summarize the Torah, he uttered a now famous reply, "That which is hateful to you, do not do unto your neighbor." But these words were only the start of the verse. Hillel's view of the Torah concluded: "All the rest is commentary. Now go and study." The commentary to which Hillel referred was obviously the Oral Law.

Hillel intended that the commentary, which a student could grasp only after exhaustive study, contained the Torah's *real* meaning. The law, far from being chiseled in stone, is the interaction between the Torah and the Jew. The Torah, Hillel was saying, is only the seed waiting to flower with the waters of commentary.

Orthodoxy repeatedly reminds us that the sages who produced this commentary were not on their own. "What a distinguished disciple will rule in the presence of his teacher," the Talmud says, "was already conveyed to Moses at Sinai." The great sage Maimonides, revered for his rationality, actually counted back forty generations to demonstrate that all commentary had been "handed down from person to person from the mouth of Moses, our teacher at Sinai." Every innovation, every interpretation, every insight, say the rabbis, has been foreordained by God.

Yet the Torah itself casts doubt on the notion that its words were directly imparted by God alone. Scholars point to the Book of Deuteronomy, which differs from the Torah's other books in that the text is in Moses' voice, not God's. Deuteronomy opens with, "These are the words which Moses spoke unto all Israel," which scholars take as evidence that it is Moses' personal recapitulation of his life.

A famous Talmudic anecdote makes a similar point. It imagines Moses transported in the second century to Rabbi Akiva's yeshiva where he witnesses a Halachic debate that, to his dismay, he cannot understand. As the debate unfolds, a disciple asks, "Whence did you derive this decision?" and Akiva replies solemnly, "It is a ruling handed down from Moses at Sinai." Moses is shocked by the assertion. The story, in questioning whether God is really behind all commentary, gently mocks rabbinic pretensions to speak in His name.

In still another Talmudic tale, a senior rabbi, failing to persuade younger colleagues on a Halachic matter, asks God to perform three miracles to support his credibility. God complies, but the colleagues are unmoved. The rabbi then asks God to speak audibly in his behalf, and the younger colleagues reject God's voice, explaining audaciously that the Torah is an earthly document, and "is not in heaven." At that point, the Talmud says, the Prophet Elijah solicits God's response. God, relates Elijah, "smiled and said, 'My children have overcome me.'"

The stories suggest that God, in the Talmud's view, supports a legal system that the sages may modify to keep up with social needs. But in our own time, with society changing in kaleidoscopic fashion, the Orthodox rabbinate has allowed the law to fall behind. Claiming their hands are tied, the rabbis characteristically ignore the early sages who declared the law must be constantly reformulated to serve its age.

Scholars point out that rabbis in the eighteenth century, when the

Enlightenment inundated Western society with liberal ideas, reacted—much as the Papacy did in the same period—by trying to freeze time. New secular values filled them with dread. Overlooking the law's organic character, Orthodoxy circled the wagons to keep these new values from penetrating the core of Jewish belief. It is clear that, in seeking to preserve the theological status quo, the rabbis also aimed to preserve their own traditional powers within the Jewish community.

ꕔ   ꕔ   ꕔ

RABBIS, OF COURSE, deny a hostility to change and even boast of their capacity to make Halachic adjustments to the shifting demands of modernity. To say the least, these adjustments have been modest in recent times. They may be best illustrated in Halachic modifications of the rules for observing the Sabbath, which Judaism regards as a joyous day, but whose limits many believers find burdensome.

The Torah sets some very specific rules for the Sabbath. Exodus declares:

> For six days you are to make all your work,
> But the seventh day is Sabbath for the Lord your God
> You are not to make any kind of work,
> Not you nor your son nor your daughter,
> Not your servant, nor your maid, nor your beast,
> Nor the sojourner that is within your gates

A century or so ago, rabbinic sages ruled that the activation of electrical devices fell under the ban on kindling fires on the Sabbath. Modern rabbis have shown great ingenuity in approving automatic switches and other mechanisms to circumvent the ban. Notwithstanding the Torah, modern rabbis also authorize the hiring of a Gentile—the so-called *Shabbos goy*—to perform chores that observant Jews regard as forbidden.

Rabbi Adin Steinsaltz, an Orthodox scholar who has won the Israel Prize for Jewish studies, raises another point. In *The Essential Talmud*, he cites the dilemma rabbis face in dealing with the biblical command, "No man shall go out of his place on the seventh day." The words seem to bar observant Jews not just from performing work or attending synagogue but from leaving their houses at all.

Some Jews throughout history have complied literally, Steinsaltz says, by staying indoors. But modern sages, claiming to understand God's intent, have addressed the limitation by liberalizing the meaning of "his place." They have, he points out, contrived curious models of boundaries in space, designed to give believers a sense of lawfulness as they leave home and move about the town.

Such contrivances, says Steinsaltz, characterize current Sabbath law, which has become "an almost Gothic structure made up of thousands upon thousands of tiny and meticulously fashioned details clustered around the original form." He writes with awe not so much of the result but of the craftiness required to achieve it.

Known for his erudition, Steinsaltz is celebrated for making the Torah accessible to lay readers. Some years ago, he provoked controversy within Orthodox circles by suggesting that Jewish law was not delivered in final form at Sinai but has evolved over time. An Ultra-Orthodox rabbi denounced him for contending that the law was the creation of man as well as God. Steinsaltz also upset the sages by arguing that historical, social and economic factors had always been involved in the lawmaking process.

Steinsaltz's work questioned whether Orthodoxy was more honest to Judaism by its complicity in rabbinic casuistry than were Jews who openly rejected traditional commands. Many rabbinic rulings, he argues, may end up being faithful to the Torah's words while clearly mocking its intent.

In the years after Israel's independence, Yeshayahu Leibowitz, a deeply observant Jew as well as a scientist and philosopher, created a stir by contending that Halacha had little relevance to a modern Jewish state. It was mute, he pointed out, on such matters as military security, police procedures, and transport and communications systems. Orthodoxy would be far stronger, he said, if its rabbis accepted Halacha as *personal* commandments, of no concern to the state. Unanimously, rabbinic Judaism rejected his ideas.

Indeed, Orthodox rabbis, rejecting change on a grand scale, as Leibowitz proposed, have been no better on small issues, like the burdens imposed by Jewish law on *agunot*, "chained wives." *Agunot* are women whose husbands are permitted by law to take new wives themselves, but refuse to grant them Halachic divorces, without which they cannot remarry or bear legitimate children.

Halachically, the source of the ruling lies in Deuteronomy, which holds that, should a man choose to divorce his wife, he "may write for her a document . . . [*get*], place it in her hand and send her away from his household." The wife has no comparable power. The verse, say the rabbis, makes divorce a private matter between spouses, over which they have no control.

The imbalance is a vestige of an era of Jewish polygamy, when the Torah permitted multiple marriages to men, while restricting women to a single spouse. In the Middle Ages, the rabbis found a way to abolish polygamy but left intact the requirement that women, to remarry, needed a *get*. Today, men often refuse to give their ex-wives a *get* out of malice, or hold it hostage to a favorable settlement on children or money. Israel compounds the problem by granting to the Ultra-Orthodox a monopoly over the law governing marriage and divorce, which bars any recourse to civil authority.

Over the centuries, Orthodox rabbis have acknowledged the pain the rule inflicts on women, and even the logic of reform. But they maintain that they are powerless to legislate any change in the process.

Rabbi Abraham Ravitz, Israel's most powerful Ultra-Orthodox politician, insisted in an interview with me that the *aguna* issue was a "bluff" by the enemies of religion. Halacha is extremely attentive to women's rights, he said, and, besides, "only a few dozen" Israeli women are affected by the rule. Rabbis have tried to mitigate the burdens on *agunot*, dating back to the close-knit communities of the Diaspora, when they could ostracize or excommunicate husbands who refused to grant a *get*. But many Israelis scoff at the claim that today's rabbis use their powers to ease the hardships of *agunot*, and even Ravitz acknowledged that no plans exist to change the rule.

On the contrary, Israel's attorney general said as recently as 2001 that the situation had grown steadily worse. Rabbinic courts routinely accept denials of a *get*, even if made to evade alimony or child support. Refusal of a *get* has made many children legally illegitimate, and though the chief rabbi has recommended that religious courts name lawyers to represent the children's interests, rabbinic judges generally ignore the recommendation.

Growing numbers of Orthodox women regard the rabbis' claim of powerlessness to change the rules as no more than a means to preserve male dominance. Rabbis who take pride in having produced the *Shabbos goy* to circumvent Sabbath rules, they say, can easily find ways to cure the affliction of "chained wives."

Alice Shalvi, a respected Orthodox woman, has led the fight in behalf of *agunot*, calling for women's rights within a Halachic context. A founder of the Israel Women's Network, she says proposals for resolving the *agunot* issue have been on the rabbinic agenda for centuries. In 1993, her organization brought a set of these proposals to Israel's highest rabbinic authority. Though these men acknowledged the Halachic validity of the proposals, she said, they insisted they could act only with the consent of "the great sages of our time." The answer, she said, was no more than a ploy to avoid considering the issue.

"The Torah bids us to do justice," Shalvi said in an interview with me. "The rabbis' role is to come up with solutions to present-day problems, not to erect obstacles. Jewish law has always moved forward. Judaism has always practiced Halachic renewal in light of changes in social norms."

Shortly after her rebuff, Shalvi abandoned Orthodoxy to join a Conservative synagogue. As personally observant as ever, she has since become rector of an institute of Jewish studies within the Jewish Theological Seminary in Jerusalem. The seminary is the educational hub of Conservative Judaism in Israel.

"When my 'conversion' to Conservative Judaism was reported," she said, "I received pained responses from Orthodox women. I told them I had reached the conclusion Orthodoxy and feminist goals are irreconcilable. I made the break because I felt personally marginalized and disregarded in Orthodox ritual. But more than that, I could no longer bear the refusal of the rabbinic establishment to come to grips with the women's issues.

"I suppose I should not be surprised. You raise young men in a yeshiva environment, where women have no entry. They are taught that women can't cope, that they are impure, that the sight of their hair is lewd. It's horrible. Recently there was a call by some Ultra-Orthodox men for separate buses, and I thought 'these men must feel so afraid of sexual attraction that they need to suppress everything.' Ultra-Orthodox misogyny is so deep-seated.

"The tragedy of the *agunot* meets only with lip-service. The rabbis are simply unaware that a major revolution in our time is the emancipation of women and their attainment of access to education, income-earning, social and professional status and political power. Frustration led me to a more humane religious movement, where rabbis have preserved the age-old tradition of reinterpreting Halacha in the light of changing social norms."

Shalvi said she now applauds the Jewish principle, presented in the Talmud, of *aseh lecha rav*, "choose a rabbi for yourself." The principle, she said, encourages a pluralism of religious beliefs and legitimizes a range of Halachic attitudes and judgments.

🔊   🔊   🔊

THE SAGES WHO EMBARKED on crafting a code of law had as a foundation the experiences of the Israelites from their earliest days. The Bible provides evidence that the tribes had sound rules for the administration of justice even before they had the Torah.

Moses, while leading the Israelites in the desert, said to his father-in-law Jethro, the Midianite, "When the people come to me to inquire of God, or when some legal matter comes to me, I judge between man and his fellow, and make known God's laws and His instructions." Jethro replied that Moses, as the Israelites' sole judge, was taking too great a burden upon himself, and advised that he delegate judicial responsibilities.

Jethro also cautioned Moses to exercise care in choosing judges. "You are to have the vision," he said, "to select from all the people men of caliber, holding God in awe, men of truth, hating gain." Moses acted on Jethro's advice, establishing a judicial hierarchy. He "chose men of caliber from all Israel," Exodus says. "He placed them as heads over the people, as chiefs of thousands, chiefs of hundreds, chiefs of fifties and chiefs of tens. They would judge the people at all times.

The difficult matters they would bring before Moses, but every small matter they would judge by themselves."

In Deuteronomy, Moses reports that he also received guidance from God, Who commanded him to instruct judicial candidates: "Hear out what is between your brothers, judge with equity between each man and his brother or a stranger. You are not to recognize a face in judgment, as the small so the great, you are to hear them out; you are not to be in fear of any man, for judgment—it is God's."

How such concepts came so early to the Israelites is unclear. But, barely out of bondage, according to the Bible, they already embraced the principles of judicial integrity and equality before the law.

After crossing into Canaan, the Israelites, abandoning their no-madic ways, moved beyond the simple law that had served them in the desert. At first, it appears, each tribe took responsibility for adminis-tering the Torah's codes. But the tribes also made new law dealing in commerce and agriculture, as well as in the relations with one an-other and with their neighbors.

After David became king, the system evolved further to address the needs of the newly founded monarchy. Solomon, his son, governing an empire, sought a legal structure of still greater sophistication. As for the lesser men who succeeded these titans, they no doubt manip-ulated the law in their endless struggles to retain their thrones.

By the time of the Maccabees, several centuries later, an actual lawmaking body called the Sanhedrin had emerged. Though its pre-cise functions are unknown, it had both priests and rabbis as mem-bers, and it may have served as both legislature and high court. Rabbinic sources credit it with enacting a range of ordinances that re-sponded to the needs of the tumultuous era of Roman occupation.

In the decades leading to the destruction of the Second Temple, the schools of Hillel and Shammai are most commonly associated with emerging Judaic jurisprudence. The Sanhedrin, it seems, consulted with both of them as independent authorities, especially on issues over which it was itself divided. Little is known about the substance of the issues, but the more liberal Hillel has gone down in history as the preeminent guide. Says the Talmud, "Both opinions are the words of the living God, but the law is like the School of Hillel." Hillel was believed readier than Shammai, for example, to admit converts to Judaism, to defend the rights of women and to be flexible in ritual practices. A later sage wrote in the Talmud that "a man who wishes to impose additional restrictions upon himself by adopting the stricter practices of Shammai's school . . . can be characterized by the biblical verse 'a fool walketh in darkness.'"

In the academy at Yavneh, after the destruction of the Temple, the first objective was to collect and organize the Oral Law, transmitted by word of mouth from teacher to disciple since at least the second century B.C.E. Its sheer mass was by then overwhelming, and the diversity of authorities created great confusion. Rabbi Akiva had urged his students to "sing it, constantly sing" to assist in memorization. He and his disciples also devised categories in which to simplify access. But the sages were reluctant to inscribe their work, fearful of insulting Yavneh by acknowledging the Oral Law as rival to the Torah.

Only at the end of the second century C.E. did necessity overcome the resistance to writing down the Oral Law. Rabbi Yehuda ha-Nasi, a descendant of Yavneh scholars and the era's most erudite sage, had persuaded the Romans to revoke their decrees against Torah study. It was ha-Nasi who led his rabbinic colleagues in putting their commentary down on paper, though it continued to be called Oral Law.

Many centuries later, Rabbi Solomon ben Isaac, an acclaimed scholar known to history as Rashi, described the deliberations over the Oral Law. He compared the debate to the sparks that fly when a hammer strikes a rock. Living in France, he had the benefit of some nine hundred years of hindsight to provide a narrative of how Yehuda ha-Nasi proceeded:

> He sent for and gathered together all the scholars of Israel. Until this time, the tractates [chapters] were not arranged in order; rather, each scholar who heard something from his superior repeated it saying, 'This particular ruling I heard from this teacher.' When all were gathered, each one said what he had heard, then they discussed the reasons for the different opinions and whose opinion should be followed. They arranged the tractates [by subject]. . . . Those opinions

that Rabbi Yehuda saw fit to accept were repeated without stating the name of the author, so that they would be established as the Halacha.

The book whose birth Rashi described was the Mishna, the first written complement to the Torah. "Posterity," wrote Rabbi Steinsaltz, the present-day Talmudist, "was [now] liberated from the burden of studying vast numbers of Halachot from hundreds of various sources in order to learn the Oral Law." Once the sages around Rabbi Yehuda ha-Nasi committed the text to paper, the Mishna became the basic manual for teaching the law both in Palestine and the exile communities.

The Mishna presented rulings and dissenting judgments, suggesting that not even Rabbi Yehuda regarded its contents as definitive. Though written in Hebrew, the text contains many words of Greek and Latin origin, a sign of the evolving nature of Jewish society. The absence of dogmatism also testified to a willingness by the sages to take account of change in establishing the law. The Mishna specifically says, in fact, that its role is to present only fundamentals, leaving to later generations of Halachic sages the duty to abandon obsolete opinions in favor of new ones.

ℭ   ℭ   ℭ

THE MISHNA WAS CLOSED in about 200 C.E. with a recognition that elaboration of the law was an ongoing duty. Two schools of scholarship—one in Babylonia, the other in Palestine—were ready to seize the judicial baton.

A Babylonian school had been working on the law since the exile of the sixth century B.C.E.; under the aegis of successive Persian dynasties, its members met in several academies, notably Sura and Pumbedita. The other school, still subject to Rome's hegemony over Palestine, gathered in academies in several small Galilean towns, particularly Tiberias. Both would remain at the task for hundreds more years, but in the early generations scholars of the two institutions would routinely journey back and forth to consult with one another. In time, however, their interaction declined and ultimately they labored separately to produce two different and, in some measure, rival works.

Jewish nomenclature, confusing even to specialists, has designated both works the Gemara, to distinguish them from the Mishna. Together the Mishna and the Gemara are commonly known as the Talmud, which means "teaching." But Jews distinguish between the Babylonian Talmud and the Jerusalem Talmud, though the latter was not written in Jerusalem at all, where Rome still ruled.

The era that produced the two Talmuds is often cited as the most creative in all of Jewish history. Of the two, the Babylonian Talmud is generally judged grander and more authoritative than its Jerusalem counterpart. But both were pure Diaspora documents, produced under Gentile rule. Under these circumstances, it is hard even to understand, much less to grant, Orthodoxy's claim that the Talmud has fixed Jewish law for all time. Neither book was directed at Jews living in their own state, since nowhere had the Jews a state of their own. The Jewish society they addressed was gathered exclusively in exile. The problems the two books treated were exile problems.

These circumstances raise the question of whether exile is the essence of rabbinic Judaism itself. Until Rome destroyed the Temple in 70 C.E., the rabbis, after all, were marginal figures. Scarcely recognized by the state, they deferred to the priesthood in the hierarchy of religious authority.

Had a Jewish state survived the Temple's destruction, it would certainly not have conferred on the rabbis the power they came to exercise. Taking David's monarchy as a precedent, such a state would probably have ruled by mixing religious and secular law. The rabbis might have played a small role. But the preeminence they exercised over the Jews living within Gentile cultures they awarded to themselves. The authority of the rabbis within Judaism derives purely from the conditions of the exile.

By itself, of course, exile did not impart authority. The Jews had no other leaders; still, the rabbis needed a force beyond themselves to make their word enforceable. By claiming divine authority, they compelled obedience. A present-day scholar calls it "the doctrine of rabbinic infallibility," but it was buttressed by consensus. The willingness of the Jews in exile to defer to the leadership of their rabbis gave rabbinic law its force.

Rabbinic authority was further enhanced by the tightly knit organization of Jewish life, in both East and West, within *kehillot*, autonomous Jewish communities. The scope of the Jews' self-governing powers varied according to place and time, but by definition it included jurisdiction over personal and intracommunal matters. The law that governed within the *kehillot* was the Halacha. It was the rabbis who administered it.

Jewish laymen rarely contested rabbinic power, except around the margins. From the second until the eighteenth century, the rabbis were undisputed masters of the *kehillot*, wherever their location. And so rabbis were the dominant authority in the Jewish world.

Westerners no doubt find it difficult today to conceive of a legal system that operates outside the bounds of state sovereignty. But before the rise of the modern nation-state, the organizing concept of most societies was corporatism, which granted wide legal powers to autonomous bodies within the borders of the state. Artisan guilds, merchant syndicates, municipalities and church associations were among these bodies. Almost invariably, so were Jews.

Without disputing the state's ultimate authority, Jews, wherever they went, conventionally negotiated for themselves some level of power over their own affairs. Like other corporations, they normally paid a tax for these privileges, an arrangement that was sometimes extortionate but often surprisingly equitable. It is not surprising that the Talmud said of Jews in ruling positions within the *kehillot*, "they take the place of the king."

The central attribute of the *kehillot*, though they were often disparaged as "ghettos," was the preservation of major communal decisions in Jewish hands. From the Jewish perspective, that was their purpose. Their affairs ruled by Halacha, the *kehillot* were the institutions that kept the Gentile intrusion upon Jewish life at a distance.

In the *kehillot*, the rabbis were the chief enforcers of the law. Rabbinic courts imposed fines, corporal punishment and sometimes *herem*, excommunication, as penalties. But more often the rabbis simply relied on social pressures to insure conformity. Ordinary Jews, deriving their identity from their *kehilla*, accepted its norms, including rabbinic authority, as a matter of course.

From London to Teheran and beyond, *kehillot,* with only minor variations, followed the same code of law, the Halacha. It was the bond between Jewish communities, the force that united the Jews as a people, wherever they might be and whatever the language they spoke. Though Halacha's authority is rooted in the peculiarities of the age of corporatism, its vision of keeping Jewish society within *kehilla* walls remains intrinsic to Orthodox thinking today.

நு நு நு

THOUGH THE TALMUD was unchallenged for centuries as the basis of Halacha, law students in our own day would not easily recognize it as a legal manual. The format followed in both Babylonia and Palestine would strike law students today as undisciplined, even formless. The Talmud is not so much a book of codes as of sources, containing raw material for making law out of conditions of daily life.

The Talmud, both Babylonian and Palestinian, reflects the habits, customs, beliefs and even superstitions of the Jews of its time. It is a trove of information on history, medicine, astronomy, commerce, agriculture, demonology and magic, botany, zoology and whatever else then passed for science. It contains biblical commentary, popular proverbs and fables, accounts of traditions and manners, narratives of folklore and moral maxims. It also discusses the ceremonial, civic and moral duties of Jews. It is down-to-earth and rarely indulges in theological speculation or philosophical abstraction. It is meant as a practical *guide* to Jewish conduct.

The Talmud's basic style is dialectic. Typically, a discussion starts with a lecture by a sage, delivered in a synagogue on the Sabbath. The issue is likely to be a subject touched upon by the Mishna. The audience poses questions, provides contradictory data or simply dissents.

Later, talk adjourns to a yeshiva, where the head—known as the *gaon,* an abbreviation of the Hebrew for "head of the academy that is the pride of Jacob"—presides over further exploration by peers and students. Speeches need not be germane, so the talk commonly rambles, richly or tediously, into unrelated matters.

The Talmud offers the minutes of these discussions, in all of their formlessness. It grants little deference to established authority, giving equal attention to a range of opinion on whatever is on its agenda. The Talmud, says a present-day writer, is a *mishmash* of centuries of wise and banal utterances that have dropped from the lips of believers, most notably rabbinic sages.

It is important to note that not all the participants were full-time sages. Steinsaltz describes the yeshiva as a social center funded by the *kehilla*. Its teachers—belying Orthodoxy's present-day claim that Torah scholars must study full-time—were mostly part-timers. Its resident sages were not independently wealthy, and often worked as clerks, blacksmiths, shoemakers, carpenters and tanners, as well as farmers, physicians and merchants. Most Talmudic discussions, in fact, were recorded during the months after the harvest, the slack season for farmers. Though all the participants, needless to say, were men, the arrangement assured that diverse interests would be represented in shaping the law.

The Babylonian Talmud was still developing about 400 C.E. when work on the Jerusalem Talmud came to an abrupt halt. The Jews in Palestine had again rebelled against Rome, which punished them by closing their religious institutions once more, making Talmudic debate impossible. In an effort to leave behind a usable document, the sages in Palestine edited their work hastily, transmitting unresolved points with imprecision, preserving errors. Their material overlapped much of the Babylonian work, but the overall intellectual level of the product was inferior. The Jerusalem Talmud remained the main source of law in Palestine until the Arab invasion in the seventh century. But history remembers it as a "stepbrother," to use Steinsaltz's term, to Babylonia's grander work.

Completed about 500 C.E., the Babylonian Talmud became Halacha's most authoritative source. It guided Jews not only in their prayers, their festivals, their Sabbath observance and their defense of ritual purity. It ranged across all of Jewish life, addressing civil and criminal matters, and the concerns of family and women. It also fixed the powers of a rabbinic elite that reigned uncontested, until the eighteenth century, when the Enlightenment began nibbling away at its authority.

The Talmud, in instructing Jews how to live on earth, is not a metaphysical work. It is all but silent on such soaring questions as man's relationship to God, the nature of the soul, the final judgment and the afterlife. As befitted a people living in exile, often in harsh or hostile conditions, its objective was to provide guidance for getting from one day to the next. The Jews never attained God's vision of a "nation of priests." Instead the Talmud shaped them into a people defined by codes designed to soften the edges of Diaspora life.

The Talmud's impact, to be sure, went beyond jurisprudence. The requirement that it be studied made Jews—or at least Jewish men— literate on a scale unique in its time. Its lessons, first taught in Babylonian schools, spread to the remotest settlements of Asia, Africa and Europe, where it became, along with the Torah, a manual of Jewish learning. It imparted to Jews everywhere, notwithstanding the vernacular each spoke, a language that linked them one to the other.

The great thinker Maimonides was unstinting in promoting Talmudic authority. He wrote:

> All Israel is obliged to follow the matters in the Babylonian Talmud. Every city and every province are to be coerced to follow all the customs which the sages of the Talmud followed and to obey their decisions and follow their enactments, since all the matters in the Talmud have been accepted by all Israel. Those sages . . . have, by tradition, heard the main principles of the Torah for generation after generation, reaching back to the generation of Moses, our teacher, on whom be peace.

In attributing all the Talmud's rulings to the Torah, Maimonides was repeating the rabbinic argument that the two were equally divine. If the one came from God, so did the other. The meaning of this contention is that behind the Halacha, the Talmud's chief product, stands God Himself.

ॐ   ॐ   ॐ

LOOKING BACK, IT IS CLEAR the laws of the Jews evolved steadily and without fanfare from the time of Moses. The process, out of necessity, accelerated after the Jews went into the exile. Maimonides' words reaffirm that the Talmudic sages had no compunctions either about enacting these changes or holding them to be ordained by God.

Some of these changes departed from explicit commands from the Torah. Exodus could hardly be clearer in stating, for example, "Make for Me an altar of earth and sacrifice on it your burnt offerings, and your sacrifices of well-being, your sheep and your oxen." Yet as we have seen, when the Temple fell, the rabbis deposed the priests and abandoned the practice of sacrifice with enthusiasm.

The rabbis also gave up the *lex talionis,* though God had said very explicitly: "When two men scuffle . . . if harm should occur, then you are to give life in place of life, eye in place of eye, a tooth in place of a tooth." Though the commandment had governed legal relations within Israel for centuries, Oral Law, despite God, swept it away.

If the suppression of animal sacrifice had political implications, amending the eye-for-an-eye command surely reflected a concern for justice. The Talmud records a lengthy debate after which the sages decided that "exact" retribution was impossible. So they simply asserted the power to grant a victim compensation in money rather than blood, even while denying abandonment of the old principle.

The sages were not casual about rewriting the Torah. But like jurists throughout history, they shaped their reasoning to accommodate the desired outcome. Depending on one's viewpoint, the outcome may be applauded or deplored, but there is no doubting the willingness of the Talmudic scholars to override the Torah itself to accommodate changes in the conditions or values of the society.

The Talmud explicitly recognizes the principle of rabbi-made law. Such law is designated *de-rabbanan,* and though it is lower in the legal hierarchy than Torah-based law, called *de-oraita,* both are considered valid. Predictably, sages responded to the distinction between them by debating to which category a given law belonged. With disarming honesty, the Talmud acknowledges that, in daily life, the sages "imparted to their own enactments the force of rules of the Torah." Their practice effectively abolished difference between the two categories.

But the sages also pronounced laws for which they claimed no Torah source at all. Often they imparted the force of law to existing custom, even when it contradicted Torah commands. Sometimes they relied, in place of the Torah, on other segments of the Bible—notably Prophets—which, under normal procedures, they would dismiss as irrelevant. Occasionally they reached conclusions on the basis of free-wheeling logic, or by reasoning logically from other judgments.

According to Steinsaltz, the kashrut, Jewish dietary bans, are derived solely from the sages' personal preferences. "They have no rational explanation," he writes, "nor did the sages try to supply one." Of the laws of purity, such as the duty of women to immerse themselves in a *mikva* after menstruation, he says, "this legislation . . . contains a plethora of detail that seems to have been determined at random with no clear rationale."

Steinsaltz goes further to say that the exclusion of women from important spheres of Jewish life has no Torah endorsement at all. Over the centuries, rabbis have argued that Halacha, respectful of women's burdens in keeping a home and raising children, serves to relieve them of onerous religious duties. This argument seems strained, Steinsaltz suggests, if not hypocritical. The result, deliberate or not, is "inevitably [to] preclude them from playing a part in Jewish cultural and religious life," assuring the preservation of male religious dominance.

Among the most famous Halachic rulings was the ban on polygamy imposed by Rabbi Gershom of Mainz, a medieval Ashkenazi sage. Polygamy, though sanctioned by the Torah, was, by the Middle Ages, practiced only by Jews living in Arab lands, and Rabbi Gershom decided to cleanse Judaism of it once and for all. It was not the first or last Halachic ruling made in emulation of Christian practices. In the same era, other Ashkenazi sages adopted the Christian custom of the lighting of a *yahrzeit* candle on the anniversary of a family member's death. Both monogamy and the lighting of candles now hold a place of honor among the practices of the Jews.

Ironically, some important Halachic decisions seem to be without explanation at all. One of them—the ruling on matrilineal descent—goes to the very heart of Jewish identity. Though rabbis acknowledge that it has no Torah endorsement, the Talmud says, "Thy son by an Israelite woman is called thy son, but thy son by a heathen woman is not called thy son." It means that Judaism recognizes only the child of a Jewish mother as a natural-born Jew.

The Talmudic statement actually overturned biblical practice in defining Jewish identity. Moses' wife Tsipporah, who was a Midianite, was accepted as an Israelite, as were his sons Gershom and Eliezer. Rabbis do not dispute this point, though they argue that the sons were born before Moses made the covenant with God. Nothing in the covenant with God, however, explains why the sages in the Mishnaic era narrowed the definition of who is a Jew.

If there is a scriptural basis to the change, it is said to derive from Ezra, a book of the Hagiographa, the final third of the Bible and the last section to be canonized. Talmudic sages did not normally recognize Ezra, or any other book in the Hagiographa, as a source of law.

Written about 400 B.C.E., the book describes Ezra as a priest who returns from Babylonia with the aim of restoring the holiness of the Jews. He not only bans Jewish men from intermarrying, but commands them to give up their non-Jewish wives. The book makes clear, however, that the order is his personally, not God's. The Talmud does not reveal the sages' reasoning in leaping from Ezra's stand on intermarriage to the formulation of the matrilineal rule.

The rule provoked a controversy after World War II, when Orthodox rabbis decided that thousands of Jews whom the Germans murdered for their Jewishness were in reality Gentiles. Orthodoxy, citing matrilineality, still denies the Jewishness of many Holocaust survivors and descendants of Holocaust victims. Using powers given them by the state, it even refuses burial in Jewish cemeteries to soldiers killed fighting for Israel if they are not matrilineal Jews.

In our own time, when intermarriage is widespread, the rule has profound implications for the future of Judaism. American Reform Jews, committed to preserving the Jewish community, have reopened the question and, drawing authority from the Torah and Talmud, have ruled that a child of either a Jewish mother or a Jewish father, raised as a Jew, is legitimately Jewish. The Conservative movement considered and rejected such a ruling. Orthodoxy, maintaining that patrilinealism is heresy, never considered a change at all.

Linked to the definition of who is Jewish is the dispute over the terms for conversion to Judaism. Orthodox rabbis in Israel insist that the state recognize the validity of only Orthodox conversions, a demand that Reform and Conservative Jews see as an avenue to their delegitimation. The dispute has provoked deep bitterness in all corners of the worldwide community of Jews.

Two distinguished Israeli professors, Zvi Zohar and Avi Sagi of Bar Ilan, Israel's only Orthodox university, have researched the history of Jewish conversion and concluded that Halacha traditionally required very simple acts: immersion in the presence of three witnesses plus, in the case of men, ritual circumcision. The Talmud made clear that converts had no further duty to pledge observance to religious law. Maimonides, Zohar and Sagi wrote, later reaffirmed these terms.

Only during the Enlightenment, when Orthodoxy closed its ranks against liberal ideas, were stricter procedures contemplated. Zohar and Sagi wrote that, faced even then with rising intermarriage, rabbis were divided along lines that can only be called political. Some were "adaptationists," who favored bringing newcomers into Judaism. The others they called the "rejectionists," who wanted to keep them out.

Zohar and Sagi summarized the contending positions like this:

> The adaptationists sought to respond to modernity through compromises designed to draw intermarried Jews into the circle of community life, sanctioned by Halacha. By doing so, they accepted non-religious Jews into the community. The price of such a move was the inability to realize the ideal nature of Jewish existence in the actual life of the community.
>
> It was precisely this price that the rejectionists were unwilling to pay. They saw no significance to the existence of a Jewish community which did not follow the Torah. . . . While the rejection of non-observant converts might lead to the alienation of their Jewish spouses from the community, such a price was well worth paying, as the predicament of Judaism in modern times called for emphasizing the gap between Jews faithful to the tradition and those who betray it.

Zohar and Sagi emphasized that what divided the adaptationists from the rejectionists was not Halacha, to which both could make equal claim. The adaptationists exalted the well-being of the community; the rejectionists opted for the integrity of piety. In the dispute two centuries ago, the rejectionists triumphed, just as within Orthodoxy today, on the issue of conversion the rejectionists rule.

The procedure for Orthodox conversion since the eighteenth century has required that the convert promise to follow Halacha in everyday life. The shift has changed conversion from admission into the *tribe* of Jews, the biblical notion, to the embrace of the Jewish *faith*, an emulation of Christian and Muslim ideology. The rejectionists, wrote Zohar and Sagi, have succeeded in redefining Jews as a religious sect, a radical change from the concept historically imbedded in Jewish law.

In today's battle, Orthodoxy contends that Halacha empowers its rabbis alone to conduct conversions. Moreover, it insists it has no power to liberalize the process. Halacha imparts to rabbis a wide latitude to reinterpret the law. An entry in the Talmud says, "The statements of later scholars carry primary authority because they knew the reasoning of earlier scholars as well as their own, and took it into account." These words are an invitation to amend the law, whether the objective is to provide justice to *agunot* or to make non-Jewish spouses welcome into the community of Jews.

There is no denying that, over the centuries of exile, rabbinic Judaism's laws rendered great service to the Jews. In adapting law to the conditions of Jewish life, the rabbis were the linchpin of Jewish survival. In our own day, they hold the same powers as their predecessors, and if they choose to use them only to preserve the status quo, the responsibility lies not with God or the Torah, much less with the Talmud or Halachic codes. The responsibility lies with them.

ぐ   ぐ   ぐ

BABYLONIA, IN THE TALMUDIC era, became, as Yavneh once was before it, the spiritual hub of Judaism. Jews everywhere acknowledged the last word on commentary to the great yeshivot of Sura and Pumbedita. As the Talmud spread around the Jewish world, the wisdom of the *geonim*, the heads of these yeshivot, enhanced the authority of the Halacha.

A ninth-century *gaon* of Sura told his disciples, however immodestly but not without a grain of truth:

> There are among you who dispute the decisions of the *geonim*, the pillars of the world, saying, "Whence do they derive these things?" . . . The wisdom and the dialectic of the *geonim* is the word which God commanded to Moses. Even though they say, "So it is," failing to cite evidence in any place, one must not doubt their word, whether it refers to great or small things. A man who dares dispute any decision of theirs is like unto one who rebels against God and the Torah.

The statement illustrates why Jews call the period of Babylonian dominance, from the sixth to the eleventh century, the *geonic* era.

Oddly, the Arab conquest of the region in the seventh century only enhanced Babylonia's influence. The Arabs, far from emulating Rome in oppressing the Jews, respected their scriptures and the wisdom of their sages. For the world's oldest monotheism and its youngest, this was a period of mutual enrichment.

As newcomers to monotheist ideas, the Arabs looked on the Talmudic academies with deference. Arab scholars in Baghdad almost certainly sought counsel from the Jewish sages in the nearby academies in creating the Shari'a, Islamic law. In turn, the Mu'tazilites, a school of Islamic rationalists exposed to Greek thought, enriched rabbinic thinking with liberal notions of scriptural interpretation and with speculations promoting the doctrine of free will. Babylonia's Jews, no doubt, shared in the glory of what was then the world's most accomplished civilization.

Islam's encounter with Judaism may also explain the rise during the *geonic* era of a Jewish fundamentalist sect called Karaites ("scripturalists"), who harked back to the Sadducees in rejecting Oral Law. The Karaites shared with most Muslims a conviction that intermediaries like rabbis should not stand between God and believers. In imposing strict religious observance, the Karaites argued for a literal reading of the Torah, thereby denying the foundation of rabbinic authority. Even today Karaism, a schism still claiming to be Jewish, casts a shadow on conventional rabbinic thought in repudiating Oral Law.

But if Karaism was an irritant, a real problem for the Talmudic sages was how to communicate the authority of the law they had created to the Jews who would use it. Indeed, it is fair to say that the problem was unprecedented. The most obvious obstacle was geographic, with Babylonia landlocked and very far from the Diaspora's major communities. But the problem of communication was not limited to distance.

The Talmud's style, based on the dialectics of scholars in the study hall, often left Jews in the dark on how to transform debate into law. There was a linguistic barrier as well; much of the Talmud was written in Aramaic, Babylonia's lingua franca, intelligible to only a fraction of Diaspora Jews. Still another difficulty arose from the sages' focus on agrarian matters, in an age when most Diaspora Jews, by necessity, were living in urban centers.

From both east and west, scholars, rabbinic students and even ordinary believers braved the perils of land and sea to reach Babylonia for Halachic instruction. On occasion, ambassadors from the *geonim* visited Diaspora cities. These travelers narrowed the gap in understanding, but they left countless questions unanswered.

A partial solution lay in the ebb and flow of letters between the Diaspora and the academies. Written queries—on dietary laws, family relations, festivals and prayers, criminal penalties—regularly reached Babylonia by mail. The sages dutifully replied to them, often peremptorily, in letters that said "forbidden" or "permitted." But short or long, the answers were considered binding on the recipient.

The exchange established a literary form known as *responsa*. It still exists as correspondence between Halachic scholars, but over time the letters also became a reservoir of information on both Talmudic thought and Jewish life generally. Of the thousands and thousands of letters written, many have been published and others await publication, but bundles of them still lie, unread for centuries, in synagogue archives and libraries. Whatever historical importance they might have, however, in their day they reinforced Babylonia's role as the supreme court of Jewish law.

But even the *responsa* were not enough to penetrate all the Talmud's obscurities. Rabbis whose chief duty was to serve their *kehillot* as judges in their courts felt a special need, especially in western Europe's growing communities. The best-trained rabbis acknowledged that they, on their own, could not translate Talmudic discourse into binding law.

As early as the eighth century, Babylonian scholars recognized the importance of organizing and refining the Talmud's random talk into statutes, then compiling the statutes into legal manuals. In later years, efforts to this end shifted from Babylonia to the Diaspora, and the first widely accepted compilation was published in the tenth century in Fez, Morocco.

By then, Babylonia's academies, shadowing the Arab empire's decline, had ceded institutional preeminence. Jewish life was gravitating westward, and communities in North Africa and Spain, based on what was to become the Sephardi tradition, were claiming independent powers. Meanwhile, in France, Germany, Italy and, later, Poland and Lithuania, dynamic Ashkenazi communities were placing an austere stamp of their own on the meaning of the law.

The rift between Sephardi and Ashkenazi cultures was hardly noticed at first. But when the Crusades imposed a halt on most east-west traffic, it became clear the Jewish world was separating into two. As each evolved, sages in both continued to issue Halachic rulings. The Babylonian Talmud remained their common denominator, enabling them, whatever their differences, to preserve the essentials of Halachic tradition. But by the eleventh century, the dispersion of authority had added another layer to the need for a comprehensive Talmudic code to which Jews everywhere could refer.

Maimonides, the master sage, undertook a work in the twelfth century "so that all the laws stand revealed to the great and small." He produced in Cairo the second classic of codification, the Mishna Torah, which became the standard reference of the age. Like the codifiers who preceded him, he gave a personal twist to his reading, while denying any contradiction whatever between his work and existing

Halacha. Students, however, have counted no fewer than 120 rules that he added, plus 50 in which he decided between conflicting lawmakers. Modest as his intent may have been, Maimonides imparted a new dimension to the Talmud's meaning.

Notwithstanding Maimonides' towering reputation, his work gave birth to challengers. Rabbis questioned not only his reading of the codes but the practice of codification itself. Among them was one Samuel Ben Ali, one of the last *geonim*, who denounced any tampering with Babylonia's work. Maimonides had little patience for such criticism.

In a reply to a student troubled by Ben Ali's criticism, Maimonides comments scathingly on the decadence into which, in his view, Babylonia had fallen.

> Why, my son, should you take offense that a man whom people accustom from his youth to believe that there is none like him in his generation; when age, high office, aristocratic descent, the lack of people of discernment in his city, and his relationship with individuals, all have combined to produce this deplorable consequence that each and every individual hangs on every word from the academy. . . . How, my son, could you imagine that he should love truth enough to acknowledge his weakness? . . . This is a thing that a man like him will never do, as it was not done by better men who preceded him.

Notwithstanding an undercurrent of rabbinic concern about codification, many more volumes poured forth. After Maimonides, none was so grand as the *Shulchan Aruch*, the "set table," written by Joseph Caro. A Sephardi scholar born in Spain, Caro began his work in Turkey and finished it—the Diaspora having come full circle—among the sages in Safed in the Holy Land. Both Talmudist and mystic, he superseded Maimonides' Mishna Torah with Halacha that took account of the Jews' recent experience as victims of Christian persecution and expulsions. Caro described his work as "a collection from the flowery crown of a large and thick tree."

Published in Venice in 1565, the *Shulchan Aruch* benefited from the newly invented printing press to spread across the Jewish world with unprecedented speed. Sephardi rabbis welcomed it at once. Amended by Polish rabbis to reflect certain Ashkenazi practices, it soon became the chief Halachic authority among Western Jews as well.

Scholars have called the *Shulchan Aruch* the last major work of the hugely creative era of rabbinic Judaism that began with Hillel, passed through Yavneh and Babylonia and ended in the yeshivot of eastern Europe. As a response to exile, rabbinic Judaism was surely the key to a triumph that, against all odds, preserved the cohesion of a disparate community scattered across the face of the globe. The creativity of rabbinic Judaism provided the means to maintain Jewish identity against the relentless pressures and temptations to assimilate into the Gentile world.

The era came to a close in the eighteenth century, when the Enlightenment abruptly transformed Jewish life. Not only did the Enlightenment introduce new ideas that tantalized all Europe, including its Jews. Equally important, it was accompanied by the rise of a more rigorous nationalism and a more centralized nation-state, the corollary of which was the erosion of the *kehillot*, along with the corporate concept itself that lay at the foundation of Jewish autonomy.

In the new nation-state, Jews became citizens, presumably no different from others. The laws that governed their lives were the same laws that the Gentiles were bound to observe. The powers that the *kehillot* had historically exercised to keep the Jews apart were abolished. In many of the new nation-states, the rabbis themselves were targeted, typically by being barred from applying the age-old penalty of excommunication.

The rabbis' foe was now not only Gentile encroachment; it was also the substantial body of Jews who, for the first time in seventeen hundred years, seriously challenged rabbinic Judaism's authority. As seen through the rabbinic prism, the Jews' newly acquired freedom endangered Judaism itself.

If the historic role of rabbinic Judaism had been to preside over the Halacha's observance, the new era imposed the responsibility to protect the Halachic system from destruction. Though the yeshivot in the

European nation-states still taught Torah and Talmud, their rabbis had to acknowledge that the Halacha no longer controlled Jewish life. New Judaic sects arose, promoting Enlightenment values. The traditional rabbinic role in interpreting the law gave way to a duty to keep the ancient scriptures at the center of Jewish life. Rabbinic Judaism, to distinguish itself from its rivals, took the name of Orthodoxy, and shifted into a defensive mode. It remains there to this day.

Chapter Five

MESSIANIC ILLUSIONS

BY THE SEVENTEENTH CENTURY, modern times had arrived in Europe, the lands where most Jews now lived. The Renaissance had sown the seeds of secularism and the Reformation had broken the power of the Catholic Church. Voyages of discovery to distant continents were accompanied by the decline of feudalism and the rise of capitalism. The centralized nation-state was spreading, population was soaring. The Ottomans at Europe's furthest frontier had ceased to be a threat. The Middle Ages were over.

The Jews might have been expected to applaud their departure. The Middle Ages, after all, had not been kind to them. Anti-Semitism, always hardier in the Christian West than in the Islamic East, had taken a leap forward during the Crusades and showed relentless dynamism. In the ensuing centuries, Christians directed hatred and abuse at the Jews with unprecedented ferocity.

Throughout Europe, Jews were routinely murdered, vilified, forcibly converted, expelled from their homes. Their freedoms were increasingly restricted by decrees. Their Torahs and their Talmuds were burned in pyres. Long past, moreover, was the Second Temple era's fiery defiance of Gentile rule. The Jews' strategy for survival was a kind of tenacious passivity. Under the wing of their rabbis, they prayed that, by keeping a low profile, the Christians would somehow overlook them.

For more than a thousand years, the Jewish communities of the Diaspora had changed very little. Jews remained faithful to their rabbis and their books, to small commerce and crafts, to a communal life guided by rigid tradition. Sealed off in their *kehillot,* Jews had been unengaged—except as victims—by the issues that preoccupied the outside world. They accepted, without protest, the constraints that Christian rulers imposed on them. If they nurtured dreams of rebellion, they kept them well concealed.

As the seventeenth century opened, the Jews had no way of knowing whether the world that was emerging would be more, or less, benevolent than the one being left behind. New ideas intruded more on Jewish life and were more difficult than earlier innovations to ignore. The rabbis saw no good coming in them and reacted coldly. Not surprisingly, the rabbis reasoned that the Jews' safest course was to remain steadfast to their established way of life.

But many believers were tantalized by the messages they were hearing. These messages were not the familiar anti-Semitism. They seemed, in fact, to be its opposite. The Jewish reaction expressed not so much contempt for old practices as a loss of confidence in them. Jewish disputatiousness, long dormant, seemed reborn in popular reexamination of Judaism's meaning, as a series of great waves battered traditional rabbinic preeminence.

The first wave was stirred up by a messianic pretender named Shabbatai Zevi, who immersed Jews in a challenge to rabbinic conventions. It was followed by the rebellion of Hasidism against what many regarded as rabbinic Judaism's legalistic rigidity. Then came the uprising of the Reform movement against the rabbis' unwillingness to consider any accommodation to modern values at all.

Of the three, it is difficult to gauge the lasting impact of Shabbateanism. But the other two, Hasidism and Reform, have since imposed major changes on both the practice of Judaism and the structure of the Jewish world. They split a once cohesive worldwide community and placed the rabbinate on the defensive as it had never been before. Together, they gave Judaism a new face.

Yet the old ways survived. In our own time, in fact, rabbinic Judaism—now called Orthodoxy—seems renewed. It even bids to regain terrain that, in the turbulence of these earlier centuries, it had been forced despite fierce resistance to cede.

ᔕ   ᔕ   ᔕ

AT THE JUNCTURE of the medieval and modern eras, the Jews of Poland were enjoying a golden age. Along with adjacent Lithuania, Poland was home to nearly a million Jews, who tilled the land or worked as village craftsmen or scrambled for wealth in urban commerce. Jews enjoyed a flourishing social, cultural and religious life, conducted in Yiddish, their own tongue. Their *kehillot*, linked in federations, extended Jewish autonomy to a regional level. Their famous yeshivot carried the influence of Polish rabbis to the remote corners of the Jewish world.

Barely visible were the weak spots in the picture. Poland, overwhelmingly Catholic, had recently annexed neighboring Ukraine, an Eastern Orthodox society. Poland's nobility, to exploit the conquest, recruited Jews to be its agents in the Ukrainian countryside. Together, Catholics and Jews ran a feudal system that imposed on Eastern Orthodoxy a serfdom based on exorbitant rents and taxes. The situation was waiting to explode.

The explosion came in 1648, under the banner of Bogdan Chmielnicki, the leader of a band of Cossack irregulars. Ukraine's peasantry, whatever its anger at its Polish landlords, was whipped by Chmielnicki into a frenzy against the Jews. Anti-Semitism joined class conflict, leading to Chmielnicki's savage butchering of some one hundred thousand Jews during a campaign that extended into 1649. Many of those spared were forcibly converted to Christianity.

Five years later, Russian Cossacks invaded Poland, unleashing a new wave of anti-Semitic mayhem. A Jewish scholar of the time compared the devastation to that of the ancient Temples: "The Third destruction was just the same as the First and Second destruction." At the Poles' behest, Jews later gravitated back to the sites of the bloodshed, but the golden age was over. Entering the eighteenth century, Jewish society in Poland was tense and fearful.

The Jews' feelings of insecurity invited resurgent messianic feelings, never far from the surface in troubled times. The conception had changed since Bar-Kokhba's era: Rabbis no longer expected the Messiah to perform military feats, like liberating Jewry from heathen rule. Their focus, influenced by contemporaneous Christian thinking, was more mystical, envisaging a day when they would pass from a painful life on earth to a world free of suffering and sin. Rabbis prayed that the Messiah would lead them to redemption, restoring them to their homeland and their ancient intimacy with God.

The Jewish roots of this revised messianism lay largely in Kabbalah, the mystical tradition within Judaic thought. Kabbalah had been rising in popularity since the Jews' expulsion from Spain in 1492, when sages began gathering in Safed, a mountain town in the Holy Land. There they cultivated a belief that the Messiah's arrival was imminent.

Rabbinic Judaism had held historically that Halacha and Kabbalah were irreconcilable poles, and as the Middle Ages ended, the faith seemed torn between rationalism and mysticism, law and ritual. But the Safed rabbis narrowed the gap, offering a Kabbalah that fused genuine spirituality with Halachic legalism. Joseph Caro, author of the *Shulchan Aruch,* was among those who held that Jews, while true to Halacha, could also establish a mystical attachment to God. Many Western rabbis absorbed the lesson into their Halachic worldview. After Chmielnicki, the masses, comforted by the promise that redemption was near, were also ready to absorb this lesson.

Shabbatai Zevi, born in 1626 in the Ottoman town of Smyrna, was deeply mystical by personal disposition. Modern scholars believe he may also have been a manic-depressive. As a student of both Talmud and Kabbalah, he drew dedicated followers through his spirituality and asceticism. Aroused by the Chmielnicki massacres, Zevi made a decision to embark on the salvation of his people.

When he was only twenty-two, Zevi began calling himself the Messiah. In the face of early indifference, he made a journey through the eastern Mediterranean to confer with other Kabbalists. In Gaza, he met a brilliant young mystic named Nathan who apparently provided comfort to his troubled psyche. Proponent of ideas that were unconventional even for Kabbalists, Nathan became Zevi's gray eminence and the chief supporter of his messianic pretensions.

In 1665, in a period of high personal rapture, Zevi revived his messianic declaration, and much of the Jewish world seriously embraced his claim. In Palestine, where he first spoke out, adoring crowds composed largely of the poor surrounded him wherever he went. From there, excitement spread rapidly through the Diaspora. Relying on Nathan's calendric calculations, Zevi promised the Jews redemption within a year.

Zevi's assertions split the rabbinate. Rabbis steeped in the Kabbalah, most of them in the East, tended to embrace him. Among the Ashkenazim, whose Talmudic loyalties were less flexible, rabbis tended to skepticism, and many denounced him for undermining traditional belief. In Germany, a rabbi charged Zevi with a Christian heresy for placing faith above law. But rabbinic opposition was unable to halt the swell of popular emotion, even in the West.

The wave of enthusiasm was fed by Nathan's wondrous dispatches, the contents of which somehow penetrated to every corner of the Jewish world. From Yemen and Kurdistan to Amsterdam and Vilna, Jews alternated fasts and acts of repentance with explosions of ecstasy. They wrote and circulated poems of allegiance. Jewish merchants closed their shops and craftsmen sold their tools to prepare for the return to the Holy Land. By early 1666, apex of the Shabbatean wave, rich Jews and poor, in every country, seemed poised for Zevi to deliver on his promise.

The Gentile world, both Christian and Muslim, did not know what to make of the phenomenon. Poland's king called for a halt to demonstrations, but the crowds only grew. Finally, Ottoman authorities arrested Zevi, but from prison he issued pronouncements signed "the firstborn son of God," which accelerated the spread of the delirium.

Zevi's downfall may have begun with rabbis in Poland who, in their alarm, sent an emissary asking the Turks to bring him under control. Accounts say that by then he had fallen into a deep depression. Taken from the luxury of the Ottoman prison, Zevi was brought to trial before the sultan's court, which sentenced him to a choice between apostasy and death. Barely a year after the Shabbatean rocket ignited, it fizzled in Zevi's conversion to Islam.

The Ottomans, in return for his conversion, granted Zevi a pension and set him free. Living in Turkey, he apparently alternated for a decade between mania and depression. He received visits from Nathan and other apostles, and formed links with Muslim mystics. Finally, in 1672, the Turks deported him to Albania, where soon thereafter he died, denying to the end that he had betrayed his people.

The Jewish world, having hailed Zevi's claims of innocence, reacted to his apostasy with disbelief. Most Jews, gradually, took the position that they had been defrauded by an imposter. Embarrassed rabbis sought to restore the old order, burning the records of their naïveté.

Yet some of Zevi's faithful embraced the myth promoted by Nathan of a conversion so mysterious that its meaning eluded even Kabbalists. Denying heresy, Shabbateanism endured for another century, anomalously more tenacious in Poland and Lithuania than in the East. Many Kabbalists remained loyal to Nathan's theology and for years continued to defend Zevi's messianic claim.

Haim H. Ben-Sasson, a prominent Hebrew University historian, holds that Shabbateanism's collapse led the Jews to abandon their medieval mentality, in which mysticism flourished, to open the door to secularism. He points out that the Enlightenment successfully promoted reason over faith, and Jews did not escape its lure. Western Europe had embarked on a course that was hostile to all religion. Yet the record does not support his theory that the Jews, at that point, were ready to board the secular bandwagon.

A more powerful challenge to rabbinic Judaism came from Hasidism, which was not secular at all. Like Shabbateanism, it drew its inspiration from Kabbalah and its dynamism from a leader who, though not messianic, was deeply charismatic. Hasidism's home ground was eastern Europe, where Chmielnicki had recently roamed. A century would pass after Shabbateanism's collapse before secularism established a major beachhead in the Jewish world. Even today, in fact, Hasidism thrives and secularism's triumph among the Jews is far from complete.

In time, Hasidism and conventional rabbinic Judaism would agree that secularism was more threatening to both than either was to the other. In Israel today, the two old rivals—together called Haredim, Ultra-Orthodox Jews—continue to reject all Enlightenment values. But before reaching that decision, they would engage in decades of rancorous, often violent conflict, enfeebling rabbinic Judaism just as secularized, non-Orthodox Judaism was stepping up to claim a rightful place within the Jewish community.

꣼   ꣼   ꣼

HASIDISM MADE ITS appearance in Poland in the mid-eighteenth century, when the Jewish world, its golden age a faded dream, was disintegrating. Nationalism was rising throughout Europe. Monarchies, Poland's included, were moving toward the centralization of power. Poland's *kehillot,* once the strongest in Europe, were steadily being stripped of their powers. Some even faced financial bankruptcy.

The problem, at least in part, stemmed from bands of marauders called Haidamaks, Chmielnicki's heirs, who pillaged Jewish villages with little interference from the state. The *kehillot,* to erect defenses, borrowed from the Polish nobility and even from the church, raising taxes to unprecedented levels. The inequities strained the political fabric, inviting bribery, even in the appointment of rabbis. The privileges seized by the rich induced the working classes to turn away from traditional communal institutions.

Hasidism—its name comes from a biblical word for "the pious"—emerged amid the insecurities of this class conflict. Contemporary documents attribute the fraying of communal bonds to "causeless hatred," the term applied to the strife among Jews on the eve of the Second Temple's destruction. Though scholars note that Hasidism was born in this disordered framework, they do not agree on why.

It may be coincidence that Jacob Frank, a vestigial Shabbatean, was rallying a following in Poland at the time that Hasidism took its first steps. Deeply heretical, Frank promoted a bizarre doctrine of redemption by impurity, which included sexual license. Excommunicated by the rabbis, his band ended up as converts to Christianity.

Hasidism, whatever it holds in common with Frank's doctrines, angrily denies that it borrowed from them. It equally rejects the theory that it took ideas from a range of mystical Christian sects flourishing in the region at the time. Hasidism brought to Judaism not heresy but lusty physical expression in collective ritual. Only by chance, it maintained, did it also share with Shabbateans and deviant Christians a disdain for the fine points of religious law.

Hasidism had Kabbalah, with its emphasis on a worshiper's inner life, at its core. Kabbalah's influence shifted Hasidism away from rabbinic Judaism's dry legalisms to the attainment of bliss by personal communion with God. Hasidism disavowed the view adopted by Poland's traditional rabbis that the sins of the Jews were to blame for the Chmielnicki massacres. It rejected asceticism, which many Jews had embraced as an expression of repentance for these sins. Hasidism, arriving in troubled times, urged Jews to be pious by adopting a cheerful attitude toward life.

Hasidism's seminal figure, born in 1700, was Israel ben Eliezer, affectionately known as the Besht, an acronym for the title "Baal Shem Tov." The term, which translates as Master of the Divine Name, was popularly applied to pious Jews who distributed amulets and worked with magic to combat disease and evil spirits. The Besht, an itinerant folk healer without formal schooling, was one of them.

Because the Besht left behind little writing, his precise views are unclear. What is known about him derives chiefly from his oral teachings, published some twenty years after his death in 1760. To them were added reminiscences about him, published in 1814. Yet scarce as the sources are, the Besht's impact on Judaism has endured.

The Besht was from a poor family in a small Polish town. Left an orphan in childhood, he was employed at menial jobs until his twenties, when he embarked on Kabbalistic meditations in the Carpathian forests, where he had gone to live with his wife. At the age of thirty, he had a revelation and moved to Miedzyboz, a town where he became famous for curing illness by expelling demons from people's souls. The reputation opened doors for him to become a wandering preacher, and within a decade he had attracted many followers. Most were poor, working-class Jews, but a few were esteemed rabbis, and some were Shabbateans or ex-Shabbateans.

The Besht taught that God pervades every aspect of life, and that devotion to Him is a permanent source of joy. He declared prayer a means of making an ecstatic link with God. "Our father in heaven hates sadness and rejoices when His children are joyful," he often said. He urged Jews to cling to God not just in worship but in business and social affairs. God's presence, he said, makes physical pleasures no less a divine blessing than spiritual experiences.

In describing the Besht's mystical appeal, a disciple wrote that he took his text from the angels and taught "the language of the birds and the trees and the holy names and formulas for uniting the holy spheres." The Besht was scornful of rabbis who would not surrender their fondness for asceticism. He denounced those who were disposed to fire and brimstone and who preached grim Halachic warnings. "You think somehow that you must mortify yourself, which upsets me greatly," he once said. "Such deeds are born of a bitter darkness and lead to melancholy. God's divine presence dwells . . . rather in the joy of holy purpose."

Though he revered the Torah, the Besht departed from the conventions of rabbinic Judaism in not regarding its study as the Jew's central duty. "Warm thyself by the fires of the wise, but beware of their glowing coals," his disciples said, conveying his skepticism of rabbinic authority. Under the Besht's guidance, Hasidism became rich in stories and parables, often quite profane, which served to complement, if not supersede, the Torah in expressing principles of moral behavior.

Though the Besht shared popular messianic yearnings, he warned his followers that the Messiah would not be coming along soon. As did Christianity, he emphasized the duty of the faith to save individual souls by establishing direct links to God. In the last decade or so of his life, groups of his disciples set up congregations throughout Poland. Renouncing the austere messianism of rabbinic Judaism, they separated themselves from other Jews, bringing ecstatic shouting and waving to their worship, and even to their way of life.

These Hasidim built substantial numbers of small, simple houses of prayer, called a *shtibl*. Tables and benches, fit for communal meals, often replaced pews. Inside, the ritual practiced was informal and emotional. An opponent of Hasidism left a graphic description of the worshipers:

> Some of them are ignorant of any knowledge . . . , having studied neither the Kabbalah nor the Gemara nor the Halacha, intellectually barren and wailing aloud, prancing upon the hilltops. And in prayer they sing out loud and change voice over and over. Their behavior is strange: they dress in white . . . and they make their hands go to and fro and they sway like the trees of the forest. . . . And though they have not studied or read books, still they consider themselves wise and call their leaders "rabbi." Among them, the more of these swayings and other gestures the better, and those who perform these are glorified by their women and children, and wax great in the eyes of those who know nothing . . . This ignorant audience will praise these people to their face, saying "O pious one, O humble one."

Among ordinary Jews, such practices struck at the heart of traditional belief. The threat was most severely felt by the middle classes, whose idea of Judaism was a handsome synagogue, formal liturgy and strict religious decorum.

ᔕ ᔕ ᔕ

HASIDISM DISTURBED the rabbinic establishment not only by its religious practices but by its concept of leadership. The Besht's disciples were not alone in complaining that rabbinic Judaism had become autocratic and aloof, dedicated more to texts than to people. As functionaries of the *kehillot,* many were also beholden to the moneyed elites. The Besht called openly upon rabbis to shift their concern from scholarship and politics to everyday human affairs.

Drawing from Kabbalah, Hasidism dwelt on the sanctity of bonds between leaders and followers. These bonds implied a rabbi's responsibility for the welfare of his congregants. They also placed the mysteries of God's universe on a higher religious plane than the niceties of Halachic law.

To promote its religious vision, Hasidism called its leaders *zaddik,* a "completely righteous man," the term dating back to biblical times. Some scholars hold that the early zaddikim tapped into the messianic fervor left over by Shabbateanism. The zaddik's role, in sharp contrast to the rabbi's, was to serve believers as a personal redeemer, much like a priest of the church. His responsibility was to devote his spiritual gifts to helping Jews attain salvation through personal communion with God.

Hasidim were taught to cling to their zaddik, whose jurisdiction included their personal as well as their religious life and, in fact, made little distinction between them. The zaddik offered guidance on family and financial affairs, and provided counsel on psychic discomfort. If the coals of religious belief cooled, he fanned them. He allowed no secrets, furthermore, not even of the bedroom, which made him an overarching presence in his followers' lives.

These powers made the zaddik the hub of a circle of psychological dependency. His followers viewed him as seer and saint whose every act was imbued with religious lessons. "I did not go to the [zaddik] to learn Torah from him but to watch him tie his bootlaces," is a saying that embodies the Hasid's reverence for even the banalities of their leader's experience.

The zaddik's role constituted a rebuke to rabbis whose conception of duty was limited to mastery of the scriptures. In an age when most rabbis earned their own living, the zaddik was supported by payments made by the community. Hasidic lore regards these payments as gifts of love, uniting the zaddik with his followers. Hasidim called him *rebbe*, an affectionate Yiddish term, that they use to express deference.

Not surprisingly, their powers tempted many zaddikim into authoritarian excess. Carried away by his awesome powers, one claimed to be "master over all the decrees issued by God, [with] the power to avert all the dangers which threatened Israel." A zaddik could shape his doctrines as he saw fit and command his following according to personal whim. As Hasidism's rich literature confirms, the zaddik came in many styles: humble, comic, tolerant, wise, sybaritic. The anti-Hasidic literature that shadowed the movement talked early of the system's cult-like character and the "degeneration" of the zaddik's office.

In the democratic societies where Hasidic communities later settled, the zaddik could also be counted on to deliver the votes of his entire following to the candidate of his choice. This power has routinely
been exercised in return for some financial or political consideration.
Where it has been used, in Israel and America, it has distorted the
electoral process and added inordinate public influence to the private
authority the zaddik already possessed.

Whatever the Besht's intentions, the zaddik's office also became
hereditary. Scholars note a long-standing fascination among eastern
European Jews with genealogy. Like the priestly class in biblical
times, rabbinic families cultivated their pedigree, safeguarding it by
arranged marriages. Though traditional rabbis disapproved of the
practice, stressing the primacy of personal credentials, Hasidim
claimed that only by having the office pass from father to son could
the zaddik's sanctity be preserved.

In *The Wandering Jews*, the novelist Joseph Roth describes something of the role the zaddik played a century or so ago in eastern Europe:

> Each *zaddik* is reckoned by his supporters to be the greatest.
> The calling has been handed down from father to son for
> generations. Each one holds court and each one has his
> bodyguards of Hasidim, who come and go in his house, fast
> and pray, and take their meals with him. He has the power
> of blessing, and his blessing is efficacious. He can curse too
> and his curse will blight an entire family. Woe betide the
> skeptic who talks dismissively about him . . .
>
> Day after day, people come to him with a dear friend who
> has fallen ill or a mother who is dying, who are threatened
> with imprisonments or wanted by the authorities, whose
> son has been called up so that he may drill on behalf or die
> on behalf of strangers in their senseless wars. Or by those
> whose wives are barren and who want a son. Or by people
> who are faced with a great decision and are uncertain what
> to do.

> The *rebbe* helps and intercedes not only between man
> and God but between man and his fellow man, which is
> harder. . . . Whoever comes to him is assured of getting his
> help.

The institution of the zaddik produced powerful leaders and enduring dynasties. The zaddik in time came to define Hasidism, especially
after the seminal doctrine faded. His authority distinguished Hasidism from all other forms of Jewish worship. Though Hasidism has
long since been incorporated as a branch into rabbinic Judaism, the
zaddik continues to play that unique role today.

During the decades that Hasidism remained a small movement
confined to Poland's remote provinces, the rabbinic establishment's
opposition was sporadic. But after the Besht's death, Hasidism's
spread set off rabbinic alarms.

Taking the offensive, rabbinic Judaism charged Hasidism with
being a Shabbatean heresy. But beneath this accusation lay the
sharper edges of class conflict, which became increasingly apparent
as Hasidic majorities took control of several straitened *kehillot*. In el-
bowing middle-class leaders aside, Hasidism humiliated conventional
rabbis by placing them into the zaddik's employ.

Actual fighting burst into the open when Hasidism, about 1770, established a beachhead in Vilna, then the most sophisticated city in
eastern Europe's Jewish world. Suddenly, the traditional rabbinic elite
saw its empire in jeopardy.

Elijah ben Solomon Zalman, at that point, took charge of the anti-
Hasidic movement. Zalman was known as the Vilna Gaon, the title
given to the great leaders of the Babylonian academies. For more than
a century, Vilna had been home to a prosperous and cultured Jewish
community. It was also a hub of rabbinic learning, of which the Gaon
was the preeminent sage. He was a man of such huge erudition that
Vilna's *kehilla* paid him to study full-time. With the battle joined,
Vilna's Hasidim tried, unsuccessfully, to have his stipend revoked.

No ordinary rabbi, the Gaon recognized that Halacha alone did not
satisfy Judaism's potential. Learned in both Torah and Kabbalah, he

was among those who worked to reconcile the two. He also studied modern science and mathematics, and wrote, "A man without knowledge of the secular sciences will lack one-hundred fold in the wisdom of the Torah." He even argued in favor of biblical instruction for girls.

But the Gaon's tolerance had limits. In contrast to Maimonides, he rejected studies in philosophy, which he disqualified for its secular roots. He had even less use for the Enlightenment's advocacy of rationalism, which was just then reaching Vilna from the West. As for Hasidim, he said, "Their insides are full of heresy absorbed from the Shabbetean sect," and he called their dedication to their zaddikim "pure idolatry." Judaism's well-being, the Gaon believed, required that Hasidism be crushed.

The Vilna Gaon was among the first to warn against the dangers that modern ideas held for the traditional faith. He saw correctly that the Enlightenment from one flank and Hasidism from the other were undermining rabbinic Judaism's claims to speak for all Jews. The Gaon made an appeal to the constituency of traditional Jews to rise to rabbinic Judaism's defense.

The Gaon and an elect circle of his pupils became the spearhead of the Mitnaggedim, a word that translates as "opponents." In time, the term came to mean a formal, nonmystical, Halacha-oriented Judaism quite at odds with the early spirit of Hasidism. But in the Gaon's era, the Mitnaggedim were simply Hasidism's sworn foes, fierce partisans of rabbinic Judaism, guardians of the status quo.

Under the Gaon's direction, Vilna became Mitnaggedism's home base. His acolytes sent letters to *kehillot* throughout the region, urging them to suppress the heresy. The Vilna *kehilla*, the Gaon's benefactor, closed Hasidic prayer rooms, excommunicated Hasidim and burned Hasidic works, including those of the Besht himself. Hasidim were kept from burying their dead in cemeteries that Mitnaggedim controlled.

Mitnaggedic tactics also broke fresh ground in intracommunal fighting. Mitnaggedim denounced Hasidim to the local police, a violation of the ancient taboo against bringing Jewish differences before Gentile powers. The taboo was deeply rooted in the rabbis' historic determination to preserve Jewish autonomy in the world of exile. Ha-

lachic codes reinforced this taboo. Yet so great was their ire that Mitnaggedim defied it, and they succeeded in persuading the Gentiles to
imprison at least a few of their rivals.

Mitnaggedim, at least once, publicly flogged a Hasid in a *shtibl*
courtyard. In their campaign of denunciation, they produced a huge
number of tracts that laid out their grievances, though their words
only proved that they were better educated and thus more articulate
than their foes. Indeed, the charges they left on the record were so
lacking in real gravity that within decades, the Mitnaggedim had
abandoned the quarrel.

Whatever the class basis of the dispute, the Mitnaggedim believed
the Hasidim were most vulnerable in the realm of religious practice.
To be sure, the rabbinic establishment was sincere in fearing the collapse of a structure that had sustained the Jews in exile for nearly two
millennia. Directly at stake was the synagogue, the structure's central
institution; its control was the chief source of status in the Jewish
community. But it seemed more promising to Mitnaggedim to rally
support by attacking Hasidic rituals.

Mitnaggedim charged that Hasidim had abandoned the Ashkenazic
rite that had long united Jews in the West in behalf of the Lurianic
rite, named for a Kabbalist in Safed. They denounced Hasidic disrespect for traditional liturgy, style of prayer, hours of worship. They
found fault with Hasidism's indifference to a synagogue schedule, insisting that prayer hours were set by Halacha. One rabbi grumbled
that Hasidim "have almost forgotten the time for the afternoon
prayers, which was determined by the rabbis of blessed memory." Another complained that delays were the product of the Hasidic pen-
chant for "stories and gossip and obscenities among themselves
before prayer." A third called the absence of punctuality a "stratagem
of evil inclination," risking "the destruction of the entire Torah."

Mitnaggedic tracts dwelt most heavily, however, on the emotion
and physicality that Hasidim brought into the synagogue, the antithe-
sis of the tightly controlled decorum that rabbinic Judaism revered.
Vilna Mitnaggedim called Hasidim "a topsy-turvy generation who do
somersaults before the ark of God's covenant . . . their heads are
downward and their feet are in the air." They sneered at the Hasidic

concept of a mystical bonding with God and insisted that the Hasidic style of prayer was heresy.

Mitnaggedim went even further to denounce, for example, "changes in ritual slaughter, using honed knives," a practice that gave them reason to reject Hasidic meat as nonkosher. One tract also excoriated "neglect of Torah study and disrespect for Torah scholars. Bizarre actions. Suspicion of Shabbeteanism. Much merrymaking and partying. Greediness of *zaddakim,* causing waste of Jewish money. Miracle-working by *zaddakim.* . . . Change of dress, a great deal of pipe smoking, etc."

Hasidim, of course, had answers to these charges. They defended having their own places of prayer, saying, "It is better to pray with few men where the spirit of friendship rests among them than to pray in a large congregation with people whose hearts are elsewhere." They insisted that the Lurianic rite was faithful to ancient tradition, explaining that when the Israelites lived in the Holy Land, each of the twelve tribes prayed in its own fashion at its own gate of the Temple. Hasidim described the Lurianic rite as a composite of the prayers recited by each of the tribes.

In fixing their own hours of prayer, they maintained that their objective was to establish a proper attitude, a product of extended meditation. They needed to synchronize their thoughts with those of their rebbe, they said. They refused to be bound by a rigid schedule, which in any case, they said, was not part of Halacha at all.

In dismissing the idea of a rigid schedule for prayer, Rabbi Schneur Zalman of Lyady, a Hasidic sage and later the founder of the Habad (Lubavitch) sect, said, "The essential idea of prayer belongs to the very foundation of the Torah, namely to know the Lord, to recognize His greatness and His glory with a serene mind, and through contemplation." Directing a note of disdain at traditional rabbis, he added, "Anyone who has drawn near to God and has once tasted the fragrance of prayer knows and appreciates that without prayer, [Jews heed] the commands of men who learn by rote."

Schneur Zalman was among the leading zaddikim who, in the years after the Besht, tried to meet with the Gaon to discuss the prospects of reconciling Hasidism with rabbinic Judaism. He insisted Hasidim were anxious to live with Mitnaggedim in a state of mutual respect. But the Gaon refused even to receive the peacemakers, dismissing them in a letter that declared, "It is the duty of every believing Jew to repudiate and pursue the Hasidim with all manner of afflictions and subdue them, because they have sin in their hearts and are like a sore on the body of Israel."

Notwithstanding the strong words, the Gaon failed to halt Hasidism's spread. Poland's *kehillot*, weakened by circumstances and by the decrees of the Russian czarist state, were unable to carry out his bidding. At best, the Gaon drove some Hasidic worship underground. More often, his instructions had no impact at all.

The Vilna Gaon died in 1797, while the struggle between Hasidim and Mitnaggedim raged at a high pitch. His death did not stop Mitnaggedic violations of the Jewish taboo, however, and a year later the rabbi of Pinsk petitioned the czarist government, which by then controlled Poland, to jail Rabbi Schneur Zalman for the crime of creating a religious sect. Arrested, Schneur Zalman was taken to St. Petersburg, whence, according to one expert, it was presumed he would not return alive, but after a brief trial, he was acquitted. The day is now celebrated by Habad Hasidim as the Holiday of Deliverance, though Schneur Zalman was arrested a second time at a rabbi's behest in 1801 and acquitted again.

Scholars disagree on how much harm, over the centuries, Jews inflicted on one another in ignoring the taboo against denunciation to Gentile authorities. The Talmud contains critical references to the practice. In the Middle Ages, rabbis conventionally tried Jews who violated the taboo and, if found guilty, penalized them by excommunication. At the least, scholars point out, the practice was common enough in Jewish history to be the subject of a special Sabbath prayer:

> May it be thy will, Father in heaven, to uproot and extirpate every stock spouting poison and wormwood in Israel so that there be no transgressor in our streets who denounce and harm Israel with their slander and distort the Jewish laws before the nations of the uncircumcised, both men and women, those who seek to endanger the condition of the

community and oppress their brethren by false accusations
in order to destroy them.

Ehud Sprinzak, an Israeli expert on Jewish extremism, cites a nineteenth-century source suggesting that kangaroo courts may have executed hundreds of eastern European Jews for breaking the taboo. He quotes a document written by a Russian provincial governor in 1838 that refers to many incidents "which end with dead Jews."

This crime is especially serious since it is committed in
places designated for prayer and religious worship. The acts
assume the form of vigilante justice made by courts of Jewish rabbis and are based on their false doctrine of eliminating "mosrim," who reveal the crimes of their co-believers.
They are so successful in hiding the investigations they conduct that the identity of the victims, let alone the guilty
judges, remains unknown.

"Moser" (plural "mosrim") is the charge that opponents leveled against Yitzhak Rabin prior to his murder. The Russian document is not clear enough for scholars to gauge how extensive the practice of execution was. The absence of Jewish records suggests the unwillingness of Jews to bring the practice into the open. By the mid-nineteenth century, it seems to have vanished, to reappear only at the end of the twentieth century when rabbis resurrected it to besmirch Rabin, Israel's prime minister, leading directly to his assassination.

෧   ෧   ෧

BY THE MID-NINETEENTH CENTURY, Hasidim and Mitnaggedim, as if belying the seriousness of their divisions, had largely given up their struggle. Both accepted a wary coexistence. Among the explanations for the abrupt shift were major changes in Europe's political climate, which altered the conditions in which Jews lived.

The changes dated back to the opening of the century, when Europe was in both military and intellectual turmoil. Napoleon's armies had crossed eastern Europe, sowing the liberal ideas of the French

Revolution. Jews no less than Gentiles were tantalized by them. Czarist Russia, the chief enemy of liberalism, upheld the old order of anti-Semitism and absolutism. In choosing sides in this conflict, the rabbinate, Hasidic and Mitnaggedic alike, adopted curious standards.

Rabbi Schneur Zalman, more austere than his teacher, the Besht, was now the voice of Hasidism. "If Bonaparte wins," he declared, "the nation of Israel will enjoy much wealth and prestige. But it will come undone, and the hearts of the people will grow distant from their Father in heaven. Whereas if our Master [Czar] Alexander wins, there will be much poverty and suffering, but the hearts of the people will draw close to their Father in heaven."

Rabbi Schneur Zalman's reasoning exemplified a persistent strain among traditional leaders, who perceived a greater threat to their followers from secular ideology than from aggressive anti-Semitism. The strain remained powerful until World War II. While millions of Orthodox Jews, my own grandfather among them, migrated to safety in secular America, all but a handful of Ultra-Orthodox Jews, faithful to Rabbi Schneur Zalman's admonition, remained behind.

In choosing Czar Alexander over Napoleon, Rabbi Schneur Zalman got what he asked for. The czar, in defeating the French emperor, kept the contagion of liberalism at bay in eastern Europe. The Rabbi may indeed have taken satisfaction in drawing his followers "close to their Father in heaven." But at the same time, they sank deeper into poverty and pain. Ultimately, large numbers, unable to escape from Europe, perished in the fires of the Holocaust.

After the Napoleonic Wars, the czars relentlessly shrank the powers of the rabbis to stand against official tyranny. They snuffed out the last vestige of the autonomy of the *kehillot*. They decreed the appointment of an "official rabbi" in each community, responsible to the authorities to supervise the affairs of the Jews.

The Russian government theoretically positioned Mitnaggedic and Hasidic Judaism to compete equally for popular allegiance by empowering synagogue congregations to align with one or the other. In reality, its growing mistreatment of the Jews enervated both. Expulsions and pogroms became a normal part of Jewish life, and the rabbinic leadership, acculturated to passivity, made no effort to resist. Judaism went into a survival mode, and the rivalry between the two movements wilted.

By the middle of the nineteenth century, Hasidism, once radical, had become increasingly conservative; rabbinic Judaism, always conservative, became more so. Hasidism shed its hostility to Torah study and toned down its exuberance. Mitnaggedism, sensing less of a threat, gave up its fixation on crushing Hasidic nonconformity. As the scholar Jacob Agus put it, "Hasidism became progressively more intellectualized, ossified, less creative, less mystical, while rationalist Orthodoxy [Mitnaggedism] took over some of the insights of Hasidism." It was observed that the Mitnaggedic *rav* came more to resemble the Hasidic *rebbe* in the intimacy of his relationship to his followers. By the end of the nineteenth century, the two sects were, in their practices, barely distinguishable.

Yet the theological contrast between them had never been trivial. They defined Judaism in very different ways and each movement, convinced it was battling in the service of divine will, had done everything it could to delegitimize the other. Only in the interest of a higher cause did they agree to a compromise or, more accurately, a truce, since neither ever renounced its particular vision. Each, finally, decided to abide religious practices it had once detested.

The higher cause they chose to share was the perception that they were more imperiled by the rise of Haskalah, the Jewish expression of the West's Enlightenment, than they were by each other. Hasidic and Mitnaggedic leaders lamented together that so many Jews "grazed in foreign pastures." Secular thought among Jews, as they saw it, was a more dangerous enemy than Russia's czars.

Haskalah, it is true, had absorbed the Enlightenment's anticlericalism. Though Haskalah Jews were not prepared to abandon their Jewish identity, they did oppose the rabbinate's dominance of Jewish life. To the rabbis, however, this dominance *was* Judaism. They had enjoyed this dominance for too long to give it up it without a fight.

By the early twentieth century, Hasidim and Mitnaggedim were united in combating liberal Judaism in all manifestations. They singled out Zionism, considered its most pernicious product, as a particular enemy, and organized a political party, called Agudath Yisrael, to keep it from spreading. Stiff-necked as they once had been toward each other, Hasidim and Mitnaggedim were lured by a common rejection of Zionism into becoming political allies.

It is worth emphasizing, however, that having narrowed the political gap, they never adopted a common identity or set of beliefs. Though both now are classed as Ultra-Orthodox, they continue to lead separate existences, in Israel and the Diaspora. Each engages in practices of which the other disapproves, and in fact once regarded as contrary to Judaism's holy essence. But in the face of the enemies they share, their truce remains intact.

The lesson of toleration that the truce contains—if such it was—never spread to the Jewish community at large. In fact, Ultra-Orthodoxy's rejection of both Zionism and liberal Judaism has widened the breach between Jews. Both movements, moreover, created institutions aimed at self-estrangement. Mitnaggedim reformed their yeshivot to separate young men in their early teens from family and community, subjecting them to a monastic atmosphere dedicated to Jewish learning; Hasidim later emulated them, isolating the young disciples who flocked for wisdom to the rebbe's court. The long-standing Jewish practice of living apart from Gentiles was thus extended to keep the Ultra-Orthodox apart from other Jews. The ghetto walls are more impenetrable today than they were two centuries ago.

The result has been that, even as the Enlightenment was inviting Jews to join the larger world, Mitnaggedim and Hasidim were retreating from it. Their children are shielded from ideas that challenge conventional religious wisdom, while their rabbis narrow Halacha to serve as a barrier against foreign ideas. In Israel and the West, not only do Mitnaggedim and Hasidim live in communities of their own, but Hasidic sects, being suspicious of each other, have created ghettos to keep them apart from other Hasidim.

In a universe of computers and motor cars, Hasidim and Mitnaggedim follow remarkably the rhythms of observance of east Europe's premodern era. Each now brings the energy it once used against the other into the fight against any observance that falls short of the standards of piety it has declared to be the only true Judaism.

Rabbinic Judaism claims to trace its beliefs to the Torah, though the Torah never mentions rabbis at all. It claims that all other forms of Judaism are godless, forgetting that its own Judaism emerged from the broken mold of the Temple priesthood. What the diverse non-Orthodox beliefs hold in common, apart from a fierce Jewish attachment, is the acceptance of Jewish legitimacy in many forms. Rabbinic Judaism recognizes only its own legitimacy, as if the Jews over the course of their history had not worshiped God in any other way.

Chapter Six

THE REVOLUTION OF REFORM

SINCE THE FALL of the Second Temple, rabbinic Judaism's raison d'être had been to guide Diaspora Jewry through the turbulence of a shifting social environment. The Talmud was its toolbox; the Halacha, shifting to keep pace with change, its principal tool. Protected by their rabbis, Jews in exile lived apart. Over the centuries a few converted. But in both Christian and Islamic lands, most were satisfied to remain Jews while having little access to the society at large.

The Enlightenment, an explosion of new ideas, changed the environment in a multitude of ways. One of them was its promise to admit Europe's Jews, *as Jews,* into the majority culture. To many Jews, the sudden prospect was dazzling. Rabbinic Judaism, however, stiffened its back, hoping the Enlightenment would prove to be a fad.

The rabbis spurned a view they once routinely took, that Judaism's survival required the law to take account of changing circumstances. It is true they were baffled by the singularity of the challenge, which came as much from within the Jewish community as from outside. Yet rather than examine its potential benefits, they saw only its dangers.

The rabbis interpreted the Enlightenment as the new Hellenism and resolved to resist it in every way.

The walls the rabbis built around Judaism, however, could not stop changes from taking place within. Apart from the rush of new ideas, a population boom was straining the old social structure, inevitably imposing strains on Judaism as religion. Some rabbis perceived the need to accommodate to the pressures coming from outside the ghetto walls. But most, spurning accommodation, favored reinforcing the walls.

The Enlightenment, in fact, called into question the ghetto itself. The *kehillot* as an institution were all but dead, as was the corporatism of which they were the offspring. Europe's states wavered between Enlightenment liberalism and the absolutism of the old-line monarchies, but both dangled the prospect of emancipation before the Jews, requiring a redefinition of their relationship to Gentile society.

Some historians contend that Jewish emancipation, a product of Western civilization, rode on the same wave as the end of serfdom in Russia and of slavery in America. It consisted of the formal lifting of servitude and other personal limitations long enforced by the state. In most of Europe, for example, Jews had conventionally been denied political rights, as well as the choice of where to live and work. Emancipation offered them citizenship and the perogatives enjoyed by other citizens.

The idea both frightened and excited many Jews. They recognized that, after so many centuries of separation, emancipation would demand a new outlook. Few, even among those responsive to the challenge, understood the difficulty of reorienting to the modern world, but many had no interest in reorienting at all. At the end of the eighteenth century, only a minority, mostly in the West, seemed to aspire to emancipation, while the rest preferred the comfort of traditional ways. In Poland, for example, Hasidim and Mitnaggedim reconciled their differences largely so they could turn their backs on the Enlightenment and preserve the life they knew.

Orthodoxy to this day regards the Enlightenment as a tragedy. Rabbi Eliezer Desler, a Haredi sage, recently suggested that God punished the Jews with the Holocaust for failing to resist the Enlightenment more fiercely. He said:

The era of the Emancipation was given us by God to serve as a time for preparation for the coming of the Messiah. To this end, the yoke of exile was eased from upon us. . . . But we used the situation to mix with the Gentiles and imitate them. . . . [Yet] the Holy One Blessed Be He delays His anger. He does not punish until we have reached the limit.

In eastern Europe, Orthodoxy succeeded for a century in holding the Enlightenment at bay. It was in western Europe that it had a powerful impact. The Jews there—most notably in Germany—were lured by the prospect of shedding their ancient chains. Many even envisaged the creation of a new Judaism embracing Enlightenment ideals.

ॹ   ॹ   ॹ

AS THE MIDDLE AGES drew to an end in the sixteenth century, the worldwide population of Jews was less than a million, divided about evenly between Europe and the Islamic world. The public health revolution introduced by modern times somehow benefited Jews disproportionately, and their population grew at twice the rate of Europe as a whole. By 1800, Europe's Jewry had passed a million. By 1900, Russia alone had five million Jews, and in all Europe, despite the migration to America, Jews totaled nearly nine million. Worldwide, Jewish population soared to eleven million, a number that, by itself, was enough to shatter old ways.

Europe's Jews, even as an isolated minority, had never gone unnoticed, thanks to their central role in Christian theology. But the demographic boom, by unleashing a surge in Jewish urbanization, created pressures for admittance into occupations—in industry and the professions, for example—once limited to Gentiles. As barriers dropped, many Jews defied restraints imposed by the Jewish community, and a Jewish middle class emerged. Jews stopped being cultural curiosities in a Christian world and became major players in the hurly-burly of social and economic life.

Europe, meanwhile, was going through a fundamental transformation of its own. The Enlightenment, in loosening the faith-centered mind-set of the medieval age, suggested a new posture toward Jews.

For the next two centuries, Europe would at one moment experience a liberal wave that swept in an unfamiliar tolerance, and in its wake a self-absorbed nationalism that reinvigorated waning prejudices. In this changed atmosphere, neither Jews nor Gentiles found it easy to sort out their feelings toward each other.

Some Jews were drawn, at the same time, to a reexamination of rabbinic Judaism. Scholars point out that Maimonides began nibbling at rabbinic authority as far back as the twelfth century, advocating a synthesis of Judaism and Greek philosophy, doctrines regarded as incompatible by most sages. Known to Talmudists as "Athens versus Jerusalem," the dispute had been a thread in the fabric of Jewish cultural life since the Hellenism of the Second Temple era. At issue was the role of rationalism and of its companion, secular studies, within the body of Judaic thought.

Though Maimonides' standing surpassed that of all his contemporaries, on this issue traditionalist sages stood firm against him. They held that, whatever his dedication to the Torah, he erred in seeking a rational analysis of revelation. The sages triumphed in the debate. But the argument continued into the Middle Ages, with Maimonides' rationalist ideals remaining latent in Judaic theology.

The historian Jacob Agus contends that Maimonides' ideas contributed to the discourse of the Renaissance by promoting a rational humanism over primitive Christian dogmas. Renaissance thinkers who argued in behalf of reason and extolled earthly pleasures over a fixation on eternal salvation drew, he says, from Maimonides. Whether or not Agus is correct, the impact of these humanist ideals was felt by Europe's Jews as well as by its Christians.

Baruch Spinoza, born in 1632, picked up rationalism where Maimonides let it go, which cost him his niche in Jewish society, and nearly his life. A Jew whose family had fled the Portuguese Inquisition to settle in Amsterdam, he regarded rationalism and religion as natural antagonists. In holding that the Torah was revealed by God, he said, Maimonides was not being rational at all.

Too unconventional for conversion to Christianity yet not an atheist, Spinoza argued for reading the Bible as a source of understanding of Jewish belief at succeeding stages of development. He regarded religion as superstition and Halacha as fallacy. Man, he contended, must determine his fate in a rational relationship with God, without being diverted from his course by religious myths.

"I show," Spinoza wrote in summary of his convictions, "that the word of God has not been revealed in books but was transmitted to the Prophets as a simple idea of the divine mind, namely obedience to God in singleness of heart and in the practice of justice and charity."

Spinoza's vision frightened Amsterdam's Jews, Sephardim who had suffered much for their fidelity to Judaism, and he was brought before a religious court on charges of apostasy. The judges' verdict, after extended testimony, read: "Receiving every day more information about the abominable heresies practiced and taught by him . . . , [we] decided, with the advice of the rabbis, that Spinoza should be excommunicated and cut off from the nation of Israel."

Twenty-four years old at the time, Spinoza spent the rest of his brief life in isolation, writing on philosophy, ethics and biblical interpretation, while grinding lenses for a modest living. The rabbinic elite did whatever it could to keep his work from being published, but he nonetheless passed on a body of ideas that would influence not just Judaism but all Western thought.

Spinoza helped to shape the philosophers who built the Enlightenment. Descartes and Newton, Locke and Voltaire, Kant and Rousseau, each in his way followed in Spinoza's tracks. Near the end of the eighteenth century, Enlightenment ideology soared on the wings of the American and French Revolutions. Later, it accompanied Napoleon's caissons across Europe and into the Middle East.

In opting for reason over faith, the Enlightenment offered humanity a nonreligious identity. It made science the key to unlocking the universe and challenged the gloomy Christian concept that original sin doomed humankind to suffering. Breaking the intellectual bonds of the Middle Ages, it proposed that men and women alike be free of their clerics, and invited both Jews and Gentiles to adopt what has become the liberal Western view of the modern world.

Moses Mendelssohn, heir of Maimonides and Spinoza, imparted to Enlightenment thought a uniquely Jewish twist. Born in 1729, he was also a disciple of Descartes, and chose secular education as his vehicle for a personal journey from medieval Judaic culture to modern German society. But he remained traditionally observant, never forgetting he was Jewish and, being Jewish, an outsider in his homeland.

Mendelssohn was among the first to maintain that it was consistent to be both Jewish and German. He was offended by Germans who proposed that emancipation be conditioned on Jews' shedding their traditional religious practice. He consistently challenged the views of anti-Semites. Mendelssohn argued the unfamiliar proposition that Jews, as Jews, had every right to be German citizens.

> It is remarkable [he wrote] how prejudice has taken on the shape of all centuries in order to oppress us and to place difficulties in the way of our civil acceptance. . . . Now it is superstition and stupidity which are attributed to us: lack of moral sentiment, of taste and refined manners, inability in the arts, sciences and useful crafts, especially those in the service of war and government, unconquerable inclination to cheating, usury and lawlessness. These take the place of ruder accusations to exclude us from the number of useful citizens and to push us away from the motherly bosom of the state.

The *Jewish* Enlightenment, conventionally called by the Hebrew term *Haskalah*, emerged largely from Mendelssohn's pen. Its activists were given the name *Maskilim*, from a title of honor ("learned") used by Sephardim. The aim of the Maskilim was not only to encourage Germany to emancipate its Jews but to prepare Jews for their freedom by promoting modern values within the Jewish community.

Son of a Torah scribe, Mendelssohn attended traditional Jewish schools before winning acceptance to a German university, where he studied languages and philosophy. Rejecting Yiddish, his mother tongue, he learned German and later wrote it with flair. He even translated the Torah, aiming, on the one hand, to attract Jews to the German tongue and, on the other, to build a bridge to the Germans.

Germany's rabbinate gave him no encouragement. "A rabble of unclean birds," was one rabbi's description of the Maskilim. Few rabbis sympathized with either of his goals of funneling young Jews into German culture or having Jews reach out in comradeship to German society. Mendelssohn saw the rabbis' objections as a crass defense of their own powers.

Given the depth of his piety, Mendelssohn was not an easy target for Jewish counterattacks. "Adopt the mores and constitution of the country in which you find yourself," he wrote, "but be steadfast in upholding the religion of your fathers." Denying incompatibility between personal Judaism and modern culture, Mendelssohn legitimized Haskalah values for a key generation of European Jews.

In philosophy, Mendelssohn embraced Spinoza's ardent rationalism and Maimonides' belief in God's revelation, thus serving as a link in the chain of Jewish speculative thought. Though God created the Jewish nation at Sinai, he maintained, it was a response to fleeting political conditions; in the Diaspora, the Jews as a nation did not exist. But, he added, "Whoever is born in the faith is compelled to live and die in it." Even in becoming fully German, he believed, the Jews' obligation to religious observance would remain eternal.

Mendelssohn attacked Jewish law, which he distinguished sharply from piety. The Talmud, he said, was a relic, useful as a guide to moral precepts but without legal force. Many Jews, seeing Judaism as synonymous with the law, felt he failed to make his case. But Mendelssohn continued to argue that the only law to which Jews owed allegiance was the law of the state in which they lived.

Unlike some well-intentioned Christian thinkers, Mendelssohn had no interest in blurring Jewish-Gentile differences. "If you care for true godliness," he wrote, "let us not pretend that conformity exists where diversity is obviously the plan of Providence." Denouncing conversion, he said when God chooses to release Jews from their vows at Sinai, God will amend the holy covenant. Until then, the vows taken at Sinai remain in place.

For Mendelssohn and a rising class of bourgeois Jews, life in Germany outside the ghetto was very attractive. Some, lured by the wealth and sophistication of Germans, were tempted to abandon Jewish identity altogether. But Mendelssohn, rejecting choice, insisted there was no conflict between being a cultured German and a pious

Jew. Only much later was Germany overcome by the demonic impulses, which suggested that his confidence had been misplaced.

ᔕ   ᔕ   ᔕ

GERMANY, IT SHOULD BE remembered, was not yet a unified nation and would not be until 1870. In Mendelssohn's time, it was still composed, as it had been since the early Middle Ages, of hundreds of independent principalities. All absolutist, each regulated religious practices within its borders. Every principality, whether home to many Jews or a few, was ruled by the whim of a reigning prince. The treatment accorded the Jews varied substantially from one to another.

Inside this constitutional framework flourished the peculiar historical institution known as "Court Jews." For generations, Court Jews were a linchpin in government, a vital arm of the ruling elite, with influence in principalities all across Germany.

Court Jews, as individuals, became an institution by virtue of their talents, unusual for the time, in administration and finance. Being Jews, they could also call on a network of contacts with other Jews throughout Europe. Their services made them indispensable to their princes, with whom they often developed warm personal bonds.

Court Jews, who were often rewarded with wealth and high rank, were nonetheless recognized openly as Jews. Some had been schooled in yeshivot; many even headed the local *kehilla*. Nearly all, out of personal and community interest, were advocates of Jewish emancipation. The German historian Heinrich Schnee may be exaggerating only slightly in saying, "the emancipation of the Jews was the product of the *Hoffactoren*—the Court Jews."

To promote emancipation, Court Jews often persuaded their princes to be guided by local Maskilim, whose priority was the reform of Jewish education. Their objective was to switch Jewish students from religious to secular subjects, notably German, which they believed offered access to Enlightenment thought. Many princes, convinced such reform would benefit the state, willingly followed this advice.

Education reform, however, infuriated the rabbis. The princes, in gutting the *kehillot*, had already curbed many long-standing rabbinic powers. Educational reform would go much further, threatening the rabbis with irrelevance. The rabbis saw the Maskilim, not altogether incorrectly, as their enemy not just within the Jewish community but inside princely palaces.

In Russia, rabbinic relations with the Maskilim were even worse than in Germany. Russia's Jews, Europe's most numerous, were also the most oppressed. The czars, though not more absolutist, ruled without the liberal attitude of Germany's princes. Russia, too, had largely dismantled the *kehillot,* but it gave no compensating consideration to Jewish emancipation. The czars seemed determined to punish the Jews for being neither Russian nor Christian.

Russian Maskilim persisted in believing, long after the evidence belied it, that the conditions of Jewish life would improve if only Jews embraced Haskalah ideals. With some success, they promoted secular reform of Jewish schools and even urged financial incentives to wean Jews away from their distinctive clothing. The only results, however, were more anti-Semitic edicts from the czar's government.

Russia's Maskilim labored under another disadvantage: their Jews, unlike Germany's, had no reason to admire, much less envy, the primitive nature of Russian society. They looked on Russians, overwhelmingly poor and illiterate, with disdain. Living in fear of their Russian neighbors, they had no desire to emulate them. Later, many Jews would show their discontent by becoming politically radical and religiously secular, but in the early years of the Haskalah, nearly all saw Judaism as a refuge in a hostile Russian society.

Germany was the most open of the Enlightenment cultures. Its Maskilim, emulating Mendelssohn, debated new ideas not just with other Jews but even with Christians. Unlike France, where the Enlightenment evoked a visceral anticlericalism, Germany stayed deeply Christian. Many of its intellectuals considered themselves beneficent in holding conversion to be their mission to the Jews.

Gotthold Lessing, a close Christian friend of Mendelssohn, drew on Spinoza to argue that Judaism had lost its spiritual relevance during the Second Temple era. It was superseded by Christianity, he maintained, an advance in religious evolution. Judaism, Lessing argued, had become an anachronism, which Jews should abandon.

Immanuel Kant, the most influential of Germany's Enlightenment thinkers, also wrote as a Christian. He questioned whether Judaism, emphasizing obedience to law over spirituality and conscience, was a religion at all. The Sinai covenant, he wrote, was "a collection of mere statutory laws upon which was erected a political organization." He called Christianity a *genuine* faith, and the Jewish God an autocrat who demanded mechanical worship. Kant, like Lessing, thought he was performing a service to the Jews by urging them to convert.

Under this barrage many did convert, among them the celebrated poet Heinrich (originally Chaim) Heine, who admitted his only objective was to be accepted by Christian society. "Jewishness," Heine wrote, "is an incurable malady," though in abandoning it he did not find relief. Pursued by anti-Semitism even after conversion, he migrated to France, and shortly before he died in 1850, he wrote sadly, "I make no secret of my Judaism, to which I have not returned, because I never left it."

Heine was among many who found their Jewishness a fact that baptism would not erase. Yet in the nineteenth century, according to Argus, no fewer than a third of the members of the Berlin *kehilla* converted. By another calculation, at least two hundred thousand of Europe's Jews, most of them German, became Christian by 1900. Some observers were sure Judaism was at last on its way to extinction. Even Europe's Jews talked of being Judaism's last generation.

"A new concept of Judaism was needed," writes Agus, himself a rabbi, of the crisis, "if it was to survive as a vital faith in the Western world—a concept that would uncover its essential truth and validity, its distinctive ideology vis-à-vis Christianity and its relevance to the life of the Jewish individual."

Europe's Jews, led by the community in Germany, did react by examining new concepts. Some among them, to be sure, clung tenaciously to the old ways and took the name of Orthodoxy. But another segment reset the Jewish compass and headed in a new direction. Called liberal, progressive or, most commonly, Reform, these Jews maintained that the faith could not ignore secularism and rationalism, offspring of the Enlightenment. They vowed to preserve Judaism by absorbing into it the wisdom of the modern world.

ﺋ   ﺋ   ﺋ

REFORM JUDAISM DID NOT at first regard itself as a denomination. Nor, of course, did Orthodoxy. Both accepted unity as the Jews' safeguard against a hostile world. The two thought of Judaism as a faith that, no matter how scattered its members or how bitter its disputes, was one.

Since superseding priestly Judaism in the first century C.E., rabbinic Judaism's supremacy had been secure. Apostates were rare and, like Spinoza, routinely marginalized. Only in the nineteenth century, after the iron grip of the rabbis had slipped, did the concept of multiple Judaisms emerge.

Though Orthodoxy's doctrines had girded Judaism since the fall of the Second Temple, Reform was convinced that the changed times imposed a new imperative. Reform's vision was no more revolutionary than the vision of the sages who snatched control from the priesthood in the first century C.E. Believing Orthodoxy exhausted, the Reformers saw a duty to come to the rescue of the faith.

In Germany, a few souls sought an innovative synthesis, embracing the Enlightenment while remaining true to the law spelled out in Caro's *Shulchan Aruch*. They even initiated a movement, called Neo-Orthodoxy, in which emancipation and secular education, German culture and ritual reform were assigned a role within the framework of Mosaic law.

Many decades later, when Jews were arguing over religion's place within Zionist ideology, a movement called Mizrachi resurrected the premises of Neo-Orthodoxy. Its ideas passed into what is now called modern Orthodoxy. But in Germany in the early days, its followers, squeezed between conventional Orthodoxy, which ceded nothing, and mutinous Reform, which called for Judaism's total renovation, soon dispersed in confusion.

The first practitioner of what might be identified as Reform Judaism, though it did not yet have that name, was Israel Jacobson, a rabbinically trained Court Jew in service to the duke of Brunswick. A partisan of the French Revolution, he rejoiced when Napoleon occupied his principality in 1807, merging it into the Kingdom of Westphalia and, more important, emancipating its fifteen thousand Jews. Napoleon's minions named Jacobson head of the Westphalian consistory, with authority over the kingdom's rabbis. He was told to bring "a number of customs which have crept into Judaism more in line with changed circumstances." It was an order that corresponded with Jacobson's view that Jewish practices were inconsistent with the temper of the times.

Jacobson's reforms were aimed at narrowing the gap with the customs of Germany's churches. They required rabbis to end the tradition of breaking glass and throwing rice at weddings, described as primitive superstitions. They instructed rabbis to quit their pulpits to provide comfort to the ill and bereaved. They also required rabbis to promote Westphalian patriotism through sermons delivered in German. Jacobson also instituted ritual confirmation of Jewish children, borrowed directly from Christianity, but this innovation stirred such opposition that he had to cancel it.

Whatever Jacobson's reforms, in his own eyes his greatest achievement was probably the synagogue he built in the Brunswick city of Seesen. With a church-style bell tower and an organ, it was designed to send the message that Judaism was no longer a foreign faith, practiced by transplanted Orientals. Jacobson may have been the first to call a synagogue a *temple*, as a reminder of the lost grandeur of King Solomon.

At its dedication in 1810, Jacobson invited Christian and Jewish notables, and had Torah passages, read in Hebrew, translated into German. Proclaiming his personal fidelity to Judaism, he also announced that rituals offensive to Christians would be expunged. Conversely, Jacobson called on Christians to end their anti-Jewish prejudices. The interfaith brotherhood he celebrated at the dedication later became a basic component of Reform Judaism.

Jacobson's enterprise, however, came to an abrupt end. In 1813, as Napoleon's empire disintegrated, the Kingdom of Westphalia fell, putting Jacobson and the consistory leadership to flight. But even before, his agenda had failed to enlist much Jewish allegiance. His deviance from tradition was still too great for the community to embrace. Reformers would need more time to prepare the ideological ground.

In the succeeding decades, liberal Jewish thinkers labored to frame a theology freed of what they regarded as arbitrary digressions from essential Judaism. Predictably, it was not work on which agreement came easily. But to accuse them, as Orthodoxy did, of seeking nothing more than rites palatable to the goyim was unjustified. The first premise of these thinkers was not to supersede rabbinic Judaism, much less to Christianize Judaism, but to rebuild their faith to serve the Jews in dynamic times.

Whatever their differences, these thinkers were indisputably sincere in their quest. It led them not just into the theology but also the history and philosophy of Judaism. It took them down roads from which they later retreated, only to choose other roads. In contrast to Orthodoxy's strategy of refusing to try any new roads at all, they believed that, whatever their missteps, Judaism would only grow stronger from the journey.

ꙮ   ꙮ   ꙮ

ABRAHAM GEIGER WAS the outstanding intellect of the new movement, weaving into Judaic theology strands of liberal German thought. Born in 1810, he was the product of an observant Frankfurt family, schooled in scriptures before going on to secular studies at universities in Heidelberg and Bonn. He aspired to lead a scholarly life but, blocked by the anti-Semitism that kept Jews from university posts, he instead became a pulpit rabbi, which he remained for the rest of his life.

Geiger was the chief exponent of a school that held Jews could discover the basis of their religion in the objective study of its history. Like other thinkers of the time, he sought to demystify both Bible and Talmud, arguing that they be read as products of their age. The validity of sacred texts was not eternal, he maintained; each generation had to determine for itself those that were viable.

Geiger preached prophetic over Talmudic Judaism. This meant he shared the priority that the Prophets gave to the needs of the downtrodden and valued only ritual that promoted moral and spiritual impulses. In Geiger's eyes, Amos, Isaiah and Micah were as important to Judaism as Moses. Their ideals, rather than Talmudic law, were to him Judaism's essence. Geiger's writings on the Prophets remain an integral part of Reform Judaism today.

Geiger never aimed to sunder the Jewish community. Had he possessed Martin Luther's charisma, he might have led a powerful movement of religious change. As an intellectual, he provoked vital debate, but neither he nor any other Reform leader attracted a major personal following. Few issues, as a result, were resolved among them, and the debate over Reform's place in Judaism continues to our day.

Only inadvertently did Geiger serve as the catalyst of the breakup of Germany's Jewish community. It happened when the Jews of Breslau, a majority of them liberal, named him in 1838 as assistant rabbi and presumed successor to the aging, rigidly Orthodox chief rabbi, Solomon Tiktin. Tiktin, however, declared that Geiger's secular studies disqualified him from the post and refused even to stand with him in prayer.

The controversy engulfed all of Germany's Jewry. Tiktin's allies wrote of Geiger, "If he likes, let him call himself doctor or scholar or even preacher, but with what right rabbi?" They denounced him as a Sadducee and a Karaite, ancient opponents of the Oral Law. At one ceremony, Orthodox and Reform factions actually attacked each other with fists.

When Tiktin died Geiger did in fact succeed him, but by then the break was irreparable. The schism, though formally limited to Breslau, produced competing denominations throughout Germany. Reform and Orthodoxy each sought legitimacy at the other's expense. Reform rabbis ranged, theologically and ritually, from radical to conservative, and politically, depending on their pulpits, from weak to very powerful. Geiger put his energies into articulating a platform that would unite these fragments, but Reform's advocates offered what was still to most Jews a renegade ideology.

Geiger's chief rival was Rabbi Zacharias Frankel of Dresden, anchor of the movement's conservative wing. Frankel, like Geiger, was a member of the Wissenschaft des Judentums, the school of thinkers that saw Judaism's history as the key to understanding the faith. He coined the phrase "Judaism is the religion of the Jews," by which he meant legitimacy was derived not from scriptures but from the practices in which Jews historically engaged. He broke from Geiger in contending that traditional practices were authentic, while the changes promoted by Reform were not.

While rejecting Orthodoxy's doctrine that Halacha was the application of God's words at Sinai, Frankel equally rejected Reform's belief that Judaism could be tailored to meet the demands of the age. He argued that the manner in which traditional Jews observe the Sabbath conveys what the Sabbath is. Patterns of observance established over time, he said, similarly communicate a religious *idea*, revealing the essentials of Judaism itself.

In 1845, Geiger called a conference in Frankfurt to challenge Frankel on doctrinal questions, and the two agreed to debate the ritual use of the German language. Narrow as the question was drawn, at stake was the course that lay before Jewish liberals. Frankel argued that, in return for emancipation, Reform had bartered away the faith of generations of traditional Jews, failing to recognize the sacrifices they had made. Outvoted by the delegates, he stalked out of the meeting, which may have been his plan. He and his followers proceeded to form the Conservative movement, an effort to fuse traditional Jewish piety with ideological change.

In 1854, Reform and Conservatism, once companionable, broke irreparably over whether Geiger or Frankel would direct a new seminary founded at Breslau as seat of the Wissenschaft des Judentums movement. The seminary, which was Geiger's idea, had been built with money he raised. But Frankel, by mobilizing anti-Reform support, was elected its leader and made it the center of Conservative thought. He also saw to it that Geiger was not offered a post to teach there.

Geiger's defeat did not end the doctrinal infighting. A Neo-Orthodox movement, more conservative than Frankel, declared that the Breslau seminary's refusal to recognize Jewish law unchanged since Moses to be heresy; it founded its own seminary. Then Geiger, seeking a home for Reform theology, founded a seminary, more liberal than Breslau's. The proliferation confirmed that diverse branches from the trunk of Enlightenment Judaism were growing, each in its own direction. Reform shattered the unity of rabbinic Judaism, but now liberal Judaism was itself in fragments.

While Orthodoxy held on stubbornly to its place in the community, liberal Judaism became defined by three branches. Conservatism occupied the middle ground. Reform, it turned out, was too intellectual for most German Jews, who also found Neo-Orthodoxy too close to rabbinic Judaism. German Jews seemed most comfortable with Frankel's mix of tradition and renewal, and by the century's end, Conservatism was Germany's most popular Jewish denomination.

🔊 🔊 🔊

BY THAT TIME, the ideological contest among German Jews had been transplanted to an arena across the sea. Jews had been trickling from Germany to America since early in the nineteenth century. But after the collapse of Germany's liberal revolution of 1848, when official reaction brought emancipation to a halt, a large wave of emigration followed. Not surprisingly, most of the Jews who fled, liberals who had supported the revolution, carried Geiger's ideas of Reform in their luggage. In the years that followed, they had a major impact in shaping American Judaism.

In the late 1860s, Prussia's leader, Otto von Bismarck, with an eye to absorbing Germany's principalities into the Prussian kingdom, enacted laws guaranteeing equality for all of Germany's religions. These laws, ostensibly, were a triumph for emancipation, but, perversely, they provoked a rise of anti-Semitism, as a consequence of which more Jews fled. By 1875, most of the quarter-million Jews who lived in America had German roots. The language of their synagogues was German. Their religious disputes mirrored, in nature and magnitude, those in which Germany's divided Jews had engaged for nearly a century.

Germany's Jews, it should be noted, were not the first to settle in America. A community composed largely of Sephardim had been established as early as the seventeenth century. In 1777, a German tourist observed that, "The Jews cannot be told, like those in our country, by their beards and costume, but are dressed like other citizens, shave regularly, eat pork . . . and do not hesitate to intermarry."

In 1790, during his first presidential term, George Washington, in a letter to the Touro Synagogue of Newport, Rhode Island, wrote, "May the children of the stock of Abraham, who dwell in this land, continue to merit and enjoy the good will of other inhabitants, while every one shall sit in safety under his own vine and fig tree, and there shall be none to make him afraid." To a people accustomed to living amid hostility, the welcome that America extended was an unprecedented pleasure.

In the early nineteenth century, a majority of America's Jews spoke English as their native tongue. They had established synagogues, most of them Sephardi, in a half-dozen cities. Only in midcentury did the numerical balance shift to the Germans, whose synagogues were mostly Reform and whose rabbis were mostly trained in Germany.

The German Jews were thrilled by their new environment. They did not suffer interference by the state in their religious affairs. They were not required to commit to a religious organization, or to answer for their beliefs to any official body. Whatever prejudice they encountered, they did not have to fit their faith into the framework of an established Christian church. America, a gaggle of disparate denominations, freed the Jews to fight their sectarian battles as they saw fit.

The outstanding Jew of nineteenth-century America was Bohemian-born Isaac Mayer Wise, one of the era's few leading rabbis who was not a product of German culture. Captivated by his adopted homeland, Wise spoke of the "American phase of Judaism . . . , reformed and reconstructed by the beneficent influence of political liberty and progressive enlightenment, the youngest offspring of the ancient and venerable faith of Israel." Convinced the era of anti-Semitism was over, Wise believed the "American Judaism" that he extolled would become integral to American life, so that even Christians would want to join it.

As a Reform rabbi, Wise is remembered not as a thinker but as a tireless organizer, an effortless orator and a true believer in his capacity to shape a unique Jewish community. Pragmatic on standards of ritual and observance, he paid little attention to theology. But, like Geiger, he aspired to re-create Jewish unity on the basis of a reformulated Judaism.

In Cleveland in 1855, Wise convoked a conference of American rabbis, both Orthodox and Reform, to establish the principles for the Judaism of his dreams. Orthodox Jews were already a minority in

America, and Conservatism had not yet made an impact. Though earlier attempts to convene such meetings had failed, Wise succeeded in bringing together delegates from eight major American cities. The most important among them, apart from Wise himself, was Isaac Leeser, a German-born rabbi who was American Orthodoxy's leading voice. Since Leeser shared the ideal of unification, hopes for an agreement were high.

Wise, to promote reconciliation, offered Leeser what he considered a major doctrinal concession. The platform draft described the Bible as being of "immediate divine origin" and said "Biblical laws . . . must be expounded and practiced according to the comments of the Talmud." When Leeser endorsed the wording, Wise was sure his goal of unity had been achieved. But Leeser, on returning home, was attacked by his Orthodox colleagues for making any compromise with Reform at all, and the proposed union promptly collapsed.

In fact, the Reform establishment was no more tolerant. Wise apart, Reform rabbis were as unwilling as their Orthodox counterparts to defer to the other side's beliefs. Overwhelmingly German, Wise's foes regarded his compromises as ideological betrayal. Their leader, Rabbi David Einhorn, was a radical thinker who had recently arrived in Baltimore to head a Reform congregation. An ardent disciple of Geiger in the famous contest over the Breslau seminary, he scoffed at Wise's openness toward Orthodoxy, as well as toward the ancient texts.

Einhorn's scathing attacks ignited an enduring feud with Wise, which, personal though it was, also reflected the dilemma faced by American Judaism. The context was the general decline in Jewish observance. Jews were drifting toward the secularism that increasingly characterized American society. The challenge faced by Judaism was not just to frame an ideology congenial to Jews but to reverse this trend.

Wise's American pragmatism ran head-on into Einhorn's Germanic dogmatism, but Reform rabbis had countless opinions between their two poles. They spent hours discussing the validity of pipe organs and the separation of the sexes in the synagogue. They debated the wording of prayer books and the content of dietary laws. Some placed on the record lofty ideals, which others promptly disavowed in petitions of protest. The Babylonian sages could not have debated issues with greater finesse, or more often lost control of the substance in personal invective and hair-splitting detail.

Yet the Reform rabbinate brought deep personal belief to the debates. However scorned by Orthodoxy, Reform thinkers were searching for answers to real problems weighing on Judaism. Their diversity contrasted sharply with the other side's unanimity. Orthodoxy, certain it represented God's will, conducted no debates at all.

〈 〈 〈

MEANWHILE, DEMOGRAPHIC SHIFTS in Europe were again changing the context of the debate within Judaism, even in America. By the late nineteenth century, oppression in greater Russia had grown so intense that many thousands of Jews were emigrating to America each year. Most of these Jews, ill at ease with Enlightenment ideas, reflexively dismissed Reform in their adopted land. Their arrival put them in direct confrontation with the resident community of German Jews.

German Jews were proud of the network of synagogues they had built, as well as of the integrated life they had made in America. If the new immigrants were uncomfortable among them, they in turn sent the message that "greenhorns" were not welcome. A Jewish historian tells a typical story of aging German Jews in Richmond, Virginia, who let their Orthodox shul die rather than admit eastern Europeans to membership. The differences went beyond religion to class and culture.

Conservatives reached out more than Reform Jews to the new immigrants. Though not indifferent to social status, they were not as resistant to absorption. The problem was that the eastern Europeans— my grandparents among them—were not interested in any modern Judaism whatsoever. Orthodox to the core, they founded European-style synagogues and left to their children the option of becoming Americanized Jews.

In 1885, the American Reform movement, under a new generation of rabbis, probably widened the breach still further in pushing again to resolve doctrinal differences. Rabbi Kaufmann Kohler, Einhorn's son-in-law and successor at New York's Temple Beth-El, convened rabbis at a meeting in Pittsburgh. Wise, now an elder, was honorific chairman, his American-style pragmatism out of fashion. The goal of the German-born Kohler, as radical as his father-in-law, was to purify Reform's message.

Amid the Reformers, however, were disciples of Zacharias Frankel, who forty years before had walked out of the Frankfurt meeting to found Conservative Judaism in Germany. In Judaism, ideological issues seem never to die. At the Pittsburgh meeting, power was once again polarized, with Frankel's heirs ready to bolt rather than give in.

The Pittsburgh Platform, which emerged from a draft by Kohler, was a collection of Reform principles. At meetings over the previous decades, under Wise's guidance, Reform was said to have proposed only what Orthodoxy did not reject. In Pittsburgh, the Reform leaders regarded Orthodoxy as out of the game, and saw Conservatives as their obstacle. Kohler's goal was to vanquish Conservatism's influence.

By Reform standards, the content was not especially extreme. But it was far from the "healthy golden mean" of the counterproposal that Conservatives presented. Faithful to their middle-of-the-road views, Conservatives called for a "Mosaic-rabbinical Judaism, freshened by the spirit of progress." They received, instead, a collection of classical Reform ideas from American and German thinkers, many of them a source of controversy since the era of the Haskalah.

The Pittsburgh Platform, in part, read:

> We hold that Judaism represents the highest conception of the God idea as taught by our holy Scriptures . . .
>
> We hold that the modern discoveries of scientific researches in the domains of nature and history are not antagonistic to the doctrines of Judaism, the Bible reflecting the primitive ideas of its own age . . .
>
> We recognize in the Mosaic legislation a system of training the Jewish people for its mission during its national life in Palestine, and today we accept as binding only the moral laws . . .
>
> We hold that all such Mosaic and rabbinical laws as regulate diet, priestly purity and dress originated in ages and

under the influence of ideas altogether foreign to our present mental and spiritual state . . .

We consider ourselves no longer a nation but a religious community . . .

We recognize in Judaism a progressive religion, ever striving to be in accord with the postulates of reason . . .

We deem it our duty to participate in the great task of modern times, to solve on the basis of justice and righteousness the problems presented by the contrasts and evils of the present organization of society.

The Conservatives denounced the Pittsburgh Platform from its very first sentence, which referred to the "God idea" rather than to God Himself. It objected to the description of the Bible's ideas as "primitive." Nor was it comfortable with the suggestion, drawn from prophetic rather than Talmudic doctrines, that Judaism was essentially an instrument for the promotion of social justice.

When Rabbi Kohler boasted that the Platform was the Jewish Declaration of Independence, Conservative opponents replied mockingly, "Independence from what?" Their rhetorical answer was, "Independence from Judaism." While Reformers organized to sell their Platform, Conservatives began organizing to build permanent institutions parallel to Reform. The two have not since attempted reconciliation.

Predictably, support for the Pittsburgh Platform was not unanimous even within Reform. As always, the absence of a central authority was an invitation to rabbis to preserve their ideological autonomy. Still, the overwhelming approval of Reform rabbis gave the movement a cohesion it had never before attained. The Platform lasted as Reform's declaration of principles until well into the twentieth century. Even after several revisions, it is recognizable today as the framework of the movement.

As much as anything, the Pittsburgh Platform meant that Jews—like Christians and Muslims—would serve God in different ways and speak for their faith in many voices. Orthodoxy, of course, did not accept this outcome, and the struggle it waged was far from over. But by the twentieth century, America sheltered the world's largest community of Jews. Its denominations, being legally equal, were free to follow their own course. Though Orthodoxy did not surrender its ancient claims, it was unable to interfere with Reform and Conservative Judaism's religious designs.

In the decades immediately after Pittsburgh, the struggle lay more or less dormant. Jews seemed to recognize that America, with its traditions of tolerance, was not a favorable terrain on which to conduct sectarian wars. After World War II produced the greatest tragedy in their history, some thought the Jews might even put religious conflicts behind them. But in the war's wake, Jews founded the modern state of Israel, which came to serve as an arena for resurrecting the internecine religious struggle, in harsher terms than ever.

The twentieth-century Jewish state was not monarchic like King David's, much less theocratic like the Maccabees'. It certainly was not Halachic, which was the aspiration of Orthodoxy. But it was sovereign, which gave Jews the power to make decisions for themselves. Many took this power as an invitation to resume the combat for religious control.

Sovereignty, moreover, brought a rise in the stakes. Without Gentiles to overrule them, Jews went at the conflict more bitterly. What Orthodox Judaism saw in sovereignty was an opportunity to make up the losses of the centuries since the Enlightenment. What Reform and Conservative Judaism saw was a chance to have their legitimacy formally acknowledged. All three sought to enlist the secular state on its side, as tolerance among them seemed to grow increasingly distant.

III

THE TURBULENCE

OF RETURN

Chapter   Seven

Seeking Divine Refuge

BY THE END OF THE nineteenth century, the social values that bonded rabbinic Judaism to the Jews of Europe had largely crumbled. Most Jews, like most Gentiles, had adopted a different view of the world. The Enlightenment had triumphed.

The *kehillot* were no more, and most Jews lived and worked within the society of Gentiles. The psychological constraints that had kept the old system intact had been sapped by the contact. Jews not only spoke the languages of the Gentiles but were schooled in Gentile disciplines and regarded themselves as citizens of Gentile states, detached from the authority of Mosaic law. The rabbinic leadership's influence over the daily life of most Jews had fallen to an unprecedented low.

Only small clusters of the faithful now practiced the rigorous Judaism that had once held the community together. In its place, Jews drifted toward new forms of observance, both within tradition and outside it, or toward no observance at all. Steadily more Jews abandoned the customs that had preserved their ghettos—most visibly, the wearing by men of heavy beards and black clothing. Many Jews even

161

moved their homes beyond walking distance of the synagogue and the kosher butcher.

A century before, Moses Mendelssohn, the most eminent son of the Haskalah, had been persuaded that freewheeling Jewish intellectuals could function within the framework of ancient observance. He would have been dismayed at how mistaken he was. Mendelssohn was observant until he died; popular religious practice thereafter declined steadily. Baffled by these seismic shifts, Orthodox rabbis were able to summon no effective response.

Yet even the Enlightenment's champions could not overlook the costs to Europe's Jews that accompanied their new status. European culture, having over centuries carved out an image of Jews as inferiors, was clearly uncomfortable treating them as equals. Conversely, the Jews' tenacious dedication to their special identity—even while abandoning observance—maintained the barriers between Christians and Jews. The Enlightenment's noble theories of social integration were not up to dispelling the web of mutual suspicion that Gentiles and Jews had so long spun.

With Europe's traditions of anti-Semitism conspiring against it, the Enlightenment failed in its promise to integrate the Jews. Intolerance proved, unexpectedly, to be the flip side of emancipation. Even the poet Heinrich Heine, desperately soliciting acceptance through conversion, was cruelly excluded. Meanwhile, the Jews who remained Jews—unlike the Protestants in France or the Catholics in Germany—were unable to win popular recognition as a legitimate minority community, separate but equal.

After Napoleon, the situation of the Jews became more perilous. One society after another adopted a militant nationalism, complemented by a Christian romanticism. As popular creeds, the two promoted a primitive, tribal xenophobia.

Racism, rarely a factor in anti-Semitism before, received an unintended boost from Darwin's innovative theories, which suggested a hierarchy in human evolution. It became a view embraced by the Catholic Church. "Oh how wrong and deluded," declared a Vatican paper, "are those who think Judaism is just a religion, like Catholicism, Paganism, Protestantism, and that [Jews] are not in fact a race, a people and a nation. The Jews are Jews not only because of their religion . . . [but] especially because of their race." Old-fashioned religious anti-Semitism made way for a new malevolence based on culture and ethnicity. "You can't baptize it out of them" became a reigning witticism among Germany's Christian intellectuals.

The anti-Semitism that grew from these seeds proved even more virulent than the earlier strains. Jews, having begun the century with bounteous optimism rooted in European liberalism, arrived at its end in gloom and foreboding. A few decades later, the virulence would reach its climax with the murder of six million of them.

Joseph Roth, in *The Wandering Jews*, captured the sense of vulnerability felt by eastern Europe's Jewish communities. Unable to escape from anti-Semitism on the one hand, they felt their lives increasingly fragmented by Haskalah values on the other.

> To outsiders and enemies, Eastern Jews like to present a united front. . . . Nothing gets through to the outside world of the zeal with which individual groups fight one another, the hatred and the bitterness with which the supporters of one rabbi assail those of another, or the contempt all devout Jews have for the sons of their tribe who have conformed to the customs and dress of their Christian surroundings. Most devout Jews are unsparing in their condemnation of the man who shaves his beard—the clean-shaven face serving as the visible sign of breaking with the faith. The clean-shaven Jew no longer sports the badge of his people. He attempts, perhaps unconsciously, to ape those happy Christians who are not mocked or persecuted. Though even that is not enough for him to escape anti-Semitism.

The rabbis to whom the Jews had historically turned for guidance in times of crisis failed to adapt to the worsening conditions. Their conventional diagnosis was that God was punishing Jews for their sins. Their advice was to study the Torah more intensively. Jews whose forbears had hung on every rabbinic word found such analysis meaningless. Though few were tempted to forswear their Jewish identity, increasing numbers backed away from religion, defining themselves—as, ironically, anti-Semites so often defined them—by culture and ethnicity.

The rabbis, unable to adjust to the separation of religion from Jewish identity, also failed to perceive that the anti-Semitism of their time was more than another passing storm in the eternal cycle of Jewish suffering. Blaming the crisis on the abandonment of Torah and the decline of prayer, they ignored the rising danger. The Mitnaggedic *rav* was no better than the Hasidic *rebbe* at jettisoning old habits of mind. Their abdication forced the community to seek out new leaders, who necessarily came from the sector of secularized, Enlightenment Jews.

The founding in Paris in 1860 of the Alliance Israélite Universelle heralded the wave. Gestating since a massacre of Jews in Damascus in 1840, it was conceived by Jewish laymen as a nonreligious institution that would bridge national barriers. The Alliance proposed to use the rising wealth and influence of emancipated Jews to combat anti-Semitism, largely by promoting secular Jewish education. Rabbis took no part.

Over the ensuing decades, the Alliance became the address to which persecuted Jewish communities everywhere turned for help. With notable energy, it fought for Jewish rights, while setting up Jewish schools throughout Europe and the Arab world. Historically, its importance lay in the model it provided for Zionism and other movements that would emerge later to fill the vacuum left by the abdication of rabbinic leadership.

But the Alliance was a thin barrier. Jews expected little of Russia, where the state rolled back the meager concessions it had once granted and promoted increasingly vicious pogroms. My father sometimes conveyed to me his childhood nightmares, in which he cowered under the bed while Cossacks raged through his neighborhood. He escaped becoming a victim when his family left Bialystok for America, but others were not so lucky. Anti-Semitism spiraled out of control not just in Poland but in Hungary, where Jews were accused of the ritual murder of Christian children, and in Romania, where charges were spread that Jews sowed germs of the plague.

Clouds were also gathering in Germany, where Jews once anticipated full acceptance, but where nationalist intellectuals now took to the streets to scream anti-Semitic denunciations. And even France, Europe's most liberal society, stunned the Jews with its fraudulent charges against Captain Alfred Dreyfus, a Jewish army officer whom it tried, convicted, imprisoned and ultimately exonerated, but only after an explosion of venomous anti-Semitism had swept through the land.

⁂

OVER THE COURSE of Europe's history, it had been the habit of Jews to submit meekly to anti-Semitism's recurring epidemics, waiting for them to pass. The rabbis had always prescribed this course to their followers, and the coming of the Enlightenment did not change the strategy.

But the Enlightenment had created a class of Jews different from the forbears who had accepted rabbinic guidance without question. Some had tasted emancipation, others had only smelled its aroma, but whatever their experience their outlook had changed. Such Jews would not, the word of the rabbis notwithstanding, resign themselves to a fate prepared for them by their enemies. Instead, they confronted danger and made plans to defeat it.

Escape, of course, had a long precedent in the Diaspora, and many followed the custom. Most of those who fled crossed the Atlantic, though traditional rabbis decried those lands as godless. These emigrants helped shape a new Jewish community in America. Unforeseen, in saving themselves they also saved much of the Jewish world.

But many stayed behind and, for the first time in Jewish history, adopted a secular strategy. However different the circumstances, the centuries of practical experience of running *kehillot* no doubt served them well. Jews had diverse conceptions of how to deal with the dangers they faced, but never before had any substantial number promoted their interests as active participants in Europe's politics.

First to emerge was the Jewish socialist movement, which conducted strikes in Russia as early as the 1870s. In 1897, after a series of failed starts, the General Jewish Workers Union, known commonly as the Bund, was founded. Speaking Yiddish, the Bund signaled its autonomy from Russian socialism, with its endemic anti-Semitism.

While pursuing an end to capitalism, the Bund also took a stand against rising anti-Semitic violence.

The Bund reached its peak in the Russian Revolution of 1905, mobilizing some thirty-five thousand members. In its subsequent decline, it continued to promote Jewish cultural separatism, along with a Jewish nationalism, the realization of which it envisaged within Russia's borders. The Bund vanished completely after the Bolsheviks took power in the Russian Revolution of 1917. But its secular activism was an important legacy for eastern Europe's Jewish community.

In the same year that the Bund was founded, Theodor Herzl, a Viennese intellectual committed to Enlightenment values, convened the first World Zionist Congress in Basel. As a journalist working in Paris, he had been shaken by the Dreyfus affair and vowed to take action against the perils he saw looming ahead. The movement he initiated was, like socialism, based on a vow to transform the Jewish habit of submission into resistance to anti-Semitism.

In contrast to the Bundist dream of a universal brotherhood, the Zionists were inspired by political separatism, specifically the movements for national independence then flourishing throughout Europe. The Zionist answer to the "Jewish problem" was to end the exile by establishing a Jewish nation-state in Palestine. While Bundists proclaimed that ethnic hatreds would evaporate in an egalitarian world, Zionism insisted that anti-Semitism would be a danger no more only when Jews were "a nation like other nations."

Some historians contend that, secular as they were, both movements had deep roots in Jewish religious mysticism. Both, they argue, emerge from a promise familiar to all Jews which holds that a miracle will produce redemption, creating a utopia from which suffering will depart forever. Both, historians say, were movements in the messianic tradition.

But however common their roots, their different aims made the movements bitter rivals. The Bund, emboldened by its own early successes, was convinced that Zionism was impractical. The Zionists replied that even if the Bund triumphed, it was a fantasy to imagine that socialism would produce a culture in which Christians would live harmoniously with Jews.

Inevitably, some Jews, most of them young, found logic in merging the two ideas. Their efforts in time produced the Zionist labor movement, the Israel Labor Party and the kibbutz movement, which profoundly shaped the Jewish state. But at the start, what Herzl envisaged was a purely nationalist movement, unencumbered by either religion or social ideals.

In the contest between the two movements, the Zionists were ultimately triumphant. As history has shown, moreover, they were all too correct in foreseeing that, even after successful revolutions, anti-Semitism would persist in socialist societies. The Soviet Union offered ample proof. As for the Zionist dream of a Jewish state, the socialists also were mistaken in regarding it as a fool's illusion.

But even as the Enlightenment secularized Jewish culture, it left Judaism as a religion very much alive. Zionist ideology failed to provide a place for it, either in its political vision or, later, in the Jewish state. For more than a century, relations between Judaism and Zionism were, at best, improvised.

It would have been unrealistic of Jews to expect an easy reconciliation. The Western nations had worked for centuries to reconcile the divergent goals of church and state, and Jews had no comparable experience in politics, much less in settling complex internal struggles. Zionism never anticipated how hard it would be to narrow the gap between Judaism and the state.

The problem, of course, was that since the Enlightenment, Judaism's role in Jewish society had become increasingly contentious. Secular Zionism's triumph in founding Israel as a Jewish state only opened a new round in a long-standing conflict. Rabbinic Judaism, though no longer synonymous with the Jewish people, was not ready to be dismissed as obsolete. Its surprising durability in the modern world has left Israel with a predicament that Jews have yet to resolve.

ᔕ   ᔕ   ᔕ

HISTORY, ON CAREFUL examination, records that the first movement for return to the Holy Land was not secular at all but emerged directly from Judaic theology. A few creative rabbis, out of feelings of piety, turned their minds to establishing a Jewish state in Palestine more than a half-century before Herzl contemplated Zionism.

Rabbinic sages, as a body, had long opposed collective efforts at a return to the Holy Land. The ban was imbedded in the tradition with which Jews had lived since exile. But these rabbis were different. Alarmed at the rise of anti-Semitism, they defied their colleagues by arguing that resettlement of the Holy Land was not only practical but ordained by God.

Rabbi Judah Alkalai, a scholar of Talmud and Kabbalah, was serving in a small town in Bosnia in 1840 when the massacre of the Jews in Damascus occurred. Alkalai called it a warning. To justify a program of Jewish return to Palestine, he drew from Isaiah: "The spirit of the times has freed all the inhabitants of the earth . . . and calls upon us to say to the [Jewish] prisoners, 'Go free.'" He proceeded with solicitations to European leaders, letters to Jewish intellectuals and active planning with the Alliance Israélite Universelle.

Among the rabbis who came to his support was Zevi Hirsch Kalischer of Prussia, who argued in messianic terms for the immediate establishment of agricultural communities in the Holy Land. "We shall succeed in redemption," he wrote, "by plowing and reaping . . . , from which come blessing of life and food to all who are therein." When the settlements were on a sound economic foundation, he said, the Lord would fulfill his promise of redemption.

These rabbis, known to history as Harbingers, had a greater impact on the secular thinkers then laying the intellectual groundwork for Zionism than on their fellow rabbis. Years would pass before their ideas found even a limited place in Judaism's agenda. Meanwhile, such critics as Rabbi Naftali Berlin, head of a famous yeshiva in Volozhin, targeted them. Kalischer, he said, was close to heresy in claiming that redemption was imminent. "In our own time," he said, "we are subjugated in the Exile and subject to new edicts, [and] we must not bring up any idea of redemption in connection with the land."

Critics like Rabbi Berlin were not suggesting that Jews renounce their long-standing plans to return to the homeland. Jews, after all, still prayed for "Next year in Jerusalem." The *idea* of redemption in the Holy Land was as alive as ever. But conventional rabbinic doctrine maintained that Jews had a duty to wait patiently until the Messiah led them back. The return, they said, would come when God willed it, at the End of Days.

According to long-standing rabbinic doctrine, individual Jews or even small groups desiring to study Torah in the Holy Land, like the sages of Safed, were free to migrate. But the proposals of Alkalai and Kalischer, as most rabbis understood them, were to initiate redemption independently of the Messiah by organizing a mass return. It was the bypassing of the divine—"forcing the End," in rabbinic terms— that they found presumptuous and judged to be a sin.

The source of the doctrine that barred "forcing the End" lay in the early Talmudic era, when rabbis were establishing their credentials as the leaders of the exile community. Central to their mission, as they conceived it, was to ease the exiles' pain. The route they chose required that Jews swear to a set of "Three Oaths," a route that had a huge impact on the life of the Jews. The Three Oaths are not widely discussed in rabbinic literature, but they dominated the Jews' collective response to exile for nearly two thousand years.

The oaths were the following:

- First, not to return en masse to the Holy Land.
- Second, not to rebel against the nations in which they lived.
- Third, in return for the second, to entreat their hosts not to oppress them unduly.

Taken together, the Oaths suggest the terms of a pact between the exiles and their hosts. The Jews, according to this pact, vowed to be passive, in return for which the Gentiles would agree to be generous. The Oaths surely did not save the Jews from persecution, but it fixed their own psychological parameters. The rabbinate makes a plausible case that passivity, over the course of exile, was the key to Jewish survival. Many critics disagree. In any case, the Jews, conditioned by their rabbis, kept their part of the bargain, even when their Gentile hosts did not.

It is fair to ask why rabbis chose to include in the Oaths a ban on the Jews' return to the land of their forebears. One explanation is the belief, repeatedly expressed in rabbinic literature, that since God sent the Jews into exile to punish them for their sins, only God had the power to lead them back.

But it is also relevant to recall that when the sages replaced the priests in power after the Second Temple fell, they designated the two Torahs, written and oral, as the foundation of Jewish life. Their instruction to the exiles was to devote themselves to studying the Torah while waiting patiently for the Messiah to lead them to redemption. Whatever comfort such persistent study may have brought, it made sure the rabbis, as the Torah's stewards, remained firmly in control of Jewish life.

There were other practical reasons for the Oaths. The rabbinic claim may or may not have been valid that, by forbidding resistance, they mitigated persecution. But, as the Talmud affirms, the rabbis retained in their memories the harsh lessons of resistance to foreign authority in the Second Temple era. Judea's futile uprisings against Rome were a constant reminder of the afflictions that foolish adventures could bring down on the people, and on the rabbinic establishment.

A prominent rabbi in about the tenth century illustrates how the sages relied on the Oaths, imbuing them with divine authority to give them force. He quotes God saying,

> I made you an oath, my careful ones,
>   lest you rebel.
> Await the End of Days, and do not tremble.

Once in exile, the Jews renounced the stiff-necked response they had made not just to God in Sinai but to Rome in the time of the Great Revolt and Bar-Kokhba uprising. Though Jews squabbled among themselves over politics and doctrine, they remained overwhelmingly obedient to their rabbis in never challenging Gentile regimes.

A celebrated Jewish poet of the era of the Crusades, after a particularly heinous massacre, described the Jewish response.

> The pious wives dispatch the work
> And offer up their guileless babes.

The fathers quickly slay their sons,
And wish not to survive their dead.
To render homage to Thy unity,
The young, the fair, prepare for death,
With "Hear, O Israel!" on their lips.

The Jews' passivity in the face of persistent persecution is explained by, more than anything else, their acceptance of rabbinic exhortation to be faithful to the Three Oaths.

Avi Ravitsky, a professor of Jewish thought at the Hebrew University, points out that during the long centuries of exile when the collective return of the Jews was not at all feasible, rabbinic literature discussed the Three Oaths only sporadically. An Orthodox Jew himself, Ravitsky is the main authority on the subject. He writes that until the Enlightenment, the Three Oaths were the conventional wisdom, taken for granted, beyond challenge.

Moses Mendelssohn, ironically, argued that the Three Oaths were intrinsic to the Haskalah. The vow of loyalty to the host government and the waiver of collective efforts to return to the Holy Land, he maintained, provided the basis for the Jews to combine Orthodox piety with German patriotism.

But as the shadows of the Enlightenment darkened rabbinic authority, Orthodoxy rediscovered the Oaths and withdrew them like arrows from their quiver to discredit the heresy they perceived in the Harbingers. By late in the nineteenth century, the Oaths had become standard rabbinic doctrine for challenging Zionism.

Rabbi Hayyim Eleazar Shapira, a Hungarian Hasid, argued vigorously that migration to the Holy Land, in abandoning "faith in miraculous redemption from heaven," preempted the Messiah. He declared firmly that Zionism, in violating the Oaths, violated Halacha itself. He called the Zionists "evil forces [who] have become stronger in our Holy Land and they undermine its very foundation through their ploughshares and agricultural colonies." Efforts at "forcing the End," he maintained, were a sacrilege.

Scholars point out that in devising the Three Oaths, the Talmudic sages redefined the Messiah himself. The Messiah is never mentioned in the Bible and has been an evolving figure in Jewish lore. The biblical citations which some interpret as references to the Messiah identify him as a descendant of King David, and so destined to restore the monarchy. Jews in the immediate postbiblical period tended to see the Messiah not as God's agent but as a military savior, like Bar-Kokhba.

The Talmud is the first to impart a mystical quality to the Messiah, promising a reversal of tragedy in saying, "Messiah was born on the day the Temple was destroyed." The sages clearly drew from Christianity, which considered him divine; the very word *Christos* translates as "Messiah." In contrast, the image painted in the Talmud is of a mortal but one with a supernatural mission. The Messiah was to put an end to human history, bringing redemption by restoring the Jews to their homeland and establishing God's kingdom on earth.

The promise of the Messiah, after the Temple fell, became intrinsic to relieving the pain of exile. The promise offered Jews the vision of redemption but required them to wait patiently for it. An early Zionist thinker hypothesized that Jews became passive—adopted a "spirit of indolence," as he put it—after realizing they could not by their own devices return home. As a substitute for action, the rabbis offered messianic hope. The formula of the Three Oaths goes far to explain why, for century after century, believing Jews accepted oppression virtually without resistance.

Not coincidentally, the Jews' messianic fervor reached its highest pitch at moments of great grief: the Crusades, the Inquisition, the Chmielnicki massacres, the pogroms. Gershom Scholem, the preeminent scholar of Jewish mysticism, calls messianism a "theory of catastrophe," in presuming devastation as the prelude to utopia. The record shows that Jews have turned to it chiefly in times of severe suffering.

So why, Jews have asked, has the Messiah not appeared to rescue them? The standard rabbinic explanation is that not he but their own failings are to blame. Rabbinic Judaism, having adopted this explanation for the Temple's ruin, repeated it with each Jewish tragedy and adopted it again in confronting the Holocaust. It dismissed as irrelevant the evil of Nazism as it did the mind-set of passivity. Millions of Jews, hoping for the Messiah to appear, marched—to use the biblical metaphor—"like sheep to slaughter." Orthodoxy attributed it to God's punishment for Jewish sins.

Rabbinic Judaism, particularly Hasidism, even insisted that Jewish passivity toward the Nazis had been heroic. Those who rebelled in defiance of the rabbis, most of them secular, were anti-Halachic. The handful of rabbis who fought Nazis were described as emulating Gentiles. One Haredi rabbi issued a blanket denunciation of resistance, saying it betrayed "a lack of heroism, a lack of capacity to live and suffer" and, somehow, hastened the deaths of many thousands of Jews.

After World War II, many survivors asked in bewilderment, "Where was God?" Orthodoxy had the answer. It was what the Israeli writer David Landau calls the "crime-and-punishment" explanation of every catastrophe that has befallen the Jews. Orthodoxy attributed the devastation to divine wrath.

Some rabbis, chiefly Hasidim, specifically cited Zionism as the sin. Hasidism had long before abandoned the Baal Shem Tov's challenge to the rigidity of Jewish law to become Halachic dogmatists, echoing the Three Oaths to hold that a Jewish state had never offered hope to the Jews. Even during the Nazi era, they argued that emigration to safety in Palestine, no less than America, exposed believing Jews to godlessness. Some loathed Zionism enough to seek out alliances with the Arabs to prevent Israel's creation. To this day, Hasidim conventionally maintain that Israel is a heresy which exposes Jews to a vengeful God.

Rabbi Joel Teitelbaum, a celebrated *rebbe* of the Satmar sect, formerly of Romania and later of Brooklyn, called the founding of the Jewish state a terrible crime. "The prohibition against violating the [Three] Oaths and trying to advance the End applies to all Jews," he wrote, "even the righteous." Teitelbaum rated the Oath that barred "forcing the End" higher than the vows the Jews had made to God at Sinai. It was the Jews' untimely return to the Holy Land, he wrote, that was to blame for the deaths in Hitler's crematoria.

> Because of our sinfulness we have suffered greatly. . . . In former times, whenever trouble befell [the Jews], the matter was pondered and the reasons sought—which sin had brought the troubles about?—so that we could make

amends and return to the Lord, may He be blessed. But in our generation we need not look far for the sin responsible for our calamity. . . . The heretics have made all kinds of efforts to violate the Oaths, to go up by force and to seize sovereignty and freedom for themselves, before the appointed time. . . . They have lured the majority of the Jewish people into awful heresy, the like of which has not been seen since the world was created. . . . And so it is no wonder that the Lord lashed out in anger. . . . And there were also righteous people who perished because of the iniquity of the sinners and corrupters, so great was God's wrath.

Teitelbaum was a particularly radical critic of the Zionist state. Yet he remains, since his death in 1977, a hero among Haredim, who take his assertions seriously. These assertions, it need hardly be said, grate upon the efforts to reconcile rabbinic Judaism, and especially Ultra-Orthodoxy, with contemporary Jewish society.

☙ ☙ ☙

A SECULAR JEW, INDIFFERENT to the Three Oaths, Theodor Herzl convened the First Zionist Congress in August 1897, in Basel, Switzerland.

Herzl's original plan had been to locate it in Munich, and the Bavarian government raised no objection, but the German Rabbinic Association protested. Composed of opposing Orthodox and Reform wings, the Association presented an explanation for each side. Orthodoxy said: "The aspirations of the so-called Zionists . . . contradict the messianic promises of Judaism as enunciated in the holy scripture and later religious canons. . . ." Reform said: "Judaism obliges its adherents to serve the fatherland to which they belong with utmost devotion and to further its national interests with all their heart and strength." Opposition to Zionism was the only point on which the two wings of Judaism agreed.

Herzl, known as much for his wit as for his organizational skills, answered scornfully, "The latest vogue in Jewry are the Protest-rabbis. These are people who sit in a safe boat using their oars to beat the heads of drowning men who try to hang on to the sides." The "drowning men" to whom he referred were Russia's Jews, though by now he should have recognized that Germany was not a "safe boat" either. Calling Orthodoxy's messianism "sheer arrogance," he mocked Reform's claim that German patriotism was in conflict with Zionism, but the Association won. He had to change the conference site.

Herzl, without serious training in religion, was in many ways typical of the Enlightenment. He had taken to celebrating Jewish holidays with his family only after embarking on his Zionist mission. Unlike religious Jews, his interest in Palestine lay only in its potential for refuge. Herzl saw Zionism as a movement of temporal salvation.

As Herzl defined his mission, it had little to do with the holiness of the land. He was even willing, until the scheme collapsed for lack of popular support, to accept a British offer to settle oppressed Jews in Uganda. Some of his followers at Basel went further in their secularism, envisaging Zionism as a movement to establish a society unburdened by traditional Judaism. "The material improvement of our nation," wrote J. L. Gordon, a prominent theoretician, "is tied up with religious change." Indeed, most Zionists considered Orthodoxy's messianic fixation as a drag on the Jewish future. Among their mottos was, "Israel has no Messiah, so get to work!"

Herzl, in his opening address at Basel, expressed concerns about religion, but in pragmatic terms. He called Zionism a "return to the Jewish fold." But his disdain for traditional practices emerged in his praise of "that part of Jewry which is modern, cultured, had outgrown the ghetto and lost the habit of petty trading." Herzl shared the attitude of most seculars, whose objections were not to religious Judaism as such but to its social consequences.

Unlike many seculars, however, Herzl refused to be diverted by ideology. He was aware, on the one hand, that Zionism had to change old patterns of thought to serve the masses and, on the other, that a large segment of eastern European Jewry remained loyal to its rabbis. Though he had succeeded in luring rather few religious Jews to Basel, he received a rabbinic delegation and surprised his followers by attending synagogue on the Sabbath, even reciting a Torah benediction. To Herzl, secularism was secondary to establishing a Jewish homeland.

The principal achievement of the First Zionist Congress was to adopt what came to be called the Basel Program. Its chief operating statement was: "Zionism seeks to establish a home for the Jewish people in Palestine secured under public law." In not mentioning a state, the program was meant to be vague enough to satisfy a range of opinion, including religious Jews. Few doubted, however, that Herzl's vision was of an independent state, Jewish and secular.

In the closing session, the chief rabbi of Basel tested Herzl's intentions by offering to abandon his theological anti-Zionism in exchange for assurance that any future state would keep Judaism's tenets, starting with the Sabbath. Herzl answered that, though rabbis had nothing to fear, Orthodoxy was only one of Judaism's schools. All Jewish opinion, he said, would be respected. His words signaled his backing for religious toleration, an idea that his audience applauded widely. The Basel rabbi was not satisfied, however, and Orthodoxy gave the idea no support.

But at least some rabbis perceived the Basel congress as the first station on what might be a long religious journey, and reasoned that in spurning Zionism they risked being left behind. Though most of Orthodoxy decided to accept the risk, a few rabbis did not. They saw Zionism as an extremely diverse movement, with room in it for religion. They reckoned that, by working within its framework, they could satisfy the needs of Jews and at the same time serve Judaism.

It is no coincidence that most of the rabbis who opted for Zionism lived under czarist rule. Like Jews elsewhere, Russians were divided between traditional and secular, but the oppression both suffered gave them a common vision. Some Orthodox rabbis thought Zionism had the potential for repenting its heresies, and some even saw it reunifying the riven community. These few rabbis saw the prospect, in effect, of converting the movement to Judaism. Heirs of the Harbingers, such rabbis dreamed of shaping a nationalism built not around secularism but around Jewish Orthodoxy.

Rabbi Shmuel Mohilever, born in 1824, had made an earlier move in this direction. He was a founder of Hovevei Zion (Lovers of Zion), a movement that responded to the czarist pogroms in the 1880s by setting up settlement associations throughout Europe. The movement never developed the vision of statehood that later defined Zionism but, under both rabbinic and secular leaders, it contributed importantly to providing homes for several thousand Jews in Palestine.

Mohilever, for his efforts, was charged by his rabbinic colleagues with "consorting with atheists." A prominent rabbi, in denouncing him, damned Hovevei Zion as a "new sect, like that of Shabbatai Zevi—may his name rot." But Mohilever, in refusing to be bound by rabbinic convention, succeeded in bringing religion to the settlement movement. Explaining his core belief, he said: "God prefers to have His children live in their land even if they do not observe the Torah rather than observe the Torah properly and live in the Diaspora."

Mohilever was a central figure, in 1889, in a clash of priorities that even today Israel has not fully resolved. Orthodoxy had demanded that the Hovevei Zion settlers observe a biblical command to let the land lie fallow on the seventh year. His first instinct, Mohilever said, was "to observe the *mitzvah* after two thousand years . . . to win over the hearts of the Orthodox to return to us." But on second thought, he said, the observance would devastate the settlers' lives, so he chose the expedient course of endorsing a Halachic opinion that permitted a fictitious sale of the land to Muslim buyers.

In explanation, he later wrote, "I staunchly maintain my position."

> . . . Now that the number of Jewish workers in our land has greatly increased, and their livelihood is derived from working the fields and vineyards of their brethren. . . . If we forbid them to work we will be taking food out of their mouths and they will, Heaven forbid, die of starvation.

Mohilever's decision followed the Talmudic injunction to "search for a way" to satisfy a practical requirement. But most Orthodox rabbis did not accept the injunction, concluding that the solution not only failed the Halachic test but, more important, sapped any prospect that Jewish migration would restore the holiness of the land. The ruling, considered a watershed, split Mohilever from Orthodoxy, confirming its belief that the effort of return was essentially a sin.

Mohilever lived long enough to encourage Herzl in his plans for the First Zionist Congress, though ill health kept him from attending. But in a poignant letter read to the Congress, he expressed his anxieties as a Russian Jew and as a rabbi:

> A great fire, a fearful conflagration, is raging in our midst, and we are all threatened. Our enemies have multiplied until they surpass many millions, and [they are ready to] devour us alive. If brethren put out their hands to deliver us from dire straits, are there such among us who would spurn them?

Then, departing dramatically from the conventional rabbinic interpretation of "forcing the End," he declared,

> The resettlement of our country—that is, the purchase of land and the building of houses, the planting of orchards and the cultivation of the soil—is one of the fundamental commandments of our Torah; some of our ancient sages even say that it is the equivalent to the whole Law, for it is the foundation of the existence of our people.

Mohilever's letter is said to have touched many of the secular delegates at Basel, opening them to the possibility of cooperating with rabbinic Judaism. The speech simplified the effort that Rabbi Isaac Reines was then making there to establish a religious beachhead within the secular majority.

A generation younger than Mohilever, Reines was head of a synagogue in the small Russian town of Lida. His interest in the Holy Land is said to have been aroused by his father, who once lived there. Reines had accepted Herzl's invitation to Basel with enthusiasm, and put his energies—with little success—to persuading other Russian rabbis to join him.

Reines had reluctantly concluded that Orthodoxy was becoming a negative force, distant from the practical needs of Jews, perhaps even jeopardizing its own survival. In contrast to Herzl, he was a Jewish nationalist who believed nationalism's heart lay in the Torah as well as the land. Reines rejected Herzl's argument that all opinions in Judaism were equal. His vision was to restore Orthodoxy's preeminence by having it recapture Zionism's institutions. First, however, he needed a doctrine to make it compatible with mainstream Zionism.

The doctrine he devised was far removed from that of the Harbingers, and even of Rabbi Mohilever, his mentor. Innovative as it was, it was theologically conservative, like its author, most of whose beliefs were close to those of conventional rabbis. In his writings, Reines makes clear his commitment to the messianic miracle. He consistently upheld the rabbinic ban on "forcing the End," the doctrine that stood as the wall between Orthodoxy and Zionism. Reines's genius lay in the intellectual dexterity by which he got over the wall.

"Zionist ideology," Reines wrote, "is devoid of any trace of the idea of redemption. . . . In none of the Zionists' acts or aspirations is there the slightest allusion to future redemption. Their sole intention is to improve the Jewish people's situation, to raise their stature and accustom them to a life of happiness. . . . How can one compare this idea with the idea of redemption?"

Referring metaphorically to the crisis in which the Jews found themselves, Reines went on, "If my family is trapped in a burning house, it matters not to me whether the person who rushes to their rescue is religious or secular."

Reines's formula for resolving the conundrum presented by messianism was to place Zionism in the present world and redemption in the next. Zionism, he explained, was the response of the Jews to an emergency; redemption was an eternal yearning. His clear desire to fuse the two may have created a paradox for some thinkers. But he saw the two goals, refuge and redemption, as separate from and complementary to each other.

Reines's two categories offered observant Jews the prospect of contributing to the return to the land while remaining loyal to the faith. His doctrine became the basis of the movement known as "religious Zionism." In time the movement would embrace a much more militant ideology, but in Herzl's era it became the vehicle for keeping Judaism as a part of the vision for the Jewish state.

In 1900, three years after the Basel conference, Reines and a group of rabbinic disciples published an open letter in support of the Zionist movement. It presented Zionism in narrow terms, as a solution to a practical problem that did not intrude upon the faith. But its criticism of conventional Orthodox thinking was severe. In part, the letter said:

> In recent years our situation has deteriorated disastrously. Many of our brethren are scattered in every direction, on the seven seas, in places where the fear of assimilation is hardly remote. The Zionists saw that the only fitting place for our brethren to settle would be in the Holy Land . . .
>
> If some preachers, while speaking of Zion, also mention redemption and the coming of the Messiah, and thus let the abominable thought enter people's minds that the idea encroaches upon the territory of true redemption, only they themselves are to blame, for it is their own wrong opinion they express. . . . Anyone who thinks the Zionist idea . . . is undermining our holy faith is clearly in error.

Reines's allegiance was to Zionism as a "political" movement, that is, one limited to resettling Jews in their homeland. A rival Zionist wing, called "cultural," urged, in addition to resettlement, the promotion of secularism, socialism and vernacular Hebrew, all anathema to Orthodoxy. At the Fifth Zionist Congress, the "cultural" wing won a vote favoring the spread of its message throughout the Jewish world. Seeing a threat to traditional Judaism, the cause he had vowed to serve, Reines gathered his forces.

In Vilna in 1902, Rabbi Reines convened a meeting at which he founded Mizrachi, an association to promote religious Zionism within the framework of the Zionist movement. Mizrachi's name was coined from the Hebrew words for "spiritual center," and its avowed aim was to purge "alien elements" from the agenda of its secular rivals. Reaffirming its commitment to the Basel Program, Mizrachi adopted the slogan "The Land of Israel for the people of Israel according to the Torah of Israel."

In retrospect, it is clear religious Zionism's split from the secular mainstream was, sooner or later, inevitable. But Herzl was committed to keeping Reines's group within the Zionist camp. Unlike the secular ideologues, he regarded cooperation with religious Jewry as essential to Zionism's long-term success. Though scarcely happy with the organizational discord it had stirred up, he accepted Mizrachi as a legitimate faction within the Zionist movement.

Not surprisingly, Herzl's decision satisfied neither Orthodox nor secular Jews. The Orthodox establishment denounced Mizrachi as more dangerous than secularism itself, claiming it provided the means for seducing the faithful. Conversely, seculars objected to his offering to old-fashioned superstition a beachhead on the shore of a new and modern Jewish society.

History has in part vindicated the worries of both. Mizrachi, by insisting on a place within Zionism for religious Jews, contributed to creating the Jewish state, which the main body of Orthodoxy opposed. On the other hand, it also opened the door to the influence that Orthodoxy was later to exercise, which gave the state a far greater religious orientation than the founders of secular Zionism had contemplated.

After its founding in 1902, Mizrachi spread its message quickly, establishing hundreds of branches throughout the Diaspora. In 1904, with the founding of the Mizrachi World Organization, it emerged as an international force. Most important, it became dominant in Russia, by now the Zionist heartland, where it offered to countless Jews a doctrine that satisfied both political and religious yearnings.

Russia's Revolution of 1905, however, led to a change in Mizrachi's character. The czar became even more hostile to Jews than before, forcing Mizrachi to move its base to western Europe. Orthodox rabbis there, exposed to far less oppression, lacked the incentive to make a common program with Zionism. With Herzl now dead, Reines lost control of the organization and Mizrachi, under new leadership, became more Orthodox and less nationalist.

After World War I, Mizrachi moved on to Palestine, where it represented Orthodox interests in the growing Jewish community, the *yishuv*. Secular Jews by now substantially outnumbered the 50,000 or so religious settlers of earlier migrations. A Mizrachi party—later to become the National Religious Party—was founded to serve as the movement's political arm. Its members set up a network of religious schools and yeshivot; they founded Bar Ilan University, where higher religious and secular learning met on common ground. Mizrachi became involved in religious kibbutzim and moshavim, as well as construction companies, banks and newspapers. Its representatives served in the *yishuv*'s self-governing bodies; Mizrachi's rabbinic students fought in the wars of independence against the British and the Arabs.

In 1948, Rabbi Yehuda Leib Hacohen Fishman, who in 1902 sat with Rabbi Reines at the Vilna Conference, became a signer of Israel's Declaration of Independence. His presence symbolized religious Zionism's success in making its presence felt within the new Jewish state. Mizrachi never attained its goal of converting the Zionist movement to religious Judaism, but it served as a wedge to make the state far more religious than the delegates at Basel ever imagined it would be.

י י י

YET IN THE JEWISH STATE, the Mizrachi movement was never free of the shadow of Orthodox criticism. Whatever Mizrachi did for Orthodoxy, it was not enough. Haredim relentlessly badgered Mizrachi for failing to achieve Reines's ideal of leading Zionism back to the faith. They castigated Mizrachi for complicity in running a godless state that, they said, was no different from the states of the Gentiles. Their sneering left Mizrachi with a kind of complex, forcing its members to ask whether they had done enough for God and whether they could not do more.

It is true that since the time of Rabbi Reines, the Mizrachi movement had evolved away from conventional Orthodoxy. Reines appears solemnly in photographs in a long white beard and high black hat, indistinguishable from other Orthodox rabbis. The heirs of the Mizrachi movement are, for the most part, now described as "modern Orthodox." They are likely to keep the Sabbath, pray regularly at the synagogue and eat only kosher food. But they dress fashionably, go to movies and the theater, read worldly literature and make homes next to non-Orthodox neighbors.

While modern Orthodox parents send their children to religious schools, they make sure the curriculum imbues them with the learning needed to thrive in a dominantly secular world. Unlike Haredim, modern Orthodox Jews believe they can be traditionally pious while living their lives in the contemporary setting. Their practice recalls Moses Mendelssohn's advice to Jews to be secular citizens in public and fully pious at home. Though modern Orthodoxy favors a state attentive to Jewish law, it is wary of religious coercion. Unlike Ultra-Orthodoxy, it is generally respectful of individual religious choice.

In Israel, the issue that basically divides Mizrachi from Haredim, however, is not outward appearance; it is still the age-old messianic question. Religious Zionists have never doubted the legitimacy of Israel as a Jewish state. Ultra-Orthodoxy still objects to Israel's "forcing the End" and holds that only the Messiah can legitimize the state.

The Ultra-Orthodox rationalize their residence in a state whose Jewishness they reject by insisting that, theologically, they are still in exile. They deny any hypocrisy to their participation in the political system by contending that they follow the practice of their forebears who promoted Jewish interests in Gentile lands in any way available to them. Agudath Yisrael, their political party, has never departed from the demand that Israel be governed by Halacha. Its Council of Torah Sages, the rabbis who make policy, still maintain that without the Messiah, Israel is a Jewish heresy.

But even a quick look reveals the Haredi charge that Israel is a state like the Gentile states to be false. The trend within Western democracies over recent centuries has been to separate church and state. Israel has gone very far in the opposite direction. Notwithstanding Orthodoxy's disdain, Israel accepts Orthodox Judaism as the state's one official faith.

Israel has a chief rabbi, who is an official paid by the state. (In fact, it has two chief rabbis, one Ashkenazi, the other Sephardi, both Orthodox.) It maintains at public expense all Orthodox rabbis and their synagogues. It finances religious education at every level, run by Orthodox administrators. It empowers a system of Orthodox courts to preside over the enforcement of Halachic law in personal matters. It also sets Orthodox standards for naturalization and waives military service for students at Orthodox yeshivot.

These concessions are the direct product of Mizrachi's labors within the Zionist community. In recent years, Orthodox Jews became a crucial "swing vote" between rival secular parties, enhancing their ability to win political favors. They have shown great skill at using these powers. But the pattern of concessions long predated that change.

This pattern can be traced back to Mizrachi's early alliance with Herzl, who regarded religious support as crucial to Zionism's long-term well-being. David Ben-Gurion, who led Zionism from the *yishuv*'s early days until the state was on its feet, followed Herzl's precedent. When a Mizrachi rabbi was asked why God chose a secular Jew as His messenger, he answered that otherwise, "people might have mistakenly believed that he [Ben-Gurion] was the Messiah."

Politically, Mizrachi was wise enough not to insist upon the attainment of its religious ideals but to take from Zionism whatever concessions it could get. In the place of full theocratic rule, for example, it has achieved rabbinic control over marriage and divorce, a power many Israelis regard as excessive. But from the start, Zionism treated this power as a fair price to pay for the cohesion of the Jewish community. Whatever the complaints of Haredim, the attainable has been significant, and were Rabbi Reines alive he would surely be pleased with the results of his labors.

On the religious level, modern Orthodoxy today has little dispute with secularism. Religious tolerance characterizes their relationship. The wars of religion in Israel today are between seculars and Haredim, who press for ever larger powers to Judaize Israeli life. Proclaiming Israel a Gentile state, Haredim call for its reorganization along the lines of the *kehillot,* with rabbis enforcing religious conformity upon the entire community. Secular Zionists draw a line against this model, but so do religious Zionists, who are satisfied to follow modern Orthodox practices.

That does not mean, however, that religious Zionists—the name "Mizrachi" has largely dropped out of usage—do not have major conflicts with the state. Indeed, after the Six-Day War in 1967, religious Zionism revealed an undercurrent of discontent, which led to a decision to do more to serve God. After some seven decades of distinguished service in balancing religion with nationalism, religious

Zionism veered away from its tradition of reconciliation, and tipped over into a zealous ultranationalism.

The change came in the wake of Israel's spectacular military victory, which led religious Zionism to a conviction that God had Himself changed priorities. Religious Zionism adopted the notion that God's priority was no longer devotion to the Torah as much as devotion to the land that Israel's army had recently conquered. The perception transformed the nature of the movement; it also transformed Israel.

Religious Zionists were not unanimous in embracing the new doctrine. Many took pride in the movement's long service to the state. Satisfied with the moderate teachings Reines had left to them, they declined to be swept into a stream that had so abruptly changed its course. But most were drawn to the new militancy, and embraced the soil of Israel as the divine challenge of a new era.

Dynamic religious movements, by their nature, require scriptural endorsement, and religious Zionism was no exception. Suddenly, the new militants declared Reines's moderate doctrines out of date and insisted on giving their allegiance to a far more radical theology. This theology originated with Rabbi Abraham Isaac Kook, a younger contemporary of Reines. In the early years of the twentieth century, the two shared the commitment to settling the Holy Land. Neither expected the Jews to wait for the Messiah to lead them home, but they had different ideas of the role the Messiah would play.

Reines had founded Mizrachi by taking the Messiah out of Zionism, insisting that the secular quest for refuge had no bearing on messianic redemption. Kook remade the movement by putting the Messiah back. He argued, more mystically, that by settling the land the Jews would hasten the Messiah's arrival. His doctrine, making land more important than Torah in service to God, was largely overlooked until the Six-Day War, when it became religious Zionism's ideology. Today, Rabbi Reines is largely forgotten. It is Rabbi Kook's emphasis on the land that has opened fratricidal rifts in the worldwide community of Jews.

Chapter Eight

CHOSEN PEOPLE, CHOSEN TERRITORY

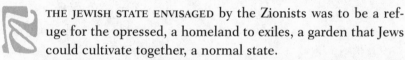 THE JEWISH STATE ENVISAGED by the Zionists was to be a ref-
uge for the opressed, a homeland to exiles, a garden that Jews
could cultivate together, a normal state.

The goal, though not modest, was limited. The Zionists had con-
sented to split the land with the local Arabs, and in 1947, with the
combined votes of the West and the Communist bloc substantially
outnumbering the Muslim opposition, the United Nations General
Assembly endorsed its partition into two states, Jewish and Arab. The
Arabs rejected the outcome and the Jews later had to fight for their independence. Even after they won, they remained besieged by Arab
neighbors. Still, in the early years, the signs pointed to Israel's becoming as normal as the Zionists had dreamed.

The massive victory in 1967 against the collective might of the Arab
world, however, lured Israel into a new course. No longer besieged, Israel suddenly became a regional military power, the ruler of a foreign
people, a headstrong nation-state on the model of Europe a century
before. So basic was the transformation that a few Israeli writers took
a page from French history to call the post-1967 state the "Second Israeli Republic."

The Jewish state after the Six-Day War occupied the hills on which David had trod and the desert in which Moses had made the covenant with God. More significantly, it held dominion, as had its Israelite forebears, over the natives on the land, whom the ancients had never subjugated and with whom they had never reconciled. Israel, since the Six-Day War, has been paying the costs of its victory.

Few Jews foresaw the problems that lay in Israel's transformation. The victory had been too intoxicating. Many rejected a simple military explanation, preferring to see it as supernatural, divinely determined, a giant step toward messianic redemption. Even the name of the war, evoking God's creation, had a mystical resonance.

Hardened secularists were as vulnerable as the pious to hidden meanings. On the war's third day, General Mordecai Gur led his forces in the capture of Jerusalem's Old City, which the Jews had not ruled since 70 C.E., the year of the Temple's destruction. Gur declared in his dispatch, "The Temple Mount is in our hands," words that rang with religious emotion. A famous photo showed Gur's toughened paratroopers showering kisses of joy on the Wailing Wall, the Temple's remnant. To celebrate, the army's chief rabbi blew the shofar, like a latter-day Joshua.

Moshe Dayan, the thoroughly secular and normally aloof minister of defense, shared the religious exhilaration. "We have returned to all that is holy in our land," he declared. "We have returned never to be parted again."

Within weeks, the Muslim quarter adjacent to the Wall had been cleared to create a huge plaza. Asked why the plaza's carnival atmosphere had replaced the mournful intimacy in which prayers had been recited for centuries, Teddy Kollek, Jerusalem's mayor, answered, "The old place had the character of exile. It was a place for wailing. This made sense in the past. It isn't what we want for the future." Israel has since abandoned the old name, since "wailing" was no longer fitting, in favor of the more commonplace designation Kotel, an abbreviation for "Kotel Ma'aravi," Western Wall.

Shortly after the war, seventy-two noted intellectuals, many of them mainstream Zionists, founded the Land of Israel Movement. In a highly publicized manifesto, they put aside historical differences to proclaim a nationalism based on divine imperative.

> The Israeli army's victory in the Six-Day war located the people and the state within a new and fateful period. The whole of the Land of Israel is now in the hands of the Jewish people. Just as we are not allowed to give up the State of Israel, so we are *ordered* to keep what we received there from the army's hands: the *Land* of Israel.

One might well ask by whom was Israel *ordered*. The answer, these thinkers made clear, was God. The Movement promptly became a force in Israeli politics.

Few Israelis failed to see a divine message in the fact that on the war's eve, the country, facing a huge Arab alliance, appeared at the edge of destruction. Yet a few days later, Israel was in possession of towns whose names leaped from Torah scrolls—Hebron, Beth-El, Jericho, Shechem (Nablus). To religious Jews, the modern seaside cities of Tel Aviv and Haifa had about them a touch of Hellenism. The hills of the interior, home of the biblical tribes, were the Jewish heartland. With God's help, they noted, this land had fallen to Israel's might.

"In the land of the Bible," an Israeli scholar wrote, summing up the war's transcendental nature, "the Israelis met the Israelites."

Jews spoke exultantly of the victory as a "miracle." They had long used the term to describe the recapture and purification of the Temple after the Maccabee triumph over the Seleucids in biblical times. It was also the term Jews used to represent their messianic expectations. Religious Zionism's rabbis, historically modest in their messianic expectations, were the lustiest in proclaiming sacred meaning. The victory, they said, meant the messianic *process* was reaching fruition, even if the Messiah himself was absent. National borders that went beyond those of ancient Israel were, to them, proof of the Messiah's hand.

Mainstream Zionism, meanwhile, having long tried to curb the Jewish appetite for territory, saw itself losing control. In 1948, David

Ben-Gurion, its leader, had agreed to the partition, reasoning that sharing the land was more likely than conquest to win the international community's endorsement, which was essential to the state's survival. He also hoped to avoid protracted warfare with the Arab world. Most Jews agreed then that a state with modest borders was better than no state at all. Suddenly, this view looked timid.

The chief dissenters from Ben-Gurion's logic belonged to a faction within Zionism known as Revisionism, modeled in the 1920s by its founder, Vladimir Jabotinsky, on the authoritarian nationalism then thriving in Europe. Jabotinsky dismissed Gentile opinion, whether Arab or Western, as irrelevant to Jews. He urged them not to shrink from using force to achieve statehood, and to agree to nothing less than Israel's historic frontiers.

So rancorous were the differences with the mainstream that Revisionism, in 1935, seceded from the Zionist movement altogether. During the War of Independence, the two rival factions actually fought a small but vicious civil war—known as the *Altalena* affair—in which several dozen Jews were killed. Israel's victory over the Arabs, and mainstream Zionism's defeat of Revisionism, appeared in 1948 to scrub the national agenda clean of expansionist dreams.

It is ironic that mainstream Zionism, through its victory in 1967, achieved Revisionism's territorial aims. Israel's foes insist that expansion had always been the national goal, and that Israel had provoked the war to attain it. Their view contradicts Israel's postwar offer, in defiance of the Revisionists, to trade the occupied land for peace. At the time, the Likud Party, Revisionism's political arm, was too weak to realize its long-standing aims. But when the dust of combat had settled, Revisionism had an unexpected ally.

The ally was religious Zionism. Since Herzl's time, religious Zionism's raison d'être had been to direct the Jewish state toward greater piety. Then, overnight, it emerged as the engine of Israeli territorialism. It called the six days of fighting the War of Redemption and declared the triumph to be God's sign that every inch of the land was holy. After decades of playing secularism's Sancho Panza, it became the spearhead of territorial messianism. Religious Zionists were unprecedented among Zionists in their zealotry. Unlike Revisionism's secular vision, their inspiration was built purely on devotion to God.

The course chosen by religious Zionism was an eerie reminder of the Holy Land in the last days of the Second Temple. Its militants evoked the Zealots, who led the Jews into the catastrophic war against Rome. Its leader recalled Rabbi Akiva, who had served as mentor of the ill-starred Bar-Kokhba. Rabbi Abraham Isaac Kook was himself a mild-mannered scholar, but the lessons that religious Zionism drew from him divided the Jews, provoked the Arabs and alienated much of the rest of the world.

Yet religious Zionism's shift to Revisionist goals did not mean the mainstream offered a sharp alternative. Though one wing of traditional Zionism favored exchanging territory for peace, another argued that national security forbade any but the most modest withdrawal. Mainstream Zionism's ambivalence made clear that even seculars had difficulty, once the land was in Israel's hands, giving it up. As time has passed, giving it up has become harder still.

The obduracy of the Arab states aggravated the problem. Meeting in the fall of 1967 in Khartoum, Sudan, the Arabs adopted a defiant stand of "no recognition, no conciliation, no negotiation" with the triumphant enemy. Many later abandoned this intransigence, and peace agreements were reached with Egypt and Jordan. But the fluidity that seemed present in Israel right after the war soon hardened, particularly toward Palestinians, whose homeland covered biblical terrain. One can debate whether the opportunity for agreement ever existed at all, but the alliance of religious Zionism and Revisionism prevailed. Since 1967, overall peace between Jews and Arabs has failed to surmount the obstacles that both sides have placed in its way.

Most Israelis agree that, in the years since the war, mainstream Zionism has lost the dynamism of its youthful days and, divided over the territories, grown unsure of itself. Revisionism, meanwhile, has probably become a shade more pragmatic. But religious Zionism, still convinced of its divine mission, is no less fierce many decades later than it was in the wake of the great victory of 1967.

By the early 1970s, religious Zionism had left far behind the conciliatory outlook of Rabbi Reines and Mizrachi. Guided by Rabbi Kook's militant ideology, it drew power from its fervor for the land, combined with single-minded mastery of Israel's complex political system. Though still small in numbers, religious Zionism became, after the Six-Day War, Israel's most dynamic political force.

🦊 🦊 🦊

ABRAHAM ISAAC KOOK was born in 1865 into a mixed Hasidic-Mitnaggedic family in a small Latvian town, where he received the customary Orthodox education. He did his rabbinical studies at the famous yeshiva at Volozhin. In his twenties, he served as the rabbi of tiny congregations in Latvia and Lithuania.

But at an early age, Kook had left his fellow students of the Talmud behind to explore the mysteries of the Bible and the Kabbalah, and even to examine European culture. He wrote religious works and also poetry, often secular in tone. While conventionally pious, he was also modern in accepting the idea of worldly progress, satisfied that its vitality came from God. His son and disciple, Rabbi Zvi Yehuda Kook, once described him as both "among the most devout rabbis" and a "free-thinking philosopher, impeded by nothing."

Though Kook did not attend the Zionist congress in Basel in 1897, he learned from friends who were there of Herzl's argument that establishing a Jewish refuge in the Holy Land had "nothing to do with religion." He later learned that Rabbi Reines held a similar view. While excited by the program adopted at Basel, he was troubled by the prospect that Jews might end the exile without a commitment to God.

Kook was basically a religious thinker, but he was also a practical man who directed his theology to practical ends. This was especially true of his thinking on migration to Palestine. To correct the flaws he perceived in Herzl's secular vision, and Reines's theology, he formulated his own doctrine of the Jews' return, daring to confront head-on the rabbinic ban on "forcing the End." "Nothing in our faith," he wrote in a direct challenge to traditional Orthodoxy, "either in its larger principles or in its details, negates the idea that we can begin to shake off the dust of exile by our own efforts."

But the goal of return, he said, must be "to prepare our people for redemption." The Jewish people, he wrote in a grand theological sweep, must "establish a religious center . . . and above all a great Sanhedrin from which Torah and instruction shall issue forth . . . and all the great sages of Israel will make decisions, when we have been planted on our land."

In 1903, Kook irritated eastern Europe's Orthodox rabbinate by describing settlement of the Holy Land not just as an option but as a duty. "Who can refrain from taking part? Who will not lend a hand? Who will oppose those laboring for the common good? . . . Perhaps it is the secret of divine wisdom which decrees that the beginning of the growth of the salvation of Israel should come through our own efforts." The next year Kook himself migrated to Palestine.

Kook's first post in the Holy Land was as rabbi of Jaffa, where he served a scattering of secular agricultural settlements. Though not known as an iconoclast, he infuriated rabbinic leaders by working with the pioneers. Orthodox rabbis were not alone in their suspicions of him. On the other side of the religious fence, the pioneers were annoyed at his conviction that holiness was as important to Zionism as refuge.

Kook was himself ambivalent toward the pioneers. "Ours is an amazing, astonishing generation," he wrote of them, "practically without parallel in our history. It is a combination of opposites, a mixture of light and darkness, both degraded and exalted, utterly guilty and utterly innocent. . . . 'Impertinence waxes, the son knows no shame before his father . . .' but at the same time kindness, honesty, fairness and mercy are on the rise, and the spirit of knowledge and idealism is ascendant."

Whatever his reservations, however, Kook believed the pioneers did more to enrich than to diminish Judaism. He believed they would in time return to the faith, bringing with them a passion for social justice that was lacking in conventional piety. The pioneer generation, he said, was an example of "the irony of history," in which improbable candidates advance Judaism's interests. He cited King Cyrus II of Persia, who invited the Jews to return from exile in Babylonia to rebuild the Temple. He also pointed to Herod, the Jewish king who, ruling at the behest of pagan Rome, rescued the Temple from disrepair.

Herzl, Kook said, was also an unknowing agent of a divine plan. "There are people who do not have the slightest idea of what an important role they play in the scheme of Divine Providence," he wrote. "They are called but do not know Who is calling them. . . . Only when the time comes will the hidden meaning be revealed." On another occasion he wrote, "God sees into the heart, but we mortals can only see what is out in plain view. . . . We must punish with utmost stringency those who violate religious law, and if the Holy One has hidden considerations, He will do as He sees fit." It was a cornerstone of his theology that secular pioneers, far from being heretics, were inadvertent instruments of God's will.

Interestingly, many pioneers, far from being flattered by his approval, considered him presumptuous in claiming to know them better than they knew themselves. The novelist Amos Oz wrote, "Zionism began among people who rebelled against the dominion of religious law. . . . [Kook] is trampling on the spiritual autonomy of others, and it has always made me feel insulted and bitter."

Once in Palestine, Kook broke new theological ground on the nature of messianism. Putting aside its dependence on a living redeemer, he reconceived it as a *process* leading to redemption.

Kook was not the first to introduce this notion. But earlier sages, Reines included, had argued that collective repentance was a precondition of the Messiah's arrival, while Kook attached redemption to change in the *external* world. "The time when Israel returns to Jerusalem and its stronghold," he wrote, turning the traditional sequence upside down, "is the very root of the coming of the Messiah." He proclaimed Zionism vital to the aspiration of Jewish redemption.

Kook thus departed significantly not just from conventional Orthodoxy but also from Rabbi Reines's argument that creating a refuge in the Holy Land was a purely political act, religiously neutral. Kook, contending that God *commanded* the return from exile, made Zionism religiously positive. His theory negated the Three Oaths, rejecting passivity, the strategy of waiting patiently for a messianic miracle. Kook invited Jews to take destiny in their own hands by embracing Zionism, and make a miracle on their own.

In practice, Kook's updated messianism, like Reines's before him, was a sincere effort to bridge the gap between religious and secular Jews. But Haredim would not be dislodged from their belief that Zionism was a heresy and seculars had virtually no interest in the Messiah at all. The doctrine did not bring the two camps closer.

Kook's theology of return, moreover, was more distant from secular Zionism than it first appeared. Zionism, to him, was a failure in not recognizing that the Jews were resettling the land for the Torah's sake. He tolerated secularism, he made clear, because he considered it an aberration that would be superseded by submission to an unconscious Jewish impulse to build a holy society. Kook had no use for the Zionists' "normal" Jewish state, which he said would be Gentile at its roots. The Jewish state was an ideal, he wrote, emerging from a divine plan. "Our state, the state of Israel," he said, must serve as "the pedestal of God's throne in this world."

Kook was in Europe attempting to sell his theology to rabbis there when World War I broke out. Stranded, he stayed briefly in Switzerland, then took a pulpit in London, which is where he was when Britain issued the Balfour Declaration, the groundbreaking promise of a Jewish homeland. Though both Orthodox and nonobservant Jews largely ignored it, Kook perceived it as a further step forward in God's plan for redemption. Confident of his interpretation, he worked to persuade Jews everywhere to build on Britain's offer.

In the wake of the war, the British assumed mandatory authority in Palestine. In 1921, Mizrachi, the religious Zionist movement, urged Britain to reinstate the chief rabbinate, an office that had existed under the Turks, hoping to use it as a counterweight to secularism. The British, for their own reasons, agreed and Kook, on returning to Palestine, was named Palestine's first Ashkenazi chief rabbi.

The chief rabbinate imparted to Orthodoxy much of the jurisdiction—over marriage and divorce, for example—that it had enjoyed, both in Europe and in the Muslim East, in the era of Jewish autonomy. Kook made it a platform for speaking against secularism, but, more audaciously, he used it promote Jewish nationalism, whether against Britain or the Arabs. Even more daringly, he took it as an opening to urge reconvening the Sanhedrin, the Jewish governing body lost in the ruins of the Second Temple. The Sanhedrin will, he said, "examine every issue, every ruling and custom, and act in accordance with the Torah." Kook's course as chief rabbi was to promote the restoration of a holy state.

Unfortunately for Kook, the chief rabbinate was a political as well as a religious office and, as a politician, he was ineffective. Mizrachi, his basic constituency, was by itself too small to give muscle to the agency. Secular Zionism, though grateful for his efforts to yoke piety to its cause, was wary of his religious goals. As for Orthodoxy, it saw him as an agent of Zionism and had no allegiance to him at all.

Kook remained in the office until his death in 1935, never able to rally the community behind him. His political legacy was largely hollow, which describes the chief rabbinate to this day. He established a yeshiva with a religious Zionist agenda, known as Merkaz HaRav, but while he was in charge it had few students, scant resources and little prestige. A quasi-political movement he founded to infuse Zionism with spirituality sputtered and died. During his lifetime Kook's ideas won little public notice and, but for a circle of disciples, he would have been lost to history.

It was only posthumously that Kook emerged as a force. His theology of return had added a layer of religious mysticism to Zionist nationalism, spawning a crusading ideology. In time, it produced a fanaticism such as Judaism had not known since Second Temple days. Kook could not have foreseen—and might not have endorsed—this militant course. A century earlier, much of Europe became enthralled to a comparable mystical nationalism, which ended with the bloody disaster of World War I. The use to which religious Zionism put Kook's ideology suggested a similar peril.

❧ ❧ ❧

ON THE NINETEENTH anniversary of Israeli independence, Rabbi Zvi Yehuda Kook, son and principal disciple of Rabbi Abraham Isaac Kook, delivered a homily in the large central hall of Merkaz HaRav, the yeshiva whose leadership he had inherited. It was three weeks before the Six-Day War.

Witnesses recall that as he talked he began suddenly to sob. He then interrupted his text to declare, "Where is our Hebron, Shechem,

Jericho and Anathoth," biblical sites then controlled by the Arabs, "torn from the state in 1948 as we lay maimed and bleeding?" Little had been heard about territorial expansion since Israel's independence. Kook's audience, composed mostly of rabbinic students, seemed stunned by the words.

Rabbi Kook, the father, had never talked about the borders of the Jewish state. Rabbi Kook, the son, however, held views that overlapped those fashioned in the 1920s by Revisionism. The rabbi's point of departure was religious, while Revisionism's was secular. But both subscribed to an ideology that aimed, as a minimum, at Jewish control of Palestine from the Jordan River to the sea.

Since the War of Independence the mainstream Zionists who governed the state had been content to let the border question rest. Until the Six-Day War, neither Revisionism nor the younger Rabbi Kook had succeeded in getting territorial expansion onto the public agenda.

The territory Israel captured in the war suddenly reopened the question. It was at that point that Kook and his homily came to public attention. The nationalist spin he gave to his father's theology immediately made him religious Zionism's spiritual guide, and his followers proceeded to characterize the homily as "prophecy." With the help of a scratchy tape recording, it became the core of religious Zionism's ideology.

If the victory transformed Israel, it also transformed Rabbi Kook. Already seventy-six, he had not been widely influential or respected during his career. He relied heavily on his father's credentials, but his interests were much narrower, and he had no independent scholarly reputation. The yeshiva he directed, which promoted a nationalist theology that some called "Kookism," was intellectually marginal. Only after the war did its teachings have an impact.

Kook's influence spread through a cadre of disciples who had graduated from Merkaz HaRav. Most had begun their education in a youth branch of the Mizrachi movement, known as Bnai Akiva, dedicated to pioneering on the land. Later, as rabbis, they would be recognized not for their Torah wisdom but for their militance in promoting settlement of the occupied territories.

A study of Kook's sermons at Merkaz HaRav reveals his advocacy of a religious nationalism that far exceeded the limits envisioned by his father. Securing territory, he said, was a divine commandment equal to traditional piety. A writer noted that Kook transferred the holiness of the sacred to the holiness of the profane. Another said Kook substituted the worship of land for the worship of God.

Though the son's works were derived from the father's, they were clearly different. The father's vision was universal, directed at the creation of a holier world; the son was narrowly Jewish, fixated on the Jewish state. The father would never have shifted the focus of his students from Torah to territory. The son did so eagerly. "The Bible and the Talmud," wrote Kook, the son, summarizing his ideology, "speak of planting trees in the Holy Land and not of establishing yeshivot."

Kook, the father, held that the Jewish state would lead the people to redemption, the ultimate expression of holiness. His son came close to regarding the state as redemption itself. He considered the anniversaries of Israel's independence to be religious holidays, on which he delivered major sermons from his pulpit. On the twenty-seventh, in 1975, he told his disciples:

> There are those who speak of the "beginning of redemption" in our time. We must perceive clearly that we are already in the midst of redemption. We are already in the throne room, not just in the antechamber. The beginning took place more than a century ago, when Jewish settlement in the Land of Israel was renewed.
>
> True, the society and the state are not run in full accord with the Torah. But we must learn to separate the wheat from the chaff, to distinguish between the precious essence embodied in the fact of Jewish sovereignty in the Land of Israel and the incidental flaws that have accumulated along the redemptive path.
>
> The principal overall thing is the state. It is inherently holy and without blemish. All the rest is details, trivia, minor problems and complications. . . . Naturally, we look forward to the time when the whole nation will belong to the Torah and commandments. But the state is holy in any case.

Similarly, the son leaped far beyond the father on the territorial issue. The elder Kook had sanctified the movement to settle the land; he had no position on its dimensions. The son was much clearer not just on the extent but on the rights and duties of possession.

> Not only must there be no retreat from a single kilometer of the Land of Israel, God forbid, but on the contrary, we shall conquer and liberate more and more, as much in the spiritual as in the physical sense. . . .
>
> We are stronger than America, stronger than Russia. With all the troubles and delays we suffer, our position in the world, the world of history, the cosmic world, is stronger and more secure in its timelessness than theirs. There are nations that know this, and there are nations that in their uncircumcised hearts do not know it, but they shall gradually come to know it! Heaven protect us from weakness and timidity. . . . In our divine, world-encompassing undertaking, there is no room for retreat.

It is fair to attribute some of the differences between father and son to the times in which they lived. The father had the luxury of envisaging an ideal, the state that he hoped would be realized. By the time the son reached maturity, though its size and character were still in flux, the state's existence was no longer in doubt. Kook showed singular dedication to the state's power. He extolled the virtues of the army and encouraged his young disciples to seek positions of military command. He received in the yeshiva prominent generals—"even," as one historian indelicately put it, "pork-eaters and skirt-chasers"—with ceremonies customarily reserved for the Torah itself.

As for Haredi rabbis, who instructed their students to obtain military exemptions, Kook is said to have had only disdain. He signaled his feelings, whenever rabbinic critics of Zionism or the state called on him, by not rising from his chair to greet them.

> How is it [he wrote] that the movement for concrete redemption in our time, including the settlement and conquest of the Land of Israel and the abandonment of exilic

existence, did not originate with the religious? How is it that some religious spokesmen even withheld their support for Zionism and the movement for redemption? . . .

They failed to recognize it was not that we mortals were forcing the End but rather that the Master of the House, the Lord of the Universe, was forcing our hand; that it was not human voices that broke down the wall separating us from our land but the voice of the living God calling upon us to "Arise!"

Kook took an equally disdainful view of the Ultra-Orthodox rabbis who claimed that the Holocaust was God's punishment of the Jews for "forcing the End." He sided with secular Zionists who contended that the Holocaust, in provoking worldwide sympathy, was the grim price paid by the Jews for their sovereignty. On these grounds, he described the Holocaust as a blessing in disguise. At the same time, he castigated the Haredi leaders who had rejected refuge in pre-state Palestine, thereby prolonging the exile and exposing their followers to destruction.

God's people [he wrote] had clung so determinedly to the impurity of foreign lands that, when the End Time arrived, they had to be cut away, with great shedding of blood. . . . [The catastrophe] was a deeply hidden, internal, divine act of purification to rid us of the impurity of exile . . . a cruel divine surgery aimed at bringing the Jews to the Land of Israel against their will. . . . This cruel excision [produced] the rebirth of the nation and the land, the rebirth of the Torah and all that is holy. . . . It is an encounter with the Master of the Universe.

It took audacity by Kook to thrust his finger in Orthodoxy's eye by describing the Holocaust positively. Carrying his father's messianism to a logical conclusion, he maintained that God Himself brought it on to uproot the culture of exile and hasten redemption.

Still, Kook's chief impact on Jewish history lay not in his own theology but in his transforming the theology of his father into a language of action. If he lacked his father's originality, he nonetheless imparted a fresh focus to his father's ideas. It was the son who made Kookism into a summons to arms.

Hours after Gur's battalions captured the Old City, the students at Mercaz HaRav rose to this summons by carrying their rabbi exultantly past the tanks and artillery pieces to the Wailing Wall. There Kook declared: "By divine command, we have returned to our home, to our holy city. From this day forth, we shall never depart from here."

Kook, over the ensuing weeks, laid out his father's vision to a constituency hungry for a new sense of purpose. He re-created religious Zionism from a well-meaning complement to secular Zionism into a radical nationalism imbued with faith. His disciples took to calling his ideas "Torah Zionism" or the "Zionism of Redemption."

Too frail by war's end to be religious Zionism's political chief, Kook served as its ideological prod. As a childless widower, soon to be disabled in speech and movement, he was an unlikely inspiration. But his piety, modesty and personal austerity proved charismatic, winning him affection that extended beyond his narrow circle. His disciples treated him like a Hasidic *rebbe,* a holy man whose wisdom-filled words demanded obedience, a link between themselves and God. While he rarely offered advice on private matters, he showed no such compunction about public questions. His instructions to resist withdrawal from a single grain of holy soil, even if ordered by the Israeli army, set a powerful precedent to which his followers clung in the political crises that ensued.

Kook, it should be noted, never claimed his judgments were derived from Halacha. He never, in fact, claimed to be a Torah scholar at all. Yet his followers deemed his learning sufficient to give Halachic authority to his words. His rabbinic disciples, predictably, were themselves soon issuing rulings, most of them on the disposition of territory. Lacking Kook's modesty, they held these rulings Halachically valid, and binding on all Jews.

🖋 🖋 🖋

ON THE EVE OF PASSOVER in 1968, a year after the Six-Day War, Rabbi Moshe Levinger, a disciple of Rabbi Kook, registered a group of ten families in the Park Hotel, a small Arab-owned lodging in Hebron. Their ostensible purpose was to celebrate the religious holiday. In fact, their carefully calculated operation was political, and became the leading edge of the great wave of Jewish settlement of the territories that were occupied in the war.

Levinger, a doctor's son born in Israel in 1935, was raised within the Bnai Akiva movement, where many of the children of religious Zionists were trained. He joined Nachal, the army program for observant youths, and after his discharge he enrolled in rabbinic studies at Merkaz HaRav. Rabbi Kook became his mentor. Levinger, after taking an American-born wife, served in religious Zionist synagogues in two small Israeli communities. The victory in the Six-Day War, however, drew him away from the pulpit to an uncharted course in the biblical heartland.

Restoring Jewish rule to Hebron, a city in the Judean hills south of Jerusalem, stood near the top of religious Zionism's goals. Hebron is the site of the Machpelah cave, said to be the patriarchs' burial place. It was the first capital of King David, who was anointed there. Jews lived in Hebron throughout most of history but were driven out by bloody rioting in 1929. A few families went back, but violence drove them out again in 1936. Hebron was incorporated into the kingdom of Jordan in the war of 1948, but religious Jews always vowed to return.

By the time Levinger appeared, religious Zionists were already calling the West Bank "Judea and Samaria," as if use of the biblical names confirmed their right to live there. The government still barred Jewish settlement, but in visiting, Levinger violated no law. When Passover ended, however, he proclaimed his refusal to leave and announced his readiness to defy civil law to stay. Levinger explained that he was settling in Hebron in response to God's decree of Jewish sovereignty over the entire Land of Israel.

When Israelis from every sector of the society, stirred by the emotions of victory, rallied to Levinger, the Labor Party government was stunned. By then, it was itself operating at the edge of international law. It had annexed Arab Jerusalem and had announced its intent to resettle the Etzion Bloc, a series of villages where Jews had taken heavy casualties in a battle in 1948. It had also begun to implement the Allon Plan, a program to establish settlements along the Jordan River as a trip wire against invaders.

But Levinger's action went beyond government plans. The cabinet claimed that its own moves—except for annexation of Arab Jerusalem—were all in the interest of security. The door to negotiations with the Arabs, it declared, remained open. To this, Levinger sneered that Zionism was infected with the "virus of peace." He claimed the right to defy civil limitations, insisting he was subject to God's law alone.

Aware of the drift of public opinion, the government gave in, the first step in what became a pattern of acquiescence to religious Zionist pressure. It allowed Levinger not only to settle in Hebron but to establish a yeshiva there. It authorized his people to carry arms, bolstering a sense of domination, adding to the local population's fears. Predictably, relations between Jews and Arabs quickly degenerated.

That fall, several Jews were wounded by a bomb at the Machpelah cave, where Jews and Arabs had come into conflict over rights to pray. In an assertion of authority over the Arabs, the government announced construction of a new Jewish town on the heights above the city. Called Kiryat Arba, Hebron's biblical name, it soon became home to five thousand settlers, many of them territorial zealots. Levinger, though without a formal position, was their chief.

"We had to stay here in Hebron," Rabbi Levinger said to me in an interview some years later. He was an incongruous leader, spindly and unkempt, with bad teeth, thin and disordered hair and a scraggly beard. Yet behind his thick glasses were eyes lit with a fiery charisma. He and I talked in his home in the ruins of an ancient synagogue in the heart of the Arab marketplace, an arena of almost daily strife between Israelis and Palestinians. His wife sat nearby, and his children played around us.

"We have to live in every place in the Land of Israel, in our country," Levinger said. "Hebron is more important than Tel-Aviv. We did not have permission from the cabinet to stay, but why did we need permission? In the Torah it is written that Eretz Yisrael belongs only to the Jews. Why do the Jews need permission to live in their own country?"

Whatever his eccentricities, Levinger proved gifted in making him-

self and his followers the vanguard of Zionist renewal. Even in flout-
ing the law, they were widely perceived by the Israeli public as agents
of Zionist idealism. Many Israelis felt apprehension about where Levinger's tactics were taking the country, but at the same time they
grudgingly admired what he was doing.

Mainstream Zionism, though basking in the prestige of victory, had
no plan for dealing with this problem. It had made Israel a force with
which even great powers had to reckon. Its enemies in the Arab world
were in disarray. The territories it occupied were on the whole remarkably quiet. Its stated policy was to observe international law, but
it did not intend to restore the prewar status quo. Mainly, it failed to
grasp the magnitude of the change the war had wrought. To preserve
national unity, it emulated Herzl in indulging religion, but without
recognizing the unprecedented scope of the demands. The petty obstacles it placed in Levinger's way only broadcast its nervousness. Religious Zionism, having defeated the government at Hebron, prepared
further challenges to the mainstream's resolve.

ﾒ   ﾒ   ﾒ

ON YOM KIPPUR OF 1973, Egypt, with Syria's support, ended the Arab-
Israeli lull by launching a surprise attack with the objective of revers-
ing the results of the Six-Day War. Israel's army repulsed both Arab
armies but its losses, compared with 1967, were far more severe. Israel accepted a cease-fire while its foes were still in possession of land
it had won six years earlier. The Jewish state no longer seemed invul-
nerable.

After the war, Israelis were not forgiving of their leaders for being
taken by surprise. They accused the government of complacency, the
Labor Party of decay, the army of dereliction. In agreements brokered
by the United States, they were forced to relinquish some territory in
Sinai and the Golan Heights, leaving them queasy about their future.
The intoxication of 1967 gave way to sullenness in 1973.

Mainstream Zionism, already in retreat before the settlers' creeping
assaults, emerged from the Yom Kippur War with its confidence in tat-
ters. Its institutions sagged under the weight of popular criticism.
Characteristically, Haredim interpreted the defeat as divine punish-

ment. Religious Zionists, in contrast, saw it as a divine command to push their policies harder. The war's lesson, they said, was God's impatience with timid Zionist values. They perceived an opening in the mainstream's palpable weakness.

After the cease-fire, Rabbi Kook issued a proclamation calling for the country to reach out to its full biblical borders. To most religious Zionists, these borders, roughly the boundaries of David's kingdom, meant the land from the Jordan River to the Mediterranean Sea. They demanded that the government erase forever the demarcation line of 1948, which separated Israel from Judea and Samaria.

But some of the faithful understood borders in even grander terms. They held Israel to the promise made by God to Abraham in Genesis: "To your offspring I assign this land, from the river of Egypt [the Nile] to the great river, the river Euphrates." The Revisionists' anthem had long celebrated this verse as their territorial goal. As late as 2001, a religious Zionist referred in a major magazine to "my right to return to those parts of the Land of Israel that lie east of the Jordan River."

Rabbi Kook himself was equivocal in defining the holy borders, but whatever his intent, he issued a fiery proclamation that Jews had to be ready to give up their lives to repossess the land. Kook's proclamation became the manifesto of Gush Emunim (Bloc of the Faithful), an organization formed by graduates of Merkaz HaRav to satisfy religious Zionism's territorial imperative. The organization emerged after the Yom Kippur War as a loose network of ardent activists, both men and women, whose ideology assured them that annexation of the land was a greater duty than obeying the law.

Gush Emunim became the vanguard of territorialism. It scoffed at what it insisted were the government's officious legalisms, the product of heretical liberal values. It treated secular law as empty shouting in the face of God. Unlike the Haredim, it did not dispute the state's legitimacy. But it regarded the state, the Zionist state, as no more than a set of bureaucratic institutions that functioned to achieve irrelevant secular ends.

In contrast to the Zionist vision of a "normal" state, Gush Emunim cultivated a mystical concept of statehood. The state would be a resurrection of David's kingdom, which God would entrust to the Jews for the purpose of reestablishing divine rule over holy soil. It would be a Maccabean theocracy, both militant and pious. A state that failed these tests might be politically legitimate, but in betraying God it would forfeit the right to popular obedience.

Gush Emunim's militants, unlike Haredim, were not traditionalists. Mostly native-born, they wore jeans and identified themselves by knitted *kippot,* usually attached by a hairpin. Though some wore heavy beards to advertise their piety, many were not pious at all. Yet in aspiring to a lost golden age in which God reigned, they were fundamentalist. Among Israelis, they were unique in basing their actions on what they believed were the priorities of God, Torah and the Messiah.

The militant core of Gush Emunim may never have numbered more than a few hundred, or a few thousand at most. But its motivation and intensity gave the organization political power that was significantly disproportionate to its numbers.

Rabbi Levinger was the militants' tactical master and guide. He did not conceal the anti-Arab violence initiated by the settlers to promote their cause, nor did he deny that Jewish rule of the territories was inherently oppressive. In a bizarre talk some years ago with professors at the Hebrew University, he presented his justification. A charitable reading of it would be that he reached back for his ideas to the Kabbalist concept of *tikkun olam,* a Jewish duty to heal the world.

> If we meet the Arabs' demands for withdrawal, we will only encourage their degeneration and moral decline, whereas enforcing the Israeli national will on them will foster a religious revival, eventually to be expressed in their spontaneous desire to join in the reconstruction of the Third Temple. We Israelis must penetrate the casbahs of cities of Judea and Samaria and drive our stakes therein for the good of the Arabs themselves.

In 1975, Levinger demonstrated his tactical mastery in facing down then Prime Minister Yitzhak Rabin over the installation of an illegal settlement in Samaria. Supported by a small army of militants, Levinger staged a sit-in at an abandoned railway depot. When Rabin proposed to remove them with troops, he found the public indifferent and the cabinet unwilling to accept spilling Jewish blood. Rabin back-tracked completely. To save face, he endorsed a "temporary" arrange-ment that allowed thirty families to move into Kadum, a nearby army base. The "temporary" setup produced the settlement since known as Elon Moreh, which remains to this day.

Soon after the Kadum episode, a dozen families defied the govern-ment by pitching tents illegally on a bleak mountaintop near Jerusa-lem. Their daring recalled to many Israelis the exciting days of Zionist pioneering. The settlement, now the Jerusalem suburb of Ma'ale Ad-umim, chipped further at mainstream resolve.

In the election of 1977, Menachem Begin, head of the right-wing Likud Party, defeated Rabin to become prime minister, shifting settle-ment policy from Labor's reluctant consent to his own enthusiastic support. Successor to Jabotinsky as Revisionism's leader, Begin re-jected Orthodoxy's vision of a Halachic state. But as an observant Jew, he was also at ease cooperating with religious Zionism in pursuit of the common goal of expanding Jewish rule.

Begin set his political course early by visiting the home of Rabbi Kook, who bestowed blessings on Likud's territorial program. Then, wearing a *kippa* and holding a Torah, he joined Rabbi Levinger at the new settlement and vowed, in defiance of Rabin and secular Zionism, to build "many more Elon Morehs." Religious Zionism thus slipped comfortably into a ruling coalition with Revisionism, isolating main-stream Zionism. Israel's political spectrum soon after split sharply into two, a loose Labor-led bloc sympathetic to trading land for peace and a Likud-led bloc committed to hard-line territorialism. The schism between them has hardly narrowed since.

But Likud's ideology could not always be reconciled with religious Zionism's. Likud was an old-fashioned political party, capable of mak-ing deals in the national interest. Religious Zionism, having grown out of Rabbi Kook's messianism, was driven by a mission that was not readily compromised for practical ends. The difference became clear when Egypt's president, Anwar al-Sadat, made a famous visit to Jeru-salem in 1977, during which he offered Israel a peace treaty in return for its withdrawal from Egyptian territory in the Sinai.

Begin, attracted by the prospect of neutralizing Israel's most powerful enemy, accepted Sadat's proposal in negotiations conducted under American auspices at Camp David, Maryland. To widespread surprise, Begin even agreed to the principle of Palestinian self-rule, much like the Jewish autonomy in the era of exile, in the West Bank and Gaza.

Religious Zionism, Begin's ally, was furious. It rejected Begin's defense that the Sinai had never been within the boundaries of the biblical kingdom. It also had no use for his claim that self-rule would be no greater than what the *kehillot* had once enjoyed. Guided by Rabbi Kook, religious Zionism held that the deal was a retreat from holy soil, unacceptable to God, and thus heresy.

Notwithstanding the opposition, Begin signed the treaty in 1979. The first phase of withdrawal came due some months later, when Israel was required to relinquish land that included the Sinai settlement of Neot Sinai. The settlers movement, long known for violence against Arabs, for the first time now threatened Jews.

Organized by Gush Emunim, about a thousand settlers laid barbed wire in a circle around Neot Sinai. Armed with pipes, stones, torches and guns, they issued warnings to whoever approached. Two cabinet ministers, trying to mediate, were shoved and spat upon. When soldiers came near, they were heavily stoned and some were injured. Only after Begin agreed to pay an indemnity, which many Israelis considered extortionate, did most defenders relent. Some, however, threatened suicide, while others prayed until they were dragged away in tears. Finally Gush Emunim, in return for forswearing rebellion, extracted from Begin a vow to evacuate no more occupied land. In the ensuing years, Begin kept the vow faithfully.

ᗰ   ᗰ   ᗰ

BY NOW, RABBI MEIR KAHANE had raised the level of anti-Arab violence in the territories. Kahane, founder of America's notorious Jewish Defense League, had led his followers to Israel after the FBI threatened to prosecute him for unlawful political demonstrations in New York. In Israel he organized Kach (Thus!) and proclaimed a plan to evict all Arabs from the Holy Land.

Raised on Revisionism in America, Kahane understood Judaism as a militant faith. Regarded as an outsider by most Israelis, he rejected Kook's complex theology and shaped an ultranationalism based on his own reading of the Torah. God's glory, Kahane maintained, was a function basically of Jewish might. Though his territorial goals were the same as religious Zionism's, he was far less constrained in promoting them and, in fact, offered Gush Emunim a new model of militant guerrilla warfare.

Kahane naturally agreed with Gush Emunim that Begin's peace treaty was betrayal and, after Neot Sinai, the two separately adopted strategies to negate it. Kahane targeted the Dome of the Rock, a major Arab shrine, with a missile, for which he was convicted and briefly jailed. Gush Emunim turned loose its vigilantes, some of whom organized a campaign to kill and maim Arab leaders in the territories.

Levinger, meanwhile, prepared for the defense of Yamit, the last major town in Sinai that Israel was pledged to evacuate. Building on the experience at Neot Sinai, he and his followers assembled an arsenal and took positions facing twenty thousand Israeli soldiers. Civil war seemed to loom.

After a protracted confrontation, Begin again defused the crisis by paying a heavy ransom. He also repeated his public vow that, should negotiations reach Judea and Samaria, he would give up no territory. The land, he said, was more important than peace. But even as Begin was resolving the Neot Sinai confrontation, plans were being laid in the Gush Emunim camp for a heightened level of lawlessness.

In 1980, the Jewish Underground, a secret society of Gush Emunim activists, booby-trapped the cars of three mayors of Arab towns, leaving two of them severely maimed. In 1983, gunmen killed three students and wounded thirty in Hebron's Islamic college. Only police vigilance stopped a third plan, for random bombings of buses on Arab streets. Disciples of Rabbi Kook openly applauded the attacks. In the synagogues of religious Zionism, worshipers debated whether "Thou shalt not kill" applied to Arabs at all. Both Labor and Likud turned an unseeing eye, and the police put little effort into finding the perpetrators.

More ambitiously, the Underground assembled explosives in preparation for blowing up the Dome of the Rock, which Kahane had tried to do and failed. Its chief planner was a young mystic named Yehuda Etzion, who said later that God, angry at the mosques that stood on the site of Solomon's Temple, had punished the Jews with the Sinai treaty. Etzion was convinced his plot was a shortcut to redemption. But even by Israel's tolerant standards, the idea was excessive. A few rabbis argued that Gentile wrath at such an act would force God to dispatch the Messiah, but the security services arrested the plotters before their theory could be tested.

During the trial, even Gush Emunim distanced itself from the plotters. Its rabbis denounced them for "false messianism." Twenty-seven of the accused were convicted and briefly imprisoned. Etzion served five years, the longest term. But Gush Emunim, of which he was a founding member, expressed no real remorse.

Years later I met with Etzion at his home in the West Bank settlement of Ofra. Boyish-looking and slim, then in his forties, he communicated without sanctimony his vision of Judaism. Sitting before a drawing board and a computer, he told me he had since put aside violent tactics but remained faithful to the ideology that had made him famous.

"The Temple Mount is the foundation of Israel's national life," he said. "Life without the Temple is like spiritual death, like living in the Diaspora rather than the Jewish state. We Jews meet God on the Temple Mount. Redemption begins there. Without it, we will be like every other nation on earth, and eventually we won't exist at all."

Etzion told me he belonged to a small group whose short-term goal was reversal of the government's ban on Jewish prayer on the Temple Mount, but its long-term goal was unchanged: to rebuild the holy Temple. When I asked whether he had abandoned violence permanently, he shrugged and said he was not yet clear on how long the rebuilding would take. But he added that, whatever the delays, Jews no longer considered his vision *meshugge*, "crazy."

"The mosques on the Temple Mount," he said, "are the wrong buildings in the wrong place. I was involved in the bombings of the mayors, and that was a distraction from our aims. The Temple Mount is the heart of our issue, and I don't believe what we proposed was wrong. The Jews will always be at war with the Muslims and the world. When the nation of Israel is good enough in God's eyes to rebuild the Temple, that will be the basis of global peace."

Levinger was among the rabbis investigated but not charged in the Temple Mount plot. After the trial, he still carried a submachine gun around Hebron, and regularly broke Arab windows and overturned vegetable carts. When he killed an Arab shopkeeper in a fit of anger, he was tried, convicted and given a prison sentence of five months. On the day it began, in May 1990, a crowd of settlers cheered him to the prison gates in a convoy of flag-becked cars.

🗿   🗿   🗿

ALTHOUGH THE TWO MAJOR parties alternated in leading Israel in the 1980s, the government—driven by religious Zionist agitation—tightened its grip on the territories. Labor, the weaker, succeeded in barring annexation to keep alive the prospect of compromise, but it acquiesced in the growth of settlements. Likud, less ambivalent, carried out Begin's vow to preserve Israeli rule of every square inch.

Whichever party was in charge, the government provided incentives to the settlers. Religious Zionism no longer needed its vigilantes, since the army functioned as its arm by keeping the Arabs under control. In fact, as more religious Zionists infiltrated the officers' corps, the army began to look much like the movement itself. Dozens of new settlements were founded, and each served as an additional barrier to withdrawal.

By 1990, population in the territories had surpassed one hundred thousand, and it would rise a decade later to twice that number. If one takes into account the sectors formally annexed to Jerusalem, the number, in fact, reached four hundred thousand. Most settlers were middle class and many were secular. The later migrants were in vast majority drawn not by zealotry but by the government's economic incentives. But whatever the motives, they constituted a huge voting block, with political and economic interests that overlapped religious Zionism's ideology. In successive elections, the settlers' votes sent large numbers of hard-liners into the Knesset, and in 1984 they elected Meir Kahane himself.

Meanwhile, Israel's military preeminence in the region quieted the insistence of the Western powers, particularly the United States, that it cede territory for peace. The Arab states had grown no stronger. Without threats to global stability looming on the horizon, proposals for Israeli evacuation of the occupied territories receded steadily from the international agenda.

The militants of religious Zionism, comfortable in their settlements, appeared in these years to lose their earlier vigor. Time also tarnished their heroic image. Rabbi Levinger softened his edge and Rabbi Kook, who died in 1984, was succeeded by disciples who, though no less ideological, lacked his influence. It seemed as if religious Zionism was taking redemption for granted.

But if religious Zionism failed to notice, changes were happening in Israel. In 1982, the Israeli army invaded Lebanon, setting off massive pro-peace demonstrations. In 1987, young Palestinians initiated the *intifada*, the first direct challenge to the occupation. Baffled by the stone throwing of thousands of street protesters, Israel's army failed to put the revolt down.

Then, in 1991, the United States, in response to Iraq's invasion of Kuwait, organized a military coalition that included Arab powers. In recognition of the Arabs' help, Washington acceded to their demand to confront the status quo, sponsoring a conference in Madrid on Middle East peace. Likud, reluctant to attend at all, managed to block any decisions but, prodded by America, Israel could not slow the momentum toward new negotiations.

Israelis, weary of the political stagnation of the 1980s, went to the polls a year later. Labor's candidate was again Yitzhak Rabin, still smarting at his humiliation by religious Zionism at Kadum in 1975. A military hero and a committed secular, Rabin was known for being both tough toward Arabs and practical about peace, a combination that made him seem ideal for the times. Religious Zionism, smelling danger, awoke from its lethargy and went on alert.

GOD, WITNESS TO MADNESS

AN UGLY DARK CLOUD separated Israel from the sun in late October 1995. Prime Minister Yitzhak Rabin, having reached agreement with the Palestinians to exchange territory for peace, had become the target of unprecedented vituperation. A scent of violence thickened the air.

Rabin, who held a thin Knesset majority, had begun to implement the Oslo Accords, which Israel had signed two years before with the Palestinians. He had already transferred Jericho and part of the Gaza Strip to Palestinian rule, and he was preparing the army for withdrawal from part of the northern West Bank. Religious Zionism's long campaign to keep the occupied land entirely in Jewish hands seemed to be ending in failure.

But religious Zionists were not giving in gracefully. Revisionists remained their faithful ally. Their antipeace alliance, moreover, had been reinforced by the addition of most Haredim and many Sephardim. Surpassing the peace forces in zealotry, religious Zionist militants incited lawlessness by vilifying Rabin as a traitor. Their rabbis joined the clamor by denouncing him as an apostate.

Islamic extremists, oddly, were also in the coalition. Though uninvited, they were linked to their Jewish counterparts by the common objective of scuttling the peace agreement. By murdering and bombing Jews, they weakened the hopes for a new Israeli-Palestinian relationship in the minds of the secular majority. Their savagery added to the poison darkening Israel's atmosphere.

In its issue of November 2, the French journal *Le Nouvel Observateur* captured the trembling hatred directed at Rabin.

> Three Kabbalists chant a deadly curse—known as *pulsa da Nura,* in Aramaic—designed to take down Yitzhak Rabin. It is read out loud by a group of Jews, covered by their prayer shawls, in front of the prime minister's Jerusalem home. . . . A Hasidic rabbi is quoted in the daily H*a'aretz* as declaring, "I'd have no regret if Rabin wound up being killed."

Rabin was aware, of course, of the murderous cloud suspended over Israel. But like most secular Zionists, he took seriously only the danger from Arabs. As a soldier in the Haganah, he had fought against Revisionists in the mini–civil war known as the *Altalena* affair. But that had happened nearly a half-century before, and he preferred to believe that mayhem committed by one Jew against another would not recur.

Being secular, Rabin knew shamefully little about religion. Neither Rabbi Kook nor redemption was in his lexicon. He thought of religious Zionists in the benign terms that characterized them before 1967. He had failed to grasp from his humiliation at Kadum the lesson that the movement had become extreme, even fanatical. Rabin refused to take seriously the danger of a religious assassin.

But on November 4, Yigal Amir, a young Orthodox Jew, shot Rabin dead. Rabin had just spoken before a hundred thousand supporters at a peace rally in downtown Tel Aviv. Unnoticed by bodyguards, the killer had strolled into the lot where the prime minister's car was parked, then fired two bullets into his back. Amir said later, with pride in a mission well done, that his rabbis had sanctioned the killing.

In retrospect, it is clear the anger that produced the assassination had been simmering not just since 1967 but since the schism between religious and secular Jews during the Enlightenment. Though the breach seemed harmless for many decades, it had never healed. The Six-Day War only reopened it. When Rabin signed the Oslo Accords, religious Jews seemed to lose all interest in bridging their differences with Jewish secularism.

As withdrawal from the occupied territories approached, mutual respect and moderation receded. Religious Jews emitted a defiant self-righteousness, to which seculars seemed unable to respond. Jews on both sides, notwithstanding the frequently disastrous consequences, assumed the stiff-necked posture that God had encountered at Sinai.

Underestimating the virulence of religious extremism cost Rabin his life. But it also cast doubt on the state's guiding vision: the age-old longing of the Jewish people to make a life together in their ancient homeland. The assassination compelled Jews to ask whether they, rather than external forces, were not their own worst enemy. It was not just the crime but the popular support behind it that raised the question of whether Jews, having created the state, possessed the civility they needed to preserve it.

᧸   ᧸   ᧸

BRITAIN'S MANDATE IN PALESTINE began with the dual promise of the Balfour Declaration: to bring the Zionist dream to reality and, at the same time, to safeguard the rights of the local Arabs. It soon became clear that the two aims were incompatible, and Britain, as mandatory power, fulfilled neither. When Britain left, Jews and Arabs were on their own. Their failure to resolve the problem of living together was shared by many parties, Jewish and Arab. It has been an enduring thorn in relations between the two communities. It has also corrupted relations among the Jews themselves.

Open fighting between Jews and Arabs broke out after the United Nations in 1947 voted to divide Palestine into two states. Both sides were convinced they deserved it all, and each believed Britain favored the other. But the Jews accepted partition and the Arabs did not. The war that ensued in a way resembled the Maccabean uprising, in which the Jews triumphed not because they were so strong but because their enemies were so weak. The war ended in catastrophe for the Palestinian Arabs and left the two peoples more divided than before.

The Zionist leadership, in victory, proceeded with its plan to declare an independent state. The date was set for May 14, 1948, the day of Britain's scheduled departure. Israel's Declaration of Independence tells much about the Jewish state, then and since. Like Zionism itself, it had roots in both traditional Judaism and the Enlightenment's liberal values. It thus bore witness to the tension between secularism and religion, by now nearly two centuries old.

The Declaration proclaimed the "natural right of the Jewish people to be the masters of their own fate," a phrase that embodied the Enlightenment vision of self-determination. It also decreed the Right of Return, resonating with the ideal of messianic redemption, in pledging a state "open for Jewish immigration and the Ingathering of the Exiles." Then, in vowing "complete equality of social and political rights to all its inhabitants irrespective of religion, race or sex," it adopted the language of secular democracy, which echoed Herzl's vision of "a nation like all nations."

The vows were a complex of contradictions. How could Israel bestow preferences on Jews while offering equality to others? What would the relations of the Jews be with the Muslims within its borders? How could the state promise redemption to believers in the context of secular democracy? Since God told Moses that Israel would be a "holy nation," could it then be "a nation like all nations"? The Jewish state, to its grave discomfort, has yet to resolve these contradictions.

To deal with them, the writers of the Declaration, most of them secular Zionists, inserted a provision that a constitution was to be written within five months. It is true that not all countries need a written constitution. England never had one. Nor is it ordained that a society must immediately resolve its contradictions. Few do. But if a country is to survive, it must hammer out a foundation of common values, which all of its citizens, or nearly all, willingly accept. That has not happened to this new nation of Jews, at least not yet.

On the contrary, the rift was too wide between the religious and secular communities for the two to endorse common governing principles. As for the Arab community, it was not involved in the proceedings at all. To this day Israel, without a constitution, is ruled largely by improvisation, with relations between its two major cultures, as well as the place of its minority cultures, still far from settled.

Tom Segev, a popular Israeli historian, illustrates the rift in his anecdote about a dispute over the Declaration between David Ben-Gurion, the Zionist head, and the Orthodox religious delegation. With the Union Jack poised to descend, the founders still could not agree on the legal foundation for the Jewish claim to statehood. Orthodox leaders insisted on citing God's promise "to the Jewish people in the Torah." Ben-Gurion replied that Jewish ethnicity and history were justification enough.

With the Sabbath only hours away, the religious delegates announced they would depart at sundown, even if no draft had been completed. Ben-Gurion was aware that in Washington forces were gathering that considered a Jewish state contrary to U.S. interests. Proposing to declare Palestine an international trusteeship, they would have snatched away the Zionist dream just at its point of realization.

Ben-Gurion, never indecisive, settled the matter. He selected the term *Zur Yisrael*, "Rock of Israel," a biblical synonym for God, as the foundation of the state. English translations of the Declaration render the phrase as "placing our trust in the Almighty." Though both secular and religious delegates grumbled, the assembly approved the wording unanimously just as the sun went down.

Ben-Gurion later called the term a "nice compromise of Jewish fellowship." But he immediately recognized the constitution which he had proposed as a "national powder-keg" and, right after the Declaration, he disavowed it. "There is no need at this time," he said, "to resolve the problems of opinion and belief, over which we shall remain divided for a long time to come." A confrontation could best be put off, he believed, because time was on the side of reconciliation.

Like most Zionists of his generation, Ben-Gurion anticipated the decline of religion in Jewish life. He was sure most Jews would follow the West toward secular liberalism. Members of his generation were convinced the Ultra-Orthodox community, shattered by the Holocaust, would in time melt away. They also believed that religious Zionism would become more Zionist, and less religious. If rabbinic Judaism survived at all, they imagined, it would become a social curiosity, a vestige of a bygone age.

It is worth recalling that America's Founding Fathers, in forging a constitution a century and a half before, similarly chose procrastination. Slavery already plagued North-South relations but the drafters, persuading themselves that it would in time wither away, left the problem unaddressed. Instead it grew only stronger and more divisive, and a terrible war was required to resolve the issue.

Only in small part was Ben-Gurion's prediction correct. Most Israeli Jews, like European Christians, have since drifted further from observance. As style of life and political institutions grow more Western, Israel becomes more "a nation like all nations." But the generation of 1948 failed to predict the tenacity with which Haredim would rebuild their prewar community. It did not imagine that the pious Jews arriving from the Islamic world in time would become allies of Haredi Orthodoxy. Least of all did it anticipate the zealotry adopted by religious Zionism after the Six-Day War. In foreseeing traditional Judaism's demise, Ben-Gurion's generation was dead wrong.

Before long, Israelis observed that their society was suffused with more religion than it had been under Ben-Gurion. All sides, moreover, were digging in. The relationship between Judaism and the state, constitutionally unresolved, was choking the cultural air that Israelis breathed.

Orthodox Jews, resentful by then that the state had not embraced redemption, claimed that Zionism has lost its purpose. But Zionism's purpose, as the Declaration of Independence made clear, was never religious. Its model was Western society, where citizens were free to speak, gather, vote and worship. Its purpose implied, more than anything, a democratic homeland where Jews could be free, productive and secure. By this measure, Zionism by the 1970s had delivered on its promises very well.

Israel's very success, in fact, permitted Orthodoxy the luxury of challenging its secular nature. Internal violence became routine in Israel in the 1970s because Orthodoxy maintained that stability was not enough. If secular Zionism failed to display a comparable zealotry, the explanation is the "normality" of its agenda, which emphasizes tolerance of religious diversity. Disorder in Israel derived from Orthodoxy's insistence on transforming the society from the liberal goals it shared with "all nations" to a radical Judaization, based on piety and territory.

The causes to which both Haredim and religious Zionists devoted their ardor, it might be noted, were basically political. Orthodoxy held that God's concern was the rule of Mosaic law, which its rabbis were to administer. Religious Zionists maintained that God's first priority was Jewish rule over the entire Land of Israel. It is true that Jewish differences are legitimate subjects of debate, and debate is a Jewish habit. But instead, convinced of God's favor, religious activists all too often abandoned debate in behalf of the tactics that culminated in the killing of Yitzhak Rabin.

꿔   꿔   꿔

HISTORICALLY, ULTRA-ORTHODOX culture had a reputation, at least partly deserved, for abstaining from violence. During the long centuries of exile, rabbis leaned on the Three Oaths to bar aggression against Gentile authorities. Living under Zionism, Ultra-Orthodox generally limited their opposition to talk. Religious Jews were known as passive people. Yet, from time to time, signs would appear suggesting that violence was not totally foreign to them.

Segev, the popular historian, draws on police records to note that as far back as the 1940s, Haredi activists in Jerusalem commonly stoned and spit on Sabbath violators, both Jews and Gentiles. Their rabbis, moreover, defended them, claiming a religious duty to punish sinners.

Ehud Sprinzak, the Israeli specialist in religious violence, points out that since the 1950s, Haredim have engaged routinely in disorderly protests against such secular activities as coed community centers, Sabbath sports events and public swimming pools. He says they physically harass single women living alone. Further, he contends that, though Haredi society is tightly closed to outside scrutiny, it maintains "chastity guards" to punish sexual deviants, usually on rabbinic orders, and resorts regularly to physical attacks to enforce moral codes.

Sprinzak says that among rival Haredi courts fistfights, property damage and even personal assaults are common. In 1984, Rabbi

Menachem Porush, an Ultra-Orthodox Knesset member, was badly beaten by youths of another sect for insulting their leader.

Haredim customarily interpret Halacha broadly enough to justify these practices. Secular Jews, both in Israel and outside, generally defer to their claims to be the *real* Jews, identifying them with Jewish authenticity and history and long-departed Jewish grandparents. Tolerant of, even bemused by, Haredi idiosyncrasies, most Jews accept the right they claim to enforce, even coercively, the Halacha.

But Haredim are far from consistent. Obdurate on some Halachic matters, they can be quite flexible when their own interests are involved. After World War II, for example, their rabbis, having long placed obstacles to the flight of Jews from eastern Europe—obstacles that stoked Holocaust furnaces—suddenly changed position. With Orthodoxy's survival in doubt, Zionism in 1948 offered them a refuge, giving them, at last, reason to soften their hostility to the Jewish state.

The Orthodox rabbinate, it might be noted, did not dissolve with gratitude. Most rabbis objected to any concessions to Zionism. When Ben-Gurion refused outright to promise them the "state according to the Torah," the rabbis threatened to testify against establishment of the state at the United Nations. Ben-Gurion denounced the tactics as extortion, and only on the eve of the arrival in Israel of thousands of Haredim did the two reach a compromise.

"Just as it is impossible to favor the state in good faith," stated Agudath Israel, the Ultra-Orthodox political party, in a tepid endorsement of compromise, "so too is it impossible to oppose it. Otherwise, the name of God would be profaned as all blame is attributed to us, Orthodox Jewry, for thwarting the state's establishment."

Ben-Gurion's deal with Orthodoxy is known anomalously as the "status quo agreement." In return for its political—but not religious— recognition of the state, Orthodoxy received privileges in excess of its pre-1948 powers. Ben-Gurion designated the Jewish Sabbath and other holy days as official days of rest. He accepted rabbinic jurisdiction over marriage and divorce, rabbinic administration and public financing of religious schools and the application of kosher dietary laws in all state institutions, most notably the army. He also granted, after a last-minute request, the exemption of yeshiva students, as well as all Haredi women, from military service.

The agreement was the high point of secular-religious harmony in Israeli history. Caught up in the day's emotion, large numbers of young Haredim fought for Israel in the War of Independence. Two Haredi rabbis signed the Declaration of Independence. For its part, Ultra-Orthodoxy modified its claim to be "living in exile" to "living in exile among the Jews," a change designed to suppress discord. Most important, Ultra-Orthodoxy accepted Ben-Gurion's offer of a cabinet seat, signaling its presence in the political system and opening the door to spoils that proved crucial to rebuilding the Haredi world.

Unforeseen at the time were the implications of the student military exemption. At first it applied to only some two hundred students, all heads of families. By studying the Torah, Haredim argued, these students were as crucial as soldiers to safeguarding Judaism. Ben-Gurion dismissed the argument but considered the number too small to matter. Only after independence did Haredi leaders initiate a fight to preserve the exemption.

"Studying the Torah is essential to our students," said Rabbi Abraham Ravitz, the Knesset's most powerful Haredi politician and a ferocious partisan of Haredi privilege. A large man dressed in black, with a great unkempt beard, he defended the exemption in talking with me in his austere Jerusalem apartment. "Their goal is not to be doctors or engineers but to study, which we religious people regard as the most enriching thing in life. We must care for these students. They are the point of our yeshivot and essential to the state. At the end of days, thanks to them, Israel and all the world will be at peace."

Menachem Friedman, a specialist in Haredi culture at Orthodoxy's Bar Ilan University, sees the exemption from another perspective. It may have saved the life of what was perceived to be a dying world, he says, but it also changed the character of this world. Friedman, with Samuel C. Heilman of the City University of New York, writes that the exemption served as an irresistible incentive for building an empire of yeshivot. The protection from the draft provided by the yeshivot draws increasing numbers of Haredi men, who then spend their most productive years within. The exemption, he says, redefined Haredim from a community traditionally known for its piety into a "society of scholars," though secular Israelis see it as a society of draft-dodgers.

Since 1948, the state has sustained this society with funds both for the yeshivot and for their feeder schools. It also subsidizes young Haredim who marry and raise families. The money, among the spoils of the status quo agreement, is now being disbursed to a fifth generation. More than two hundred thousand students are enrolled in state-funded yeshivot, a rise of thirty percent over five years. One scholar calculates that the system serves more students than, in their heyday, attended all of eastern Europe's yeshivot.

Haredi leaders insist their resistance to military service is based solely on the corruption of secular society. In Israel, secular culture credits the army for shaping common social values; those are the values from which Haredim seek protection. Most Haredi men, studying Torah, never learn to earn a living. Fewer than half enter the workforce, depending for a living on the state, as well as private charities, parents and their wives. Haredim see the system of exemptions as crucial to preserving the Orthodox character of their community.

Secular Israelis assume that if the exemption were abolished, the yeshivot would quickly empty out. Whether or not they are right, Friedman says, Haredi society is producing huge numbers of children who require ever more schools and who exhaust the capital of the community by not going into paid work. The system can survive, he says, only with constantly rising infusions of money, but Israeli society is growing impatient. Haredim concede that the system is in trouble but have not looked seriously for a solution.

Haredi politics, instead, focuses on keeping the present arrangement intact. Sensitive to the rising chorus of secular objections, the government in 1999 proposed a compromise by which students might voluntarily leave the yeshiva to earn a living in return for serving a symbolically short army tour. The Haredi leadership refused change, claiming it violated God's will.

Friedman and Heilman say one product of the system is Haredi isolation. In Western countries Haredim must work—as they did throughout history—giving them at least some exposure to life outside the walls. In Israel, Haredi men, cloistered until they are too old for the draft, emerge too old to learn a trade. A majority of Haredim is now without experience outside, sharing no values with the nation at large, increasingly "ghettoizing" Ultra-Orthodox culture. Even Rabbi Ravitz regretfully acknowledges the trend. It has made Haredim increasingly fearful, he said, and paradoxically led them to demand more of secular society.

Friedman and Heilman write that so suspicious have Haredim become that they respond only to critics who call for greater religiosity. Many critics belong to extremist sects, fundamentalists who still totally reject Zionism. These critics rebuke Haredi leaders for participating in the Zionist system at all. To justify themselves, they say, Haredi politicians dig ever deeper into what Americans call the "pork barrel," focusing not on what benefits the country but on what perpetuates a deformed system.

Haredi politicians win their demands with the support of their block-voting constituencies. Israel's electoral process awards a political party a seat for every 1.5 percent of the total vote. Haredim make no pretense that civic responsibility is involved in their balloting. "When they tell us to vote," a Haredi said of his rabbis, "it is a *mitzvah* and not an option." Block voting explains much about how Haredim win victories over the secular majority. With the Knesset's two party blocs in close balance, Haredi voters tip the balance, giving them power grossly disproportionate to their numbers.

ℳ   ℳ   ℳ

As their community regained its strength in the decades after World War II, Haredim diversified their goals. While they focused inside the Knesset on their military exemptions and the yeshivot, outside they promoted other values, sometimes violently. In the 1970s, Haredim campaigned to eliminate secular elements from their neighborhoods, particularly in Jerusalem. They bought out some families and businesses and squeezed out others by boycotts. But they also broke windows, flattened tires and set fires. The government, intimidated by the show of power, barely reacted, encouraging them to be bolder.

By the 1980s, Haredi students engaged routinely in street protests against the drafting of girls, against archaeological digs that, they said, desecrated ancient cemeteries, and against bus shelters that displayed lewd advertising. They also stoned cars, like my own one Sabbath night.

The police commonly arrested and even handcuffed Haredim for such acts. But they rarely required them to desecrate the Sabbath by riding in a car to the station house, and so the process descended into theater. The police adopted the role that American police often played in the Vietnam War protests. In Haredi eyes, arrests made their protesters into heroes, even political martyrs.

Such protests would not have been possible without rabbinic endorsement. The rabbis, who in exile had restrained Jews under the terms of the Three Oaths, sent the message that "living in exile among the Jews" meant the bars were down. Rabbis now actively supported agitation. This agitation was not terrorism; it did not aim to cause grave injury, much less to kill. Often, in fact, Haredim apologized when they inflicted wounds. As a result, Israelis rarely took these actions as serious violations of public order.

Yet the principle the rabbis proclaimed to justify the agitation *was* serious. "Our Torah is our only constitution," many declared. "Under no circumstances can we respect the Zionists' laws." Haredim, they insisted, were exempt not just from the army but from the normal obligations of citizenship. This message, while widening the social rift, also weakened the legal pillars of the state.

The Orthodox, moreover, convinced a religious tide in Israel was rising, were no longer satisfied with the concessions Ben-Gurion had granted them. Faithful to the conviction that a Jewish state should be governed by Halacha, Orthodoxy demanded more.

Yeshiva students in the 1980s began routinely provoking, with little police interference, clashes at the Western Wall with women and with Reform and Conservative Jews. Convinced it was defending the faith against apostates, Orthodoxy demanded reversal of a supreme court ruling allowing women to read from the Torah at the Wall. Haredim in the Knesset proposed a bill to classify the Wall as a synagogue, which would have made violations of Orthodox practices punishable by prison.

Meanwhile, women, tired of discrimination, pushed in the opposite direction, calling for equal treatment under law. Secular Jews, seeking escape from rabbinic authority, clamored for the right of civil marriage and divorce. Reform and Conservative Judaism, though still a minority, were drawing more Israelis to their schools, synagogues and community centers, and demanded recognition by the state.

Rabbi Ravitz, the influential Haredi politician, acknowledged that these challenges were troublesome but saw no need to submit to the challengers' wishes.

"I don't see Halacha in conflict with the rights of women," he told me. "I have seven daughters, and they study different subjects from my five sons, who study mostly Torah, but they are educated. They have a modern life, even though in some ways it's like my grandmother's life. We Orthodox have different rules for women.

"The *aguna* ['chained wives'] problem, which bothers women so much, is one we're dealing with. It's hardly a great problem, since it affects only a few dozen women. But the claim that Halacha won't change on women's questions is a bluff.

"As for the Conservative and Reform movements, if they said simply they were bringing their people to love Jewish life, we'd have no quarrel. Orthodoxy wouldn't agree with them about a lot of things, but we wouldn't have to fight. We could live with them. But they want to do marriage, divorce and conversion their way, and it's not Jewish. The people they convert cannot be Jewish. What they want will change the whole society. I don't believe in pluralism. Judaism is not what everyone wants it to be."

In recent years, Orthodoxy, while insisting its goals are only defensive, has mobilized politically to crush the challenges to its religious preeminence. The framework in which it has moved is state sovereignty, an attribute denied to Jews for two thousand years. In its absence, every religious opinion has been free to assert its legitimacy, a profound source of Orthodox anguish. What Orthodoxy demands, ironically, is that the Jewish state, of which it deeply disapproves, serve as arbiter of disputes within Judaism. Its actions envision Israel as the Vatican of the Jewish world.

By the 1980s, Ultra-Orthodoxy had built an alliance with religious Zionists and Sephardim. Though each group had its own priorities, together they gave the Knesset a powerful religious bloc. Labor, the wounded flag bearer of secularism, was weakened further by the arrangement. Likud, the dominant party of the era, was willing to support Orthodox objectives. Conditions appeared favorable to seek a major victory. Orthodoxy chose to wage the campaign over the issue of religious conversion.

The issue was called "Who is a Jew?" Older than the state, the question had been politicized by the Right of Return, Israel's vow to be open to all Jews. But who, under law, was a Jew? For centuries, the only definition of a Jew, derived from Halacha, was whoever is born of a Jewish mother or is converted to Judaism. After World War II, this limitation raised questions about the entry of thousands of survivors of those selected by the Nazis as Jewish enough to kill.

In Israel's first days, the Right of Return was granted, over Orthodoxy's protests, to whoever professed to be Jewish. In response to the protests, the Knesset enacted a new law, more liberal than Halacha, but which limited eligibility to a child, grandchild or spouse of any Jew, and to the spouse of a child or grandchild of any Jew. Though Orthodoxy swallowed the change, it denied to immigrants in these categories the right, among others, to Jewish marriage and burial. Such immigrants, it argued, fell short of being real Jews.

In the 1980s, after simmering for decades, the issue reached a boil with massive arrivals from Ethiopia and the Soviet Union. By then, the state enforced Orthodoxy's definition of a *born* Jew but rejected its definition of a Jew *by conversion*. According to Orthodoxy, in accepting Reform and Conservative conversions, the state indirectly legitimized heresy. Orthodoxy not only denied the validity of Reform and Conservative conversions; it did not acknowledge either as Judaism.

To close the loophole, Orthodoxy demanded that Israeli law recognize only conversions performed "according to Halacha," which would have authorized only Orthodox rabbis to perform them. The issue then became "Who is a rabbi?" and, had Israel's government agreed to the change, it would have gone beyond treating Orthodoxy as preeminent to denying to Reform and Conservative Judaism any status at all. Such, of course, was Orthodoxy's intent. But non-Orthodox Jews, particularly in America, were outraged at their prospective delegitimization. Each side denounced the other for tearing the Jewish people apart.

The dispute was nothing more than the conflict Jews had failed to resolve since the Enlightenment. Orthodoxy claimed to be the only Judaism; pluralism, it said, was Gentile. Reform and Conservatism said that Judaism, far from being monolithic, could be expressed in different forms. Orthodoxy called its challengers heretics. Reform and Conservatism replied that they were preserving Judaism's principles by giving them meaning within the context of the real world.

Under pressure from Jews both in Israel and abroad, the government went back and forth and, in the end, backed away from a showdown. Instead, it named a body, the Neeman Commission, which founded, as a compromise, a school in which rabbis from the three branches followed their own agendas to instruct candidates for conversion, which was formalized in an Orthodox ceremony. The liberal rabbis cooperated in the project, and Orthodox rabbis for a time joined them in an atmosphere of mutual wariness. The commission even made a few converts, mostly from among Russian immigrants. But lacking Orthodoxy's full approval, it grew more fragile and eventually dissolved.

As a temporary measure, the Neeman Commission had succeeded in reducing the political tensions created by the conversion dispute, but it did not narrow the breach between Jews. Even as the dispute subsided, in fact, the breach widened under the pressure of another issue. Peace with the Arabs had assumed a place on the national agenda, and it was fracturing Jewish society.

ᦙ   ᦙ   ᦙ

THOUGH ULTRA-ORTHODOXY lacked religious Zionism's zealotry for the land, it nonetheless weighed in to tilt the balance against peace. Its motivation was political, not ideological. It chose its course in the interest of its institutions, notably its schools. Still, the course it chose had far-reaching consequences for the Arab-Israeli conflict.

"We believe it is a *mitzvah* to be everywhere in the Land of Israel, and that Jews have a right to be everywhere," Rabbi Ravitz told me.

"But we live among so many Arabs, and human life is also a Jewish value. As Mitnaggedim, as Ultra-Orthodox Jews, we believe we can give land back, though only if it's necessary, to save Jewish lives. It's the religious Zionists, the West Bank rabbis, who say we should be ready to sacrifice Jewish lives. The question is Halachic, but we believe it must be decided within a practical context."

Haredim had once shown as much disdain for Israel's borders as they had for its claims of Jewishness. Arguing the priority of Jewish life, they were for decades more dovish than Labor, in whose cabinets their politicians served. They surely were not fixated on territorial aggrandizement, like the religious Zionists, much less the Revisionists. But suddenly they shifted. The explanation, Friedman says, lies in the labyrinth of Haredi politics, half hidden in hard-to-decipher clashes over money and power.

Ultra-Orthodoxy's break with its dovish past occurred after the Knesset election of 1988, which ended in a virtual tie between Labor and Likud. To overcome the deadlock, the two parties at first agreed to a coalition, but both were soon soliciting help from the religious parties to form a government of their own. Labor announced that, if it won, it would embark on a campaign to negotiate Arab-Israeli peace.

Haredim had always been bare-knuckled in competing for government funds. But the readiness of both Labor and Likud to buy their votes, Friedman says, renewed old rivalries between Hasidim and Mitnaggedim, and even between Hasidic *rebbes*. The deadlock, moreover, led directly to the rise of Shas, a new political party representing Orthodox Sephardim, thereby changing the face of Israeli politics.

The Labor-Likud deadlock was broken in a bizarre drama by Rabbi Eliezer Schach, a diminutive ninety-two-year-old Mitnaggedic sage. Schach had no use whatsoever for secular Zionism. "Remember what an old Jew is telling you," he once said in reference to the Zionist heresy, "God is patient but He keeps a tally. And His patience ran out . . . when six million died." Schach warned that Israel's secularism could provoke God into another Holocaust at any time.

Schach was not a hawk; on the contrary, his concern for Jewish life made him rather dovish. But as a Mitnagged, Schach set as his highest priority the reversal of the growing power of Hasidic *rebbes* in politics.

To achieve this end, he formed a basically Mitnaggedic party, which Labor tried to win over with the promise of a major allocation of funds. But Haredi politicking over the contest between Labor and Likud was intense, and Schach's decision was understood to be crucial.

Schach announced his answer in a celebrated appearance before twenty thousand psalm-singing Haredim in Yad Eliahu, a Tel Aviv sports stadium that Friedman calls, ironically, "the High Temple of Israeli secular culture." Scalpers sold tickets at the gates. Inside, the tension was electric. Schach's speech, telecast to millions, lasted only ten minutes, and it was laced with abstruse references, which a scholar retained by the television network interpreted to the audience.

It opened with Schach's promise of "a few just and honest words . . . words of the Torah . . . without any political implications." But Schach then proceeded to lash out at the kibbutzim, symbol of secular Zionism, communities "which know not what Yom Kippur or Sabbath is," and he asked, "Can these people be considered Jews?" In insulting the Jewishness of secularism, Schach targeted Zionism itself. With passion he switched to Yiddish and revealed his real purpose. "Some turn one way and some the other, but what do we have from Labor? . . . Have they not separated from our past to seek a new Torah? . . . We must cut ourselves off from the parties that have no link to Judaism."

Schach had declared Labor, in effect, a party of goyim, but Friedman insists that this was not the real basis of his choice. He surmises that Schach, in the end, extorted a more generous bounty from Likud, which earned him the leadership of the Haredi bloc. Though the bloc had only 10 percent of the Knesset votes, it was enough to tip the scale and Likud formed the new government.

Many analysts charged Schach with overkill in his attack on Zionism. *Ma'ariv*, the Israeli daily, published a cartoon depicting the old rabbi climbing to the podium over soldiers' graves, a reminder of the Haredi military exemption. Engraved on the tombstones were: "Died in the Yom Kippur War," and above them Schach's statement, "In the kibbutzim, they know not what Yom Kippur is."

But Schach, unchastened, only repeated his insults. His decision joined the Haredi parties to the alliance of the religious Zionists and Likud, forming a bloc that remains intact. The new member, Ultra-Orthodoxy, gave a decisive parliamentary edge to the right-wing camp.

The shift did not end the Haredim's differences with religious Zionism. Theologically, the two remained far apart in their views of the Jewish state and the messianic component of redemption. But in becoming political allies they adopted a common view on key issues of the Israeli-Arab conflict, and they both now hold that they were guided in their course by divine will.

~ ~ ~

THE PROCESS BY WHICH Israel's Sephardim joined the religious Zionists and Haredim in the new bloc was also a complex web. Sephardim had long been wary of the Ashkenazi character of Haredi culture. During the centuries in which they thrived in Islamic lands, they saw Europe's Jews as cold, bloodless and uncultured, and their own civilization as superior. But Sephardim, like their Arab hosts, had missed the Renaissance, then the Enlightenment, and had failed to keep up with the changes brought on by Western thinking. By the time they reached Israel, they no longer laid claim to being Judaism's aristocracy. Most, in fact, arrived as paupers.

Sephardim, on the whole, were serious believers but not pious like Haredim nor zealous like religious Zionists. Their rabbis were more lenient than Ashkenazim in prescribing Halachic duties. Friedman and Heilman describe Sephardim as having "a kind of hybrid marginal culture which made it possible to go to a traditional Sabbath service on Saturday morning and then attend . . . a football game the same afternoon, without being troubled by feelings of duplicity." It took some time for Sephardim in Israel to incorporate their social values into their politics.

Sephardi attitudes, going back decades, were marked by a deep grudge against the Labor Party, a vestige of the hardships etched into memory from the early immigrant days. Israel's founders, almost all of them Ashkenazim, had not treated Sephardim well. They confined them in fetid refugee camps, then squeezed them into urban slums or shipped them off to remote development towns. They failed to find them jobs and assigned them marginal soil to till. Worse, they dismissed Sephardi cultural values, and Labor was even accused of kidnapping Sephardi children to raise as Ashkenazim.

Ben-Gurion was among the offenders, often describing Sephardi communities as primitive. He considered Zionism a Western movement, and was convinced the new state's best citizens would come from Europe and America. The North African immigrant, Ben-Gurion once said, "looks like a savage, . . . has never read a book in his life, not even a religious one, and doesn't even know how to say his prayers." He acknowledged Labor's prejudicial practices, but even when warned that Sephardim were gravitating to the Revisionists, he was unable to change the government's anti-Sephardi tilt.

Labor, at best, faced a difficult task in integrating Sephardim. As small merchants or craftsmen, most arrived in Israel deficient in usable skills, even in literacy. By the 1950s they were already a popular majority, but also a socioeconomic underclass. Though they received sound, Western-style schooling, their failure to improve their status only hardened their animosities.

Seeing an opening to make friends, the Haredim offered religious education to Sephardi families, usually free. Though it denied the children the practical knowledge needed for jobs, this education introduced them to the Haredi world. Young Sephardim often journeyed from Haredi lower schools to Haredi yeshivot, and in the absence of their own schools drifted into the Ultra-Orthodox ranks. Most retained their Sephardi identity, but they adopted Haredi dress and a Haredi-style piety, while fueling their resentment of secularism and of the Labor Party.

In the 1970s, religious and working-class Sephardim began asserting themselves politically. In 1977, they joined in Likud's electoral campaign, imparting a new belligerence to Israel's street politics; their votes were also crucial to Likud's victory. Acknowledging this support, Likud was generous with spoils, disbursing funds to a rising Sephardi yeshiva system. When Sephardim found they were still dependent on Haredim as teachers, managers and even political advisers, however, they resolved to set up organizations, both social and political, of their own.

The inspiration for a party came from Rabbi Ovadia Yosef, a respected Torah sage. Born in Baghdad in 1920, he served for a time as Israel's Sephardi chief rabbi. Yosef's name quickly became synonymous with Sephardi politics.

In founding Shas, Yosef was helped by Rabbi Schach, the old Mitnagged, who reasoned that a Sephardi party would be an ally in his conflict with the Hasidim. Yosef, however, did not share Schach's deep-seated anti-Zionism. And though he agreed to join Orthodoxy's political bloc, he saw himself as a rival to Schach for political power.

For a time, Yosef even seemed to embark on an independent course on the peace issue. In 1989, he flew to Cairo to meet with President Hosni Mubarak, and on his return, he created consternation within the Knesset's religious bloc by announcing that he favored ceding territory for peace. His political deviation, however, was short-lived.

As Friedman and Heilman explain, the Sephardi masses, recalling unhappy experiences in the Islamic world, are deeply anti-Arab. The priority that Yosef attached to peace, moreover, was second to that of his schools. This priority was best served by the united effort of the religious bloc. After Cairo, Yosef quickly abandoned his dovishness to join the rabbinate in supporting the hawkish Likud, which dutifully provided religious funds in return.

Still, even common political interests did not eliminate tension between Sephardim and Haredi rabbis. Sephardi students often complained of the condescension of their Ashkenazi teachers. Sephardim resented Ashkenazi criticism of their unique religious practices and, especially, Ashkenazi mockery of Sephardi rabbis.

Right after the election of 1992, when Shas won five key seats, Yosef was profoundly insulted by a mindless remark by Schach. Sephardim, Schach declared, were "not sufficiently mature to lead, either in Torah or in national affairs." Yosef at that point turned his back on the religious bloc to join Rabin, Labor's leader, in forming the new government. His move came as an unexpected shift in favor of peace.

But the aftermath turned out otherwise. Entitled to a cabinet post, Yosef selected Moroccan-born Aryeh De'eri, a talented politician, who was named minister of interior. Rabin duly delivered on his promises of funds to Shas schools. But Yosef fought constantly with Education Minister Shulamit Aloni, who held fiercely antireligious views. Even more troublesome was a police inquiry into De'eri, who resigned under suspicion of taking bribes.

Subject to a long investigation and trial, De'eri acknowledged that bribes were paid but claimed that Shas's schools, not he personally, benefited from them. Investigators, in fact, later established that yeshivot under the jurisdiction of Haredi officials were bilking the government out of many millions of dollars every year. De'eri's position, however, reflected what had by then become a freely articulated principle in Ultra-Orthodox circles. It held that if an action served God, its violation of civil law was without relevance. De'eri's claim earned him wide support in the Haredi community.

De'eri was finally convicted and sentenced to a prison term. The evidence against him, moreover, vindicated the government's charge that he had reaped personal rewards. Nonetheless, "De'eri is innocent" stickers were pasted on walls throughout Haredi neighborhoods. More seriously, Yosef adopted De'eri's argument, proclaiming Halacha an overriding authority. As the months passed, he became increasingly intemperate, calling De'eri a victim of the secular elite, the victim of trumped-up charges. He went further, in fact, calling into question the validity of the entire system of civil law.

When the case reached the supreme court, Yosef called for De'eri to be freed because the judges "know no Torah . . . , are all Sabbath violators . . . [and] are the cause of all the world's torments." Later, Yosef was investigated on suspicion of incitement to violence, but no charges were brought.

Throughout the episode, Ultra-Orthodoxy generally echoed Yosef. Agudath Israel denounced the high court as a "judicial dictatorship" that "treats [religious Jews] the same way it treats Muslims." These attacks nibbled at the legitimacy of a system that Orthodoxy had long tried to cripple, if not destroy. As Rabin moved toward peace, the Yosef crisis inflamed the atmosphere of defiance of legal authority.

Yosef finally seized on the De'eri episode to withdraw Shas from the Rabin government. The loss of five Knesset votes forced Rabin to rely on Arab parties to remain in power, exposing him to the charge by the right wing that he lacked a "Jewish majority." Shas's departure also deprived Rabin, at a crucial moment in Arab-Israeli negotiations, of vital religious cover, reinforcing religious opposition to an agreement. Shas, in abandoning Rabin, suddenly adopted religious Zionism's argument that the evacuation of holy soil equaled repudiation of divine redemption. Yosef added the final straw to the negotiating process, ensuring its collapse.

ɡ   ɡ   ɡ

YITZHAK RABIN HAD BEEN elected Israel's prime minister in June 1992 by a narrow margin. His parliamentary majority consisted of Labor and several allied secular parties. He did not invite the two small Arab parties that supported him with their votes into his cabinet. Altogether Rabin enjoyed a one-vote Knesset majority, not all of whose members were peace enthusiasts. Even after his majority was enlarged by the five votes from Shas, his government could hardly have claimed to be secure.

Rabin himself, it should be noted, had never been a dove. In his earlier term as prime minister and in the succession of cabinet posts he held, he had built a reputation as a hard-liner. But the considerations that drove him were practical rather than ideological. A few years earlier, he had concluded that there was no military solution to the conflict between Israelis and Palestinians. As minister of defense when the first *intifada* broke out in 1987, he found the army unable to master the unconventional warfare that the Palestinians waged. Only a political solution was possible, he believed, and though prepared to concede very little, he was ready to embark on a diplomatic quest.

In his inaugural as prime minister, Rabin made clear that he had also been influenced by overall changes in the world order. The fall of the Soviet Union had transformed global strategic conceptions. He noted that the condition of the Jewish people had been transformed as well.

Walls of hatred have crumbled, borders have been erased.
Superpowers have collapsed and ideologies have broken
down, states have been born and passed away, and the gates

of immigration to Israel have been flung open. And it is our duty, to ourselves and to our children, to see the new world as it is now . . . so that Israel becomes part of the changing world. No longer are we "a people that dwells alone," and no longer is it true that "the whole world's against us." We must overcome the sense of isolation that has held us in its thrall. . . . We must join the campaign of peace, reconcilia- tion and international cooperation that is now engulfing the globe, lest we miss the train and be left alone in the station.

Rabin did not say—though his words implied as much—that many Jews, accustomed to being "a people that dwells alone," were uncom- fortable at the thought of being anything else. Haredim believed that the covenant with God required them to live at arm's length from Gentiles; others felt that loneliness was the immutable Jewish destiny. Religious Zionists—Rabin called them "trouble-makers in the territo- ries"—had knowingly selected a course, proclaiming it to be divine, which in his mind doomed Israel to protracted alienation from the in- ternational community.

In the inaugural, Rabin made overtures to both the Palestinians and the settlers to reverse this course. Though neither found them generous, they opened a door. Rabin offered the Arabs limited self- government, which they considered inadequate except as a step to statehood, their national aspiration. To the settlers he promised secu- rity, while warning them against disrupting his plans to scale down Jewish rule in the territories. He would soon learn how intractable the settlers' vision was.

Still, during Rabin's first year, the territories were largely quiet. He had halted construction of settlements, displeasing the settlers, but he also dawdled in promoting peace talks. The Arabs seemed to be wait- ing; so did the Yesha Council, the bureaucracy that had succeeded Gush Emunim in representing settler interests. Zealots still preached, and Kahane's heirs followed the ideology of their late chief, who had been assassinated in New York two years earlier. But most Israelis, like most Arabs, were content not to challenge Rabin's unhurried ways.

Few then knew that, since December 1992, an Israeli delegation had been meeting secretly in Oslo with Yasser Arafat's Palestine Liberation Organization to hammer out an agreement. After nine months, the two sides produced the Oslo Accords, which granted the Palestinians self-rule in Jericho and Gaza as a first step to an unspecified final resolution of the one-hundred-year-old conflict. On September 10, 1993, Rabin, who only a week before had referred to the PLO as a "despicable organization," did what he had vowed never to do: grant to the PLO full political recognition.

Three days later, Rabin stood with Arafat beside U.S. President Bill Clinton before a huge audience and hundreds of television cameras on the White House lawn. At Clinton's urging, a beaming Arafat reached out his hand toward Rabin, who hesitated visibly, his body rigid, before taking it. Few spectators were likely to forget the drama, or fail to register the hope of reconciliation that the scene contained.

In his comments, Rabin, retreating from long-held positions, showed uncharacteristic emotion:

> We have come here to try to put an end to the hostilities so that our children and our children's children will no longer have to experience the painful cost of war. . . . Let me say to you, the Palestinians, we are destined to live together on the same soil in the same land. We the soldiers who have returned from the battle . . . we say to you today in a loud and clear voice, "Enough of blood and tears. Enough!" . . . We are today giving peace a chance and saying to you, "Enough." We wish to open a new chapter in the sad book of our lives together, a chapter of mutual recognition, of good-neighborliness, of mutual respect and understanding.

For a very secular man, Rabin ended the talk in an equally uncharacteristic manner. He pronounced in Hebrew a prayer that, he said, "Jews recite daily."

> May He who makes peace on High make peace for us and
> for all Israel.

He then asked the seated audience to join in saying, "Amen." The words resonated across the White House garden.

But Rabin's religious opponents—both at home and in the Diaspora—were swayed neither by the prayer nor by his invocation of God. In Jerusalem the night before, settlers held a rally in which the crowd chanted rhythmically, "Rabin is a traitor, Rabin is a traitor." And even as he spoke, dozens of black-suited Haredim, mostly American, marched around the White House in protest of what they called his betrayal of God in abandoning the holy soil of Judea and Samaria.

Active resistance to the Oslo Accords began soon after. It was ignited by Islamic extremists, themselves opposed to peace, who unleashed a campaign of terror aimed at both the territories and Israel proper. Militant settlers retaliated by attacking Arabs on the roads and in their villages. The reprisals were encouraged by the West Bank rabbinic council, which ruled that under Halacha such violence was legitimate.

At the same time, settlers launched a campaign of vituperation against Rabin himself. Kahane's organization led them, but it was joined by the Yesha Council and even by young Haredim from Ultra-Orthodox yeshivot. Posters labeling Rabin a "traitor" and a "murderer" became common; some pictured him in an Arafat-style *kufiya*.

Then, on February 25, 1994, five months after the signing of the Oslo Accords, an American-born disciple of Kahane delivered the most devastating blow to date against the peace effort. Baruch Goldstein, a medical doctor, lived next to Hebron in the settlement of Kiryat Arba. Neighbors later recalled that in a eulogy of a terror victim, he had angrily demanded God's vengeance. Goldstein had no history of violence; in fact, he was known as a compassionate, decent man. But he had come to believe, friends said later, that Jews could preserve their hope of redemption only by stopping the peace process.

Clad in his reservist's uniform, Goldstein rose early that day, took his assault rifle and drove to Hebron's Machpelah Cave for his morning prayers. After the service, he passed by the soldiers standing guard to enter the adjacent hall where Muslims prayed, kneeling, their heads to the floor. Switching his rifle to automatic, he began firing left and right, emptying one magazine after another, using more than a hundred rounds. He killed twenty-nine Arabs and wounded scores before worshipers finally reached him from behind and beat him to death with iron bars.

Psychologists said the attack had been prefigured by events. Since the Oslo Accords were signed, blood had already been spilled in abundance, and experts had warned of a potential cataclysm. They said religious extremists, in despair over redemption's looming collapse, might be expected to turn to mass murder.

Indeed, in the settlements many applauded Goldstein. The head of a West Bank yeshiva called the massacre a "desperate act of love for his people." The rabbi who officiated at Goldstein's funeral called him "a martyr . . . who joins the victims of the Nazi Holocaust." Most settlers, loath to praise mass murder, remained silent. Even critics conventionally softened their statements of remorse by expressions of "understanding" of Goldstein's act. Kiryat Arba turned Goldstein's burial site into a pilgrimage shrine. Some settlers declared that Rabin, having forsaken them, was actually to blame.

Rabin named a commission to look into the massacre but, skirting political pitfalls, it made no effort to establish responsibility. Goldstein, it said, "saw himself as a representative of the people of Israel, ordered to act in accordance with God's will." But it did not speculate on how the tragedy might have been averted or on how to curb the rage contained in the settlers' messianic despair.

Rabin, always puzzled by zealotry, dismissed Goldstein as "mentally ill." In his view, Arabs could be fanatics; Jews could not. His government proceeded to ban the Kahane groups and arrested a few members. But by excluding ideology from his analysis, Rabin helped divert the search for causes into the blind alley of insanity. He thus missed the condition that, the next year, would take his own life.

The Hebron massacre, predictably, triggered Arab retaliation. Hamas, a rising organization of Islamic radicals, killed several Jews with car bombs in Hadera and Afula, two small Israeli cities. When settlers, hurling charges that Rabin was selling them out, mobilized vigilante squads, the army imposed a twenty-four-hour curfew, not on the settlements but on Arab villages. It also conducted security sweeps in which dozens of Arabs were killed.

But Rabin decided such measures missed the real problem and decided to try reducing frictions between Arabs and Jews in the territories. He focused his attention first on seven families of Kahane followers who lived in trailers in Tel Rumeida, an enclave in central Hebron. Thirty-thousand Palestinians surrounded them, requiring the army to provide round-the-clock protection. Rabin proposed to remove the families to better homes in nearby Kiryat Arba.

When word of the plan leaked out, settler leaders denounced it as the first step in an irreversible retreat from holy soil. Proclaiming a hunger strike, they called on Israelis to support them with mass protests. A council of West Bank rabbis fueled the fire. "The decision of the secular regime," they announced in a statement signed for emphasis by a former chief rabbi, "cannot bind a Jew when it runs contrary to religious law." Claiming Halachic authority, the rabbis called on soldiers to resist orders to evacuate the Tel Rumeida families.

Rabin was outraged by the settlers' actions and the rabbis' seditious call. But he was also sensitive to predictions that a military effort to move the seven families would ignite a Jewish civil war. By then, Shas had departed from the coalition and right-wing extremists were proclaiming that Rabin had no right to act without a "Jewish mandate." Admitting defeat, he canceled—as he had canceled the Kadum evacuation in 1975—the Tel Rumeida plan.

The rabbis of religious Zionism had once again demonstrated that they could impose their will on Israel's democratically elected government. In its most direct challenge ever of lawful authority, religious Zionism had emerged victorious over the secular state.

🕮   🕮   🕮

WITHIN A FEW MONTHS, an even more incendiary idea was growing within Orthodox circles. Two obscure Halachic precepts, reborn in West Bank yeshivot, were placed on the rabbinic agenda. Ignored since the era of the Hasidic-Mitnaggedic wars, they were named, in Hebrew, *din rodef* and *din moser*. The first criminalizes a Jew who relinquishes Jewish life or property to Gentiles; the second indicts a Jew who turns another Jew over to Gentile authorities. Both emerged from the ancient taboo devised as a response to exile, against having Gentiles resolve Jewish disputes. The crime in both cases carried a penalty of death.

Imposing the death penalty, to be sure, constituted a major stretch of the law. Halacha specifies a range of capital sins: blasphemy, idolatry, dishonoring one's parents, witchcraft, even Sabbath desecration. Throughout history, however, Jews rarely invoked the death penalty. The Talmud describes a Jewish court that sentences one person to death every seventy years as "bloodthirsty."

Though the historical record is not clear, courts apparently laid such restraint aside during the Middle Ages, when some Jews were executed as *mosrim* (informers). The doctrine was renewed in the nineteenth century by participants in the Hasidic-Mitnaggedic feud, though the number of executions, if any, is unknown. After that, it receded into obscurity, only to be resurrected by militant rabbis on the West Bank after the Oslo Accords.

Rabin was liable to being a *rodef*, these rabbis argued, because he intended to relinquish segments of the Holy Land to Gentiles, endangering Jewish life. He may also have been a *moser*, they reasoned, because he planned to subject Jews who live in the territories to the authority of Gentile rulers.

Rabbis debated these charges in secret. Later testimony, however, makes clear that their discussions resonated among settlers throughout the territories. Suddenly *rodef* and *moser*, two long-forgotten terms, were topics of popular debate, especially in yeshivot.

"It is no longer possible," three prominent rabbis wrote in a letter circulated to colleagues worldwide, "to silence the question that bursts out of the broken hearts of many Jews. . . . Is it not the duty of community leaders to warn the head of government and his ministers that if they keep pursuing the [Oslo] agreement . . . they will be subject to the Halachic ruling of *din moser*, as ones who surrender the life and property of Jews to the Gentiles?"

By adopting the interrogatory form, the authors were able to claim, after Rabin's death, that they had raised these issues only to promote

Halachic scholarship. The impact, however, went far beyond scholarly abstraction. In distant America, for example, Orthodox rabbis, in contact with Israeli counterparts, debated the issue of Rabin's criminality with less than academic detachment.

A Halachist from New York's Yeshiva University told a newspaper that Jewish law required anyone perceived as a *rodef* to be killed. A major New York rabbi won the endorsement of a large rabbinic gathering of charges against Rabin. His conclusion was that Rabin's execution was both necessary and desirable.

In the West Bank leadership, Rabbi Nahum Rabinovitch, known both as a Torah scholar and a political radical, publicly raised the issue of Rabin's indictment. As head of a Hesder yeshiva in Ma'ale Adumim, he taught the religious Zionist doctrine that young men should serve in the army and prepare for a life that combined secular duties with religious piety. He saw no contradiction, however, in undermining Rabin, the army's commander, and he consistently urged young soldiers to disobey orders that jeopardized Jewish rule.

On Israeli radio about two months before the murder, Rabinovitch called Rabin a *moser* "who, according to Maimonides, is liable to death." He then covered himself by adding, "I didn't say it's permissible to harm him." In a later inquiry, police questioned Rabinovitch on suspicion of incitement, and he publicly expressed regret if his "harsh comments . . . made out of pain" had led to unfortunate consequences. With his rabbinic colleagues supporting him, nothing came of the police inquiry.

A few years later I talked with Rabinovitch in a spare conference room in his yeshiva in the Jerusalem suburb of Ma'ale Adumim. His line, though softer, retained a sharp edge of anger toward Rabin. Denying any responsibility for the killing, he insisted that "left-wingers" had tried and failed to make religious Zionism a scapegoat. Nonetheless, he accused Rabin of serious Halachic sins in proposing to trade land for peace, for which he insisted Rabin deserved to be punished.

"There are two hundred thousand Jews living in the territories, innocent people," he said, "and uprooting them from their homes is a crime. Halacha insists on justice, and uprooting them is injustice. It is making war against our own people. The duty of a rabbi is to oppose that."

Improbably, Rabinovitch denied that religious settlers had *ever* been responsible for anti-Arab violence. "That's propaganda the left has manufactured," he said. "Baruch Goldstein's action caused much sadness among the settlers. Even the Arabs loved him for his good deeds as a doctor and a friend, but something cracked in him and no one understands why. In fact, the physical self-restraint that the residents of the territories have shown toward their Arab neighbors is admirable."

Claiming that he personally favored peace, Rabinovitch went on: "Peace is a noble objective, but we have to know how to pursue it. It's a misconception that Israel can live in harmony with the Arabs. Our values are too far apart. It's too late for peace. Why should we Israelis give the Arabs what they failed to get in war? The best we can hope for is a truce based on our military supremacy. The government's duty is to protect the Jews who live on the land."

Rabbi Eliezer Waldman, head of the Kiryat Arba yeshiva, was personally more amiable than Rabinovitch. He and I met in his modest apartment, located in a cluster of brick high rises. We took tea in his study, surrounded by religious books and by photographs of the rabbis Kook, father and son. His mild manner, particularly in the scholarly atmosphere of his home, seemed to me to belie his long and turbulent record as a radical activist.

A founder of Gush Emunim, Waldman was known within the movement as a partisan of combining piety, political involvement and militant action. In 1981, he won a Knesset seat on the list of Tehiya, an extreme right-wing party. He was said to have given his blessings to many bombings, including the one in which Arab mayors were maimed. His yeshiva's ideology was "Eretz Yisrael Judaism," which meant promotion of territorial annexation, and he led his students personally in the fight over withdrawal from Yamit. In public statements, Waldman also endorsed the advice to soldiers to resist the evacuation of Tel Rumeida.

"There were differences of opinion," he told me, "on whether Rabin was a *din rodef,* and that shouldn't be surprising. Intellectual understanding is the product of differences, and that's what is beautiful about Judaism. It's what we're taught about the Talmud in the yeshivot. We're not God. But these differences should not cause animosity among Jews. Rabin did not live by Jewish principles, but he was not heretical. No Jew has a right to lift a hand against another Jew, and surely not against Jewish leaders. That would be against the essence of Halacha, a distortion of the law, a desecration of God's name."

Waldman told me he supported the elder Kook's teaching that the process of redemption began with the Jews' return to the Holy Land. "But redemption doesn't mean suddenly everything will be perfect," he said. "The sages always taught that the process could bring pain and failure along the way. These defeats do not diminish the undertaking. The process was initiated by God but it depends on the actions of the Jews. The heart of redemption remains the reestablishment of the Jewish state as a center of Torah study." Until they learn that lesson, he said, the Jews will not realize their aspirations.

But whatever the failures, Waldman said, he saw in Jewish settlement of the Holy Land ample evidence of God's approval. As further evidence, he pointed to the Balfour Declaration, the founding of the state, the ingathering of exiles and Israel's succession of military victories. The country's transformation from desolation to the blossoming of industry, agriculture, education, technology and science, he said, is further proof of God's intervention.

"This land was one of the most backward in the world for two thousand years," he said, "like the rest of the Middle East today. Israel is a corner of light in a region of darkness and dictatorship.

"Judea and Samaria—yes, Kiryat Arba itself—are our heartland. The Six-Day War brought us back here, and thousands and thousands of Jews, not just religious Zionists but Haredim, have settled here. The will to retain this land has largely closed the gap between observant Jews. We all agree that no soil is holier. Do we need permission of the Arabs to do what we are doing? Not at all. Was this an Arab land? Never. We were driven out, and now we're coming back."

Like Rabinovitch, Waldman said he was in favor of peace but rejected territorial withdrawal. "The very notion of trading land for peace is absurd," he said. "What nation has ever chosen to weaken its hold on its land when surrounded by enemies? Our security comes from justly being in command of our own land. Our willingness to fight for our rights is what safeguards our existence. Those who believe otherwise are endangering the Jewish people."

A few days later, I met with Rabbi Yoel Bin-Nun, who was also a pioneer in Gush Emunim. The movement was said, in fact, to have been founded in his living room. But Bin-Nun, a decade before, had fallen out with Rabinovitch, Waldman and the other radicals who were shaping Gush Emunim practices. A rare moderate among religious Zionists, he held views that made him a pariah in rabbinic circles.

Born in Haifa in 1946, Bin-Nun was a paratrooper in the Six-Day War. Later, as a student at Merkaz HaRav, he too became a follower of Rabbi Kook. But he came to the conclusion that religious Zionism was distorting Kook's teachings into aggressive racism and disrespect for law, ideas that were seriously at odds with authentic Judaism.

"Things began going wrong after the withdrawal from Yamit," he said. "This was the beginning of the Jewish terror organizations. It was the first shock to me, a sign that our vision of redemption was derailed. I condemned the terror, and the rabbis who supported it. Many of them are still angry with me."

Bin-Nun also recognized practical dangers to Israel lurking in religious Zionism's emerging ideology. In 1988, in an article in the settlers' magazine *Nekuda*, he gave voice to his alarm:

> It is no longer possible to think that we can annex the territory and at the same time deny Israeli citizenship to its [one and a half million Arab] inhabitants. We cannot live with the illusion we can expel them. . . . It is possible [for Jews] to blow things up and go it alone. [But] this can lead to destroying the state of Israel and all that the present generation has achieved. . . . At stake is not our ideology but Israel's survival.

A year later, Bin-Nun quit Gush Emunim, severing bonds that had been intrinsic to his life's work.

In the months before Rabin's murder, Bin-Nun became appalled at the talk of *rodef* and *moser* circulating in rabbinic circles. After the murder, he created a sensation when he rose at a meeting sponsored by the Yesha Council to declare: "If the people whose rulings or words led to Rabin's death do not reveal themselves, accept accountability and resign from their positions, I myself will disclose their identity."

The response to his warning included death threats and a rabbinic proposal of excommunication. Nonetheless, he delivered to the police the names of seven rabbis, Rabinovitch's among them. "Rabbi Bin-Nun is a liar, a cheat and a gossip. I think he's insane," was Rabinovitch's answer. The police conducted a brief investigation, then closed the case, citing once again a lack of hard evidence to support any charges.

"Rabinovitch is a tragic story," said Bin-Nun when we met in his house in the settlement of Ofra in the Judean hills, an hour's drive north of Jerusalem. "He basically is a liberal. He has a democratic soul. I don't know why, in the months leading to Rabin's death, he became so extreme. If he regrets it now, he isn't willing to say it.

"Waldman was different. I never knew where he stood. I could understand his words but I could not see his direction. He often changed positions. But, like so many other rabbis, he wound up following Kahane and the Kahanists."

Bin-Nun explained that when he helped to found Gush Emunim he saw it as a step on the ladder of redemption but, unlike most of its members, he never regarded Israel's borders as holy. He said he regarded his own settlement, Ofra, as no holier than the new cities of the coast. Borders, like relations with the Arabs, he said, are political issues, which every Jew sees differently. One-half of Israel prefers peace to territory, Bin-Nun said, and the other half is not permitted to impose its views on them by force. If the government enacts a law to give back land, he said, all Jews have the duty to obey it, even if some think that God disagrees. As a democracy, he said, Israel cannot leave it up to the rabbis to make its political decisions.

Rabbi Kook, envisaging redemption as a process, made clear that history has not run its course, Bin-Nun said. He acknowledged that he shared the hope that one day all Eretz Yisrael would be Jewish again, as it was under King David. But it is more important now, he said, that this dream not tear the Jewish people apart.

"Many rabbis don't agree with that," Bin-Nun said. "They even defend what Goldstein did at the Machpelah cave. Or if they are not defending, they say 'We're against the massacre, of course, but we must all understand the background.' There is no background that justifies what Goldstein did. What is horrible is that, by the same reasoning, some rabbis still defend Rabin's murder."

அ   அ   அ

YIGAL AMIR, IN HIS LONG interrogation after Rabin's murder, told investigators he had modeled himself on the biblical figure Phinehas, who had taken it upon himself to serve God by slaying two sinners. Historians say the Zealots of the Second Temple era found justification for their excesses in the praise that God, in the Bible, heaped on Phinehas. Amir told the investigators that God's approval of Phinehas had inspired him, too.

The story appears in the Book of Numbers, the fourth book of the Torah. It says the Israelites, while encamped at Shittim, on the way to Canaan, engaged in whoring with the local women. They also made offerings to foreign gods, as they had done before to the golden calf. God, angry with them again, brought down a plague in which twenty-four thousand Israelites died. To expiate the Israelite sins, Phinehas, grandson of Aaron, chose to run his spear through an Israelite and a Midyanite woman with whom he was illicitly lying.

God, according to Numbers, not only brought the plague to an end; He also bestowed on Phinehas His personal pact of friendship. He commended Phinehas, moreover, for being "zealous for his God," which is the phrase that is said to have aroused the Jewish extremists of the Second Temple era.

Notwithstanding God's personal intervention, the Talmudic sages debated the authority that Phinehas had taken upon himself to enforce God's law. The consensus they reached in both the Palestinian and Babylonian academies was that, whatever God's response, Jews were barred from emulating Phinehas's vigilantism, and rabbis, moreover, were forbidden to exhort Jews to follow the precedent. Some sages even said that had the unfortunate lovers killed Phinehas in their own defense, they would have deserved to be exonerated.

Amir, drawing on his yeshiva education, found virtue in the murders Phinehas committed, but dismissed the sages' concerns. Like Phinehas, he acted on his own, aiming to arrest not a plague but territorial withdrawal. He justified his act by claiming that nationalist rabbis had charged Yitzhak Rabin with violating two provisions of Halacha, which justified the penalty of death.

Amir, prior to the murder, had no record of violence. He belonged to no ideological movement, either religious or political. If there is a clue to his behavior, it lies in his personal roots. Amir's sense of identity may reveal something important both about his crime and about Israeli society in the era of Yitzhak Rabin.

Amir was unusual in having roots in three deeply religious but otherwise distinct communities—the Sephardim, the Haredim and the religious Zionists. What the three had in common was that each, for its own reasons, had drifted for a decade or more toward disregard for Israel's civil law. Reinforcing one another, they freed Amir of moral equivocation, enabling him, like Phinehas, to find religious virtue in cold-blooded murder.

Amir was born in 1970 in Herzliya, a Tel Aviv suburb, the second of eight children of Yemenites who arrived in Israel after independence. Though his family lived in a working-class Yemenite enclave, it had by its own efforts reached the margins of the middle class. Like most Sephardim, however, the Amirs retained a memory of harsher years, when Labor was said to have barred the way to the success of Sephardim.

Both of Amir's parents, funded by Haredim, attended Ultra-Orthodox schools. Amir's father made religion his life, as a Torah scribe. His mother, the director of a religious nursery school, was the breadwinner. She was also drawn to Jewish mysticism and right-wing politics, and once made a pilgrimage to Kiryat Arba to Baruch Goldstein's grave.

At six, Amir planted his roots in Ashkenazic Ultra-Orthodoxy by entering a Haredi school. A bright student, he enrolled at twelve, with the sons of wealthy eastern Europeans in a yeshiva in Tel Aviv. "When the administrators laid eyes on Yigal, a dark Yemeni child," his mother once said, "at first they refused to accept him. But he insisted and was finally admitted." He remained in the Haredi fold until his yeshiva graduation.

Though his yeshiva studies entitled him to a draft exemption, Amir chose a Hesder program, combining Torah study with military service. It was his first link to religious Zionism. With his classmates, he joined a combat unit and was assigned to the West Bank to help put down the *intifada*. Fellow soldiers later reported that he showed a special aptitude for inflicting pain on Arabs.

In 1993, discharged from the army, Amir registered at Bar Ilan, Israel's Orthodox university. He majored in computers and law while studying Torah on the side. One summer, he volunteered to teach Hebrew to Latvian Jews in Riga. He also took part in campus politics at Bar Ilan, known then as a stronghold of religious Zionism.

The three camps in which Amir had roots, all with a commitment to Jewish piety, had reached agreement by then that Yitzhak Rabin and his party were embarked on a disastrous course. Whether Amir shared their vision of redemption is unclear, but his father told journalists that his son talked often of a duty to advance God's plan. The plan—as Sephardim, Haredim and religious Zionists understood it—focused on defeating the Oslo Accords.

Among his fellow students at Bar Ilan, Amir was known as devout but easygoing. He was always ready to visit settlements, organize demonstrations or engage in discussion on politics or divine will. His favorite book was *Baruch Hagever*, a commemoration of Goldstein's deeds. He acquired a gun, spinning a story to the authorities to obtain a permit for it, and he began to speak openly of killing Rabin, even making dry runs at potential sites to prepare for the crime. His best friend at Bar Ilan was Avi Raviv, a declared Kahanist, who only later was revealed to be a police informer, though he never warned his handlers how dangerous Amir was.

Amir's older brother Haggai, using a skill he learned in the army, fabricated ammunition capable of piercing a bulletproof vest to use in the killing. Haggai and a few friends even joined in the planning of the crime. But they all understood that the responsibility for the assassination was Yigal's alone.

Unnoticed on the evening of November 4, Amir milled about in the parking lot where security guards and drivers waited near their cars. As "Song of Peace," an anthem of the peace movement, echoed over the rally, marking its end, Rabin made his appearance. Amir moved out of the shadows and fired twice at his back. An hour after the bullets struck, Rabin died in a nearby hospital.

The security services, it was said, had trained only for Arab violence, ignoring, as did Rabin himself, the dangers of religious Jews. Amir took advantage of the lapse. "I was afraid," he said, "an Arab might kill him. I wanted Heaven to see that a Jew had done it." Arrested at once, Amir said he fully expected to pay for the crime. He was also prepared, if necessary, to die. "What I feared most," he insisted, "was that when I pulled the trigger nothing would happen, and I would be caught and sit in jail like a jerk for the rest of my life."

When Amir was informed Rabin was dead, the police reported, he smiled and said, "I've done my work. . . . Get some wine and cakes. Let's have a toast." Later he explained, "It wasn't a matter of revenge or punishment or anger, Heaven forbid, but what would stop Oslo. I thought about it a lot and understood that if I took Rabin down, that's what would stop it. . . . I thought about this for two years and I calculated the possibilities and risks. If I hadn't done it, I would feel much worse. My deed will be understood in the future. I saved the people of Israel from destruction."

Amir told his interrogators his act had been validated by rabbinic rulings. Haggai testified that one of their friends, assigned to obtain Halachic sanction, had returned with a rabbinic decision that said: "The moment a Jew turns over his people and land to enemies, he must be killed." That, he said, satisfied Yigal. Neither Yigal nor anyone else, however, identified the rabbi, and the police acquired no evidence to confirm that there even was one.

Still, Amir continued to insist that his act was based on rabbinic authority. He said:

If not for the Halachic ruling of *din rodef*, made against Rabin by a few rabbis I knew about, it would have been very difficult for me to murder. . . . Once it is a ruling, there is no longer a problem of morality. If I were involved now in the biblical conquest of the land, as said in [the Book of] Joshua, I would have had to kill babies and children. I would have done so regardless of the problem of morality. Once it is a ruling, I do not have a problem with it. . . . But if I did not get the backing [of the rabbis] and I had not been representing many more people, I would not have acted.

Before being sentenced by an Israeli court to life imprisonment, Amir declared, "Without believing in God, I would never have had the power to do this."

Rabin's murder did not, however, noticeably change the angry atmosphere in which Israelis conducted their politics.

Secular Israelis initially blamed the murder on the incitement of the religious camp. But the police made no serious search, beyond Amir and his friends, for culprits. Amir's girlfriend was convicted for complicity but, after a clamor from the settlers' movement, received a pardon. Most mainstream Zionists followed the Herzl tradition of restraint to preserve cordial relations with Orthodoxy.

Within the religious camp, few voices called for introspection. Rabbi Yehuda Amital, dean of a West Bank yeshiva, was one of the exceptions. Like Rabbi Bin-Nun, he had begun his journey to moderation even before Rabin's murder and later placed his energies into Meimad, an Orthodox political movement opposed to religious extremism. "The murderer came from among us, from religious Zionism and Judaism," Amital said, "and we cannot say that 'our hands have not shed this blood.' . . . Political extremism has been dressed up as religion."

In a talk with me in his Jerusalem home, Rabbi Amital seconded Rabbi Ravitz, the Haredi politician, who had said that Halachic rulings on the territories had to be shaped by practical concerns. "It was very easy for rabbis of religious Zionism to quote Halacha," Amital said to me, "but they never connected it to reality. We have to live in this country with the Arabs. That's reality. I had to part from them not over what Halacha was but over their blindness to what reality was."

Few Orthodox rabbis, however, followed him in such reasoning. Religious Zionism's response was more typically that of Rabbi Rabinovitch. Washing their hands of Amir, they would accept no reproach of their own conduct. The faithful insisted the secular left was looking for scapegoats, and that religion had had nothing to do with Rabin's murder at all.

After a short interval, both Haredi and religious Zionist rabbis resumed the familiar chorus that territorial withdrawal was a violation of Halacha. When the cycle of Israeli-Palestinian violence resumed, settlers insisted the peace process had encouraged the Arabs, undermining security in the territories. They issued threats against Labor for failing to protect them, and after a change in government, they issued similar threats against Likud.

Violence now pervaded the social order. An Israeli poll found that three hundred thousand Jews—out of a total population of some five million—accepted the principle of political assassination. The language of Knesset debate became more shrill; a Jewish member proposed a firing squad for an Arab member who expressed sympathy for Palestinian resistance. Kahane's band still attacked Arabs with virtual impunity, while Israel's security services issued warnings that Jewish terrorists might again be targeting the country's leaders. Whatever hopes Israelis had that Rabin's death might restore civility to the society proved grievously misplaced.

In the election held in early 1996, Labor was defeated. Election statistics revealed that Orthodox Jews—whether Haredi, Sephardi or religious Zionists—voted overwhelmingly for the right. The triumph of the anti-peace forces brought serious negotiations with the Arabs to a halt.

Yehoshafat Harkabi, the Israeli general who retired to become a historian, had warned after Oslo that "Rabin will not die a natural death." Having acquired an appreciation of the damage that zealotry had done in Bar-Kokhba's time, he was haunted by a fear of its repetition in our own. His works contain the frequent reminder of the "causeless hatred" that the Talmud cites to describe the atmosphere in which the Second Temple fell. As he saw it, Rabin's murder raised some of the same questions that Jews faced then.

Will religious extremism destroy the Jewish state? Can the religion of the Jews, as it did two millennia ago, rejuvenate itself to keep pace with their social needs? Do the traits largely summarized by God's term "stiff-necked" immutably sap the capacity of Jews to treat one another with respect? Do the divisions of the Jews foreshadow internal war?

The early pages of this book cited the speculation of scholars that Jews, more than others, may be guided by collective memory. This memory extends back to Sinai, where we were punished for worshiping the golden calf. Orthodoxy says that Jews influenced by Enlightenment values worship the golden calf today. But cannot an equally compelling case be made that those now dancing profanely around the golden calf are the Jews who have substituted for God the worship of land and the power to rule over a foreign people?

It is true that, important as the Bible is, our collective memory is also rife with our centuries of persecution and suffering. These experiences have left lacerations that have not healed and with which we struggle constantly to cope. Our common wounds, it is clear, limit our capacity to trust and to forgive. Rabin tried to persuade us it was no longer true that "the whole world's against us." It may have been his most important message, but many Jews did not hear it.

Indeed, many of us, as products of our collective experience, remain wary of Gentiles. It is a protective trait, honed over centuries. We are quick to see anti-Semitism, quick to sound the alarm that the enemy is about to descend on us. Whatever its defensive value, this trait also impairs our ability to deal responsibly with our future. Some Jews believe we have paid with our suffering for the right to blame others for our flaws. Many attribute the predicament that Israel faces today only to the hostility of the Gentile world. How long shall our innate wariness remain an obstacle to our viewing the Jewish predicament with cool wisdom, and to our living amicably—not just with outsiders but with ourselves?

If our collective memory has enabled us over centuries to survive as Jews, it has also preserved us as the stiff-necked people God encountered in Sinai. On the little questions we can disagree without consequences. But our present disputes may be apocalyptic, tearing apart the fabric of our four-thousand-year-old civilization.

Jews in the twentieth century arrived in the land of their ancestors from every corner of the globe. It is not surprising that they brought great diversity with them, and that this diversity has tied them into a Gordian knot of conflicting values. Yigal Amir had the support of many rabbis in trying—by gunfire—to undo the knot. But the disorder within Judaism, grown worse in recent centuries, will not respond to a simple fix, particularly one linked to internecine savagery.

The principal lesson of Rabin's traumatic death may be that we Jews are running out of time. Must we resolve our basic differences, as other peoples have done, by massively spilling one another's blood? And if we do, will it still be too late? Debilitated by "causeless hatred," even the Maccabean state lasted for only a century. The Zionist state, though bulging with military might, is no less fragile. To echo Harkabi's fears, unless Jews give priority to mastering the art of living together, its duration may be as brief. After two thousand years of strenuous survival in exile, it would be a grim irony if homecoming is remembered by history not as the seed of the Jews' redemption but of their self-destruction.

Notes

Introduction: My Synagogue, Your Synagogue

5   beyond the grasp of reason, that makes us Jews . . . : An abbreviated version of this quote appears in Robert M. Seltzer, *Jewish People, Jewish Thought*, Macmillan, New York, 1980, which led me to the full quote from Ahad Ha'am, "The Three Steps," *Anthology of Contemporary Jewish Thought*, no. 1, David Hardan, ed., World Zionist Organization, Jerusalem, 1970, pp. 53–54.

5   the rise of Reform and Conservative Judaism: Zvi Zohar and Avi Sagi, manuscripts, presented by the authors, published as "Giyyur: Jewish Identity and Modernization: An Analysis of Halakhic Sources," *Modern Judaism*, January 1995, and "The Halakhic Ritual of *Giyyur* and Its Symbolic Meaning," *Journal of Ritual Studies*, January 1995.

21   relax their necks and lower their heads: Jack Miles, *God: A Biography*, Vintage, New York, 1996, p. 136.

Chapter 1: Moses versus God

22   not for acquisition but only for awakening: Sigmund Freud, *Complete Psychological Works*, vol. 23, *Moses and Monotheism*, Hogarth Press, London, 1964, pp. 132–35.

23   In *Totem and Taboo*: Freud, *Complete Psychological Works*, vol. 13, *Totem and Taboo*, p. 150.

23   Memory is what happened to *us*: Moshe Sokol, ed., *Rabbinic Authority and Personal Autonomy*, Jason Aronson, Northvale, N.J., 1992, p. 141.

23 In *The Jewish Mind*: Raphael Patai, *The Jewish Mind*, Scribner, New York, 1977, pp. 28–37.

24 "A history of God in His relation to man": Paul Johnson, *A History of the Jews*, Harper & Row, New York, 1987, p. 92.

36 my resting place: Traditionally understood as the Temple in Jerusalem.

37 a punishment for the worship of the golden calf: Louis Ginzberg, *The Legends of the Jews*, vol. 3, *Moses in the Wilderness*, Johns Hopkins University Press, Baltimore, 1998, p. 120.

38 a messianic era, which would set matters right: Cited by Warren Zev Harvey in Lawrence J. Kaplan and David Shatz, *Rabbi Abraham Isaac Kook and Jewish Spirituality*, New York University Press, New York, 1995, p. 297.

Chapter 2: Making and Losing a State

49 the Jews' sense of themselves as religiously superior: Martin Goodman, *The Ruling Class of Judaea*, Cambridge University Press, New York, 1990, p. 98.

50 And provide their portion as has been commanded: From *The Wisdom of Ben Sira*, as quoted in H. H. Ben-Sasson, ed., *A History of the Jewish People*, Harvard University Press, Cambridge, Mass., 1976, p. 194.

52 in setting up for themselves a royal dynasty: Yehoshafat Harkabi, *The Bar Kokhba Syndrome*, Rossel Books, Chappaqua, N.Y., 1983, p. 69.

54 plant the sapling first: Quoted in Ben-Sasson, *The Wisdom of Ben Sira*, p. 319.

54 he regards as a reference to *sicarii*: Harkabi, *The Bar Kokhba Syndrome*, p. 80.

56 which the Romans systematically subdued: Ibid., pp. 6–19, 72.

57 we can die nobly and as free men: Flavius Josephus, *The Jewish War*, Penguin, New York, 1970, p. 398.

57 inscription reads *Judaea devicta*, Judea subdued: Abraham L. Sachar, *A History of the Jews*, Knopf, New York, 1967, p. 120.

57 Jupiter, the symbol of paganism, reigned: Ben-Sasson, *The Wisdom of Ben Sira*, p. 317.

57 the taste of the fruit was gone: Salo W. Baron, *A Social and Religious History of the Jews*, vol. 2, Columbia University Press, New York, 1958, p. 112.

59   rally support for the impending revolt: Adin Steinsaltz, *The Essential Talmud*, Weidenfeld & Nicolson, London, 1976, pp. 29–30.

60   the destruction of the First and Second Temples: The Talmud says, "disasters recurred again and again to the Jewish people [on that date]." Rabbinic sages have ruled that Hadrian's decree to build a pagan temple in Jerusalem and the Jews' expulsion from Spain in 1492 occurred on the ninth of Av. As a catchall day of mourning, Tishah b'Av has become, after Yom Kippur, the most serious Jewish fast day.

61   I and my troops are well: Quoted in Ben-Sasson, *The Wisdom of Ben Sira*, p. 333.

63   so many are forever being killed for Him?: Quoted in Harkabi, *The Bar Kokhba Syndrome*, pp. 78–79.

Chapter 3: Deposing the Priests

73   offered on the emperor's behalf: Goodman, *The Ruling Class*, p. 152.

78   I know that you will be destroyed: Quoted in Jacob Neusner, *A Life of Rabbi Yohanan Ben Zakkai*, E. J. Brill, Leiden, 1962, p. 39.

79   desire mercy and not sacrifice: Quoted in Mendell Lewittes, *Jewish Law*, Jason Aronson, Northvale, N.J., 1994, p. 48.

Chapter 4: The Halacha Contract

88   a constant "process of renewal": Steinsaltz, *The Essential Talmud*, p. 8.

89   'My children have overcome me': Robert Gordis, *The Dynamics of Judaism*, Indiana University Press, Bloomington, 1990, p. 79.

91   clustered around the original form: Steinsaltz, *The Essential Talmud*, pp. 113–15.

91   involved in the lawmaking process: David Landau, *Piety and Power*, Schocken, New York, 1993, pp. 222–29.

93   ignore the recommendation: From *The Jerusalem Report*, August 13, 2001.

96   when a hammer strikes a rock: Jonathan Boyarin, *Storm and Paradise: The Politics of Jewish Memory*, University of Minnesota Press, Minneapolis, 1992, p. xvii.

97   they would be established as the Halacha: Quoted in Lewittes, *Jewish Law*, p. 78.

97   to learn the Oral Law: Steinsaltz, *The Essential Talmud*, p. 39.

97   abandon obsolete opinions in favor of new ones: Lewittes, *Jewish Law,* pp. 77–79.

98   "the doctrine of rabbinic infallibility": Gordis, *Dynamics,* pp. 82–83.

101 slack season for farmers: Steinsaltz, *The Essential Talmud,* pp. 58–59.

104 at random with no clear rationale: Ibid., pp. 184–94.

104 the preservation of male religious dominance: Ibid., p. 137.

104 the anniversary of a family member's death: Michael A. Meyer, *Response to Modernity: A History of the Reform Movement in Judaism,* Wayne State University Press, Detroit, 1988, p. 8.

106 the tradition and those who betray it: Zohar and Sagi, "*Giyyur:* Jewish Identity."

108 rebels against God and the Torah: Quoted by Jacob B. Agus, *The Evolution of Jewish Thought,* Abelard-Schuman, New York, 1959, p. 146.

108 the world's most accomplished civilization: My earlier study of Islam (*In the Shadow of the Prophet,* Doubleday, New York, 1998) persuades me that the scholarly cooperation between Jewish and Muslim sages in the early Abbasid period merits serious research and would yield fascinating results.

Chapter 5: Messianic Illusions

120 to open the door to secularism: Ben-Sasson, *History,* pp. 703, 707, 720.

123 rather in the joy of holy purpose: Quoted in Gershon Hundert, *Essential Papers on Hasidism,* New York University Press, New York, 1991, p. 68.

123 his skepticism of rabbinic authority: Quoted in Ibid., p. 305.

124 "O pious one, O humble one": Ibid., pp. 58–59.

125 the banalities of their leader's experience: Seltzer, *Jewish People, Jewish Thought,* p. 495.

125 the dangers which threatened Israel: Patai, *The Jewish Mind,* p. 201.

127 assured of getting his help: Joseph Roth, *The Wandering Jews,* Norton, New York, 2001, pp. 32–35.

130 a great deal of pipe smoking, etc.: Hundert, *Essential Papers,* pp. 244–66.

131 according to one expert: Landau, *Piety and Power,* p. 28.

132 let alone the guilty judges, remains unknown: Quoted in Ehud Sprinzak, *Brother Against Brother,* Free Press, New York, 1999, pp. 289–90.

133 large numbers, unable to escape from Europe: Landau, *Piety and Power,* pp. 4–5.

133   supervise the affairs of the Jews: Ehud Luz, *Parallels Meet: Religion and Nationalism in the Early Zionist Movement 1882–1904*, Jewish Publication Society, Philadelphia, 1985, p. 4.

134   the rivalry between the two movements wilted: Harry M. Rabinowicz, *Hasidism: The Movement and Its Masters*, Jason Aronson, Northvale, N.J., 1982, p. 62.

134   their practices, barely distinguishable: Agus, *Evolution*, p. 358.

135   than they were two centuries ago: Samuel C. Heilman and Menachem Friedman, "Religious Fundamentalism and Religious Jews: The Case of the Haredim," in Martin Marty and R. Scott Appleby, eds., *The Fundamentalism Project*, vol. 1, University of Chicago Press, Chicago, 1991, p. 206.

Chapter 6: The Revolution of Reform

139   until we have reached the limit: Quoted in Landau, *Piety and Power*, pp. 242–43.

141   not just Judaism but all Western thought: Agus, *Evolution*, pp. 291–307.

142   the motherly bosom of the state: Quoted in Patai, *The Jewish Mind*, p. 244.

144   the *Hoffactoren*—the Court Jews: Quoted in Jacob Katz, *Out of the Ghetto: The Social Background of Jewish Emancipation 1770–1870*, Harvard University Press, Cambridge, Mass., 1973, p. 30.

146   an autocrat who demanded mechanical worship: Meyer, *Response to Modernity*, pp. 63–65.

146   because I never left it: Quoted in Katz, *Out of the Ghetto*, p. 210.

146   became Christian by 1900: Ben-Sasson, *History*, p. 791.

146   life of the Jewish individual: Agus, *Evolution*, p. 394.

148   to prepare the ideological ground: Meyer, *Response to Modernity*, pp. 28–43.

150   an integral part of Reform Judaism today: Ibid., pp. 62–99.

150   each sought legitimacy at the other's expense: Ibid., pp. 109–14.

151   the essentials of Judaism itself: Seymour Siegel, ed., *Conservative Judaism and Jewish Law*, Rabbinical Assembly, New York, 1997, pp. 1–9.

152   Germany's most popular Jewish denomination: Seltzer, *Jewish People*, p. 606.

153 none to make him afraid: Quoted in Morris U. Schappes, ed., *A Documentary History of the Jews in the United States*, Schocken, New York, 1971, pp. 80–81.

155 conducted no debates at all: Meyer, *Response to Modernity*, pp. 225–70.

155 admit eastern Europeans to membership: Moshe Davis, *The Emergence of Conservative Judaism*, Jewish Publication Society, Philadelphia, 1965, p. 152.

156 ready to bolt rather than give in: Ibid., pp. 224–28.

156 The Pittsburgh Platform: The full text of the Pittsburgh Platform appears in Meyer, *Response to Modernity*, pp. 387–88.

Chapter 7: Seeking Divine Refuge

163 especially because of their race: David I. Kertzer, *The Popes Against the Jews*, Knopf, New York, 2001, p. 137.

163 not enough for him to escape anti-Semitism: Roth, *Wandering Jews*, p. 29.

168 redemption in connection with the land: Aviezer Ravitsky, *Messianism, Zionism and Jewish Religious Radicalism*, University of Chicago Press, Chicago, 1996, pp. 29–33.

170 Await the End of Days, and do not tremble: Quoted by ibid., p. 214.

171 With "Hear O, Israel!" on their lips: Quoted by Sachar, *History of the Jews*, pp. 188–89.

171 were a sacrilege: Ravitsky, *Messianism*, pp. 41–47.

172 chiefly in times of severe suffering: Gershom Scholem, *The Messianic Idea in Judaism*, Schocken, New York, 1971, p. 7.

173 the deaths of many thousands of Jews: Landau, *Piety and Power*, p. 137.

173 every catastrophe that has befallen the Jews: Ibid., p. 145.

174 with contemporary Jewish society: Ravitsky, *Messianism*, pp. 65, 250.

175 He had to change the conference site: Amos Elon, *Herzl*, Holt Rinehart & Winston, New York, 1975, pp. 225–27.

176 Orthodoxy gave the idea no support: Ibid., pp. 236–44.

177 the hearts of the Orthodox to return to us: Luz, *Parallels Meet*, p. 43.

177 Heaven forbid, die of starvation: Quoted in Kaplan and Shatz, *Rabbi Abraham Isaac Kook*, p. 152.

178 the existence of our people: Quoted in Arthur Hertzberg, *The Zionist Idea*, pp. 401–5.

180 in the Holy Land . . . : Quoted in Ravitsky, *Messianism*, pp. 33–34.

184 concessions long predated that change: An extensive discussion appears in Asher Cohen and Bernard Susser, "From Accommodation to Decision: Transformation of Israel's Religio-Political Life," *Journal of Church and State,* Autumn 1996.

184 he [Ben-Gurion] was the Messiah: Tom Segev, *1949: The First Israelis,* Free Press, New York, 1986, p. 259.

Chapter 8: Chosen People, Chosen Territory

188 It isn't what we want for the future: Quoted by Amos Elon in *The New York Review of Books,* October 18, 2001.

189 from the army's hands: the *Land* of Israel: Ehud Sprinzak, *The Ascendance of Israel's Radical Right,* Oxford University Press, New York, 1991, pp. 38–40.

189 "the Israelis meet the Israelites": Gideon Aran, "Jewish Zionist Fundamentalism: The Bloc of the Faithful in Israel (Gush Emunim)," in Marty and Appleby, *Fundamentalism,* vol. 1, p. 273.

192 "free-thinking philosopher, impeded by nothing": Ravitsky, *Messianism,* pp. 102–4, also Benjamin Ish-Shalom, *Rav Avraham Itzhak HaCohen Kook,* State University of New York Press, Albany, 1993, p. 4.

193 through our own efforts: Quoted in Ravitsky, *Messianism,* pp. 96–98.

193 'Impertinence waxes, the son knows no shame before his father . . .' : Kook is quoting from a Talmudic tractate.

193 spirit of knowledge and idealism is ascendant: Quoted by Ravitsky, *Messianism,* p. 107.

194 feel insulted and bitter: Ibid., p. 115.

195 "the pedestal of God's throne in this world": Ibid., p. 82.

197 the core of religious Zionism's ideology: Aran, in Marty and Appleby, eds., *Fundamentalism,* vol. 1, p. 268.

197 settlement of the occupied territories: Samuel C. Heilman, "Guides of the Faithful," in R. Scott Appleby, ed., *Spokesman for the Despised,* University of Chicago Press, Chicago, 1997, pp. 329–30.

198 But the state is holy in any case: Quoted in Ravitsky, *Messianism,* p. 136.

199 there is no room for retreat: Ibid., p. 132.

199 not rising from his chair to greet them: Gideon Aran, "The Father, the Son and the Holy Land," in Appleby, ed., *Despised,* pp. 304–10.

200 calling upon us to "Arise!": Quoted in Ravitsky, *Messianism,* p. 79.

200 the Master of the Universe: Ibid., p. 127.

201 we shall never depart from here: Quoted by Heilman, "Guides of the Faithful," in Appleby, ed., *Despised*, p. 330.

201 Halachically valid, and binding on all Jews: Aran, in Marty and Appleby, eds., *Fundamentalism*, vol. 1, pp. 314–18.

204 they grudgingly admired what he was doing: Milton Viorst, *Sands of Sorrow*, Harper & Row, New York, 1987, pp. 156–58.

205 east of the Jordan River: Emuna Alon in *The Jerusalem Report*, August 13, 2001.

205 give up their lives to repossess the land: Aran, in Marty and Appleby, eds., *Fundamentalism*, vol. 1, p. 275.

206 for the good of the Arabs themselves: Ibid., p. 292.

207 which remains to this day: David Horovitz, *Shalom, Friend: The Life and Legacy of Yitzhak Rabin*, Newmarket Press, New York, 1996, pp. 87–88.

207 "Many more Elon Morehs": Aran, in Marty and Appleby, eds., *Fundamentalism*, vol. 1, p. 325.

209 militant guerrilla warfare: Meir Kahane, *They Must Go*, Grosset & Dunlap, New York, 1981, pp. 267–68.

209 kill and maim Arab leaders in the territories: Sprinzak, *Radical Right*, pp. 51–56, 80–93.

209 more important than peace: Viorst, *Sands of Sorrow*, pp. 223–29.

209 little effort into finding the perpetrators: Aran, in Marty and Appleby, eds., *Fundamentalism*, vol. 1, pp. 287, 336–37, also Sprinzak, *Radical Right*, pp. 94–99.

210 a founding member, expressed no real remorse: Sprinzak, *Radical Right*, pp. 252–59.

211 in a convoy of flag-bedecked cars: Aran, in Marty and Appleby, eds., *Fundamentalism*, vol. 1, pp. 293, 388, also Sprinzak, *Radical Right*, pp. 140–41.

Chapter 9: God, Witness to Madness

214 by one Jew against another would not recur: Viorst, *Sands of Sorrow*, pp. 64–68.

217 because time was on the side of reconciliation: Segev, *1949*, pp. 258–62.

219 a religious duty to punish sinners: Segev, *1949*, p. 237.

220 for insulting their leader: Ehud Sprinzak, "Three Models of Religious Violence: The Case of Jewish Fundamentalism in Israel," in Marty and Appleby, eds., *Fundamentalism*, vol. 3, pp. 462–87, also Sprinzak, *Brother*, chapter 3.

220 the two reach a compromise: Menachem Friedman, in S. Ilan Troan and Noah Lucas, eds., *Israel: The First Decade of Independence*, State University of New York Press, Albany, N.Y., 1995, p. 52.

220 "thwarting the state's establishment": Menachem Friedman, in Baruch Kimmerling, ed., *The Israeli State and Society*, State University of New York Press, Albany, 1989, p. 184.

221 rebuilding the Haredi world: Ibid., pp. 184–88.

222 thirty percent over five years: *The Jerusalem Report*, August 13, 2001.

223 "it is a *mitzvah* and not an option": Charles Selengut, "By Torah Alone: Yeshiva Fundamentalism in Jewish Life," in Marty and Appleby, eds., *Fundamentalism*, vol. 4, p. 255.

224 the legal pillars of the state: Sprinzak, *Brother*, p. 91, 234–44.

228 another Holocaust at any time: Landau, *Piety and Power*, p. 143.

229 they know not what Yom Kippur is: Heilman and Friedman, in Marty and Appleby, eds., *Fundamentalism*, vol. 1, pp. 246–54, also Landau, ibid., pp. xvii-xxi, 109–17.

230 guided in their course by divine will: Landau, *Piety and Power*, p. 159.

231 the government's anti-Sephardi tilt: Segev, *1949*, pp. 156–94.

232 provided religious funds in return: Heilman and Friedman, in Marty and Appleby, eds., *Fundamentalism*, vol. 1, pp. 253–54.

237 such violence was legitimate: Sprinzak, *Brother*, pp. 229–31.

237 by stopping the peace process: Horovitz, *Shalom*, p. 209.

238 turn to mass murder: Ibid., p. 212.

241 nothing came of the police inquiry: Michael Karpin and Ina Friedman, *Murder in the Name of God: The Plot to Kill Yitzhak Rabin*, Henry Holt, New York, 1998, p. 119.

244 not our ideology but Israel's survival: Quoted in Sprinzak, *Radical Right*, pp. 163–64.

245 evidence to support any charges: Karpin and Friedman, *Murder*, pp. 120–25.

249 to see that a Jew had done it: Quoted in Sprinzak, *Brother*, pp. 282–84.

249 I saved the people of Israel from destruction: Karpin and Friedman, *Murder*, pp. 27–28, 164–65, 171–78.

249   to confirm that there even was one: Ibid., pp. 127–28, 178.

250   I would not have acted: Quoted in Sprinzak, *Brother,* pp. 276–80.

250   dressed up as religion: Karpin and Friedman, *Murder,* p. 196.

252   We are quick to see anti-Semitism: For a recent discussion see Leon Wieseltier, "Hitler Is Dead," *The New Republic*, May 27, 2002.

Bibliography

This book would not have been possible without the sixteen marvelous volumes of the *Encyclopedia Judaica*, a huge repository of information, usually offered in graceful prose, on the history, theology, rituals, art, politics, prominent personalities and what have you of Judaism. These volumes (Keter Publishing, Jerusalem, 1978) were my constant companions as I studied and as I wrote.

I also received much help from the more succinct but remarkably thorough *Oxford Dictionary of the Jewish Religion*, edited by R. J. Zwi Werblowsky and Geoffrey Wigodor (Oxford University Press, New York, 1997), as well as from *The Jewish Religion: A Companion* (Oxford University Press, Oxford, 1995) and the two-volume *New Encyclopedia of Zionism and Israel*, of which Geoffrey Wigodor was editor in chief (Herzl Press, New York, 1994).

I consulted many translations of Jewish scriptures, of which the most useful were probably *The Five Books of Moses* with commentary by Everett Fox (Schocken, New York, 1995) and *Judaism: The Tanakh* by the Jewish Publication Society (Book-of-the-Month Club, New York, 1992).

I am grateful, as well, to the sources listed below.

Agus, Jacob B. *The Evolution of Jewish Thought.* Abelard-Schuman, New York, 1959.

———. *Jewish Identity in an Age of Ideologies.* Ungar, New York, 1978.

Appleby, R. Scott, ed. *Spokesmen for the Despised.* University of Chicago Press, Chicago, 1997.

Armstrong, Karen. *The Battle for God*. Ballantine, New York, 2000.

———. *A History of God*. Knopf, New York, 1991.

———. *Jerusalem: One City, Three Faiths*. Knopf, New York, 1996.

Asimov, Isaac. *Asimov's Guide to the Bible*. Wings, New York, 1981.

Avineri, Shlomo. *The Making of Modern Zionism*. Basic Books, New York, 1981.

Baron, Salo W. *A Social and Religious History of the Jews*, 16 vols. Columbia University Press, New York, 1958.

———. *The Russian Jew Under the Tsars and the Soviets*. Macmillan, New York, 1964.

Ben-Sasson, H. H., ed. *A History of the Jewish People*. Harvard University Press, Cambridge, Mass., 1997.

Ben-Yehuda, Nachman. *Political Assassinations by Jews*. State University of New York Press, Albany, 1993.

Biale, David. *Power and Powerlessness in Jewish History*. Schocken, New York, 1986.

Boyarin, Jonathan. *Storm and Paradise: The Politics of Jewish Memory*. University of Minnesota Press, Minneapolis, 1992.

Buber, Martin. *Tales of Hasidim*. Schocken, New York, 1991.

Bulka, Reuven P., ed. *Dimensions of Orthodox Judaism*. KTAV Publishing House, New York, 1983.

Cahill, Thomas. *The Gifts of the Jews*. Doubleday, New York, 1918.

Caspit, Ben, and Ilan Kfir. *Netanyahu*. Birch Lane Press, Secaucus, N.J., 1998.

Cohen, Arthur A., and Paul Mendes-Flohr, eds. *Contemporary Jewish Religious Thought*. Free Press, New York, 1987.

Cohen, Mark R. *Under Crescent and Cross: The Jews in the Middle Ages*. Princeton University Press, Princeton, N.J., 1994.

Corbin, Jane. *The Norway Channel*. Atlantic Monthly Press, New York, 1994.

Dan, Joseph. *The Teachings of Hasidism*. Behrman House, West Orange, N.J., 1983.

Davies, W. D. *The Territorial Dimensions of Judaism*. University of California Press, Berkeley, 1982.

Davis, Moshe. *The Emergence of Conservative Judaism*. Jewish Publication Society, Philadelphia, 1965.

Diamond, James. *Homeland or Holy Land*. Indiana University Press, Bloomington, 1986.

Dubnow, S. M. *History of the Jews in Russia and Poland*, 2 vols. Jewish Publication Society, Philadelphia, 1918.

Eisenbert, Azriel. *The Synagogue Through the Ages*. Bloch, New York, 1974.

Ellis, Joseph. *Founding Brothers*. Knopf, New York, 2001.

Elon, Amos. *Herzl*. Holt, Rinehart & Winston, New York, 1975.

———. *Jerusalem: City of Mirrors*. Little Brown, Boston, 1989.

———. *The Israelis: Founders and Sons*. Holt, Rinehart & Winston, New York, 1971.

Elon, Ari. *From Jerusalem to the Edge of Heaven*. Jewish Publication Society, Philadelphia, 1996.

Ezrachi, Yaron. *Rubber Bullets*. Farrar, Straus & Giroux, New York, 1997.

Fisch, Harold. *The Zionist Revolution: A New Perspective*. St. Martin's Press, New York, 1978.

Freedman, Samuel G. *Jew vs. Jew*. Simon & Schuster, New York, 2000.

Freud, Sigmund. *Complete Psychological Works*, 24 vols. Hogarth Press, London, 1964.

Friedman, Robert I. *The False Prophet*. Lawrence Hill, New York, 1990.

———. *Zealots for Zion*. Random House, New York, 1992.

Gilbert, Martin. *Israel, A History*. William Morrow, New York, 1998.

———. *Jerusalem in the Twentieth Century*. Wiley, New York, 1996.

———. *Jerusalem: Rebirth of a City*. Viking Penguin, New York, 1985.

Ginzberg, Louis. *The Legends of the Jews*, 6 vols. Johns Hopkins University Press, Baltimore, 1919.

———. *On Jewish Law and Lore*. Jewish Publication Society, Philadelphia, 1955.

Glazer, Nathan. *American Judaism*. University of Chicago Press, Chicago, 1989.

Goldberg, Harvey E., ed. *Sephardi and Middle Eastern Jewries*. Indiana University Press, Bloomington, 1996.

Goldman, Ari. *Being Jewish*. Simon & Schuster, New York, 2000.

Goldsmith, Emanuel S., Mel Scult, and Robert M. Seltzer. *The American Judaism of Mordecai M. Kaplan*. New York University Press, New York, 1990.

Goodman, Martin. *The Ruling Class of Judaea*. Cambridge University Press, New York, 1987.

Gordis, Robert. *The Dynamics of Judaism: A Study in Jewish Law*. Indiana University Press, Bloomington, 1990.

————. *Understanding Conservative Judaism*. Rabbinical Assembly, New York, 1978.

Gorenberg, Gershon. *The End of Days: Fundamentalism and the Struggle for the Temple Mount*. Free Press, New York, 2000.

Grant, Michael. *The History of Ancient Israel*. Phoenix, London, 1997.

Greenberg, Louis. *The Jews in Russia: The Struggle for Emancipation*. Schocken, New York, 1976.

Harkabi, Yehoshafat. *The Bar Kokhba Syndrome*. Rossel Books, Chappaqua, N.Y., 1983.

————. *Israel's Fateful Hour*. Harper & Row, New York, 1988.

Hartman, David. *Israelis and the Jewish Tradition*. Yale University Press, New Haven, Conn., 2000.

————. *Conflicting Visions*. Schocken, New York, 1990.

Hayes, Christine E. *Between the Babylonian and Palestinian Talmuds*. Oxford University Press, New York, 1997.

Hertz, Aleksander. *The Jews in Polish Culture*. Northwestern University Press, Evanston, Ill., 1988.

Hertzberg, Arthur. *The Zionist Idea*. Doubleday, New York, 1959.

————. *The Jews in America*. Columbia University Press, New York, 1997.

————. *Jewish Polemics*. Columbia University Press, New York, 1992.

Hertzberg, Arthur, and Aron Hirt-Manheimer. *Jews*. Harper, San Francisco, 1998.

Heschel, Abraham J. *The Prophets*. Harper Perennial, New York, 2001.

Hirsch, Richard G. *From the Hill to the Mount*. Gefen, Jerusalem, 2000.

Horovitz, David. *Shalom, Friend: The Life and Legacy of Yitzhak Rabin*. Newmarket Press, New York, 1996.

Howe, Irving. *World of Our Fathers*. Harcourt Brace Jovanovich, New York, 1976.

Hundert, Gershon D. *Essential Papers on Hasidism*. New York University Press, New York, 1991.

Isaacs, Ronald H., and Kerry M. Olitsky, eds. *Critical Documents of Jewish History*. Jason Aronson, Northvale, N.J., 1995.

Ish-Shalom, Benjamin. *Rav Avraham Itzhak HaCohen Kook: Between Rationalism and Mysticism*. State University of New York Press, Albany, 1993.

Johnson, Paul. *A History of the Jews*. Harper & Row, New York, 1987.

Josephus, Flavius. *The Jewish War*. Penguin, New York, 1970.

Kahane, Meir. *They Must Go*. Grosset & Dunlap, New York, 1981.

———. *Time to Go Home*. Nash, Los Angeles, 1972.

Kaplan, Lawrence J., and David Shatz. *Rabbi Abraham Isaac Kook and Jewish Spirituality.* New York University Press, New York, 1995.

Karpin, Michael, and Ina Friedman. *Murder in the Name of God: The Plot to Kill Yitzhak Rabin*. Henry Holt, New York, 1998.

Katz, Jacob. *Out of the Ghetto: The Social Background of Jewish Emancipation 1770–1870*. Harvard University Press, Cambridge, Mass., 1973.

Keller, Werner. *The Bible as History*. Bantam, New York, 1981.

Kertzer, David I. *The Popes Against the Jews*. Knopf, New York, 2001.

Kimmerling, Baruch, ed. *The Israeli State and Society.* State University of New York Press, Albany, 1989.

Landau, David. *Piety and Power*. Hill & Wang, New York, 1993.

Laqueur, Walter. *A History of Zionism*. Schocken, New York, 1978.

Leibowitz, Yeshayahu (Eliezer Goldman, ed.). *Judaism, Human Values and the Jewish State*. Harvard University Press, Cambridge, Mass., 1992.

Lewittes, Mendell. *Jewish Law*. Jason Aronson, Northvale, N.J., 1994.

———. *Religious Foundations of the Jewish State*. Jason Aronson, Northvale, N.J., 1994.

Liberles, Robert. *Religious Conflict in Social Context: Resurgence of Orthodox Judaism in Frankfurt am Main*. Greenwood Press, Westport, Conn., 1985.

Lustick, Ian S. *For the Land and the Lord*. Council on Foreign Relations, New York, 1988.

Luz, Ehud. *Parallels Meet: Religion and Nationalism in the Early Zionist Movement 1882–1904*. Jewish Publication Society, Philadelphia, 1988.

Mahler, Raphael. *Hasidism and the Jewish Enlightenment*. Jewish Publication Society, Philadelphia, 1985.

———. *A History of Modern Jewry 1780–1815*. Schocken, New York, 1971.

Mendels, Doron. *The Rise and Fall of Jewish Nationalism*. Eerdsmans, Grand Rapids, Mich., 1992.

Meyer, Lawrence. *Israel Now: Portrait of a Troubled Land*. Delacorte, New York, 1982.

Meyer, Michael A. *Response to Modernity: A History of the Reform Movement in Judaism*. Wayne State University Press, Detroit, 1988.

Miles, Jack. *God: A Biography*. Vintage, New York, 1996.

Mintz, Jerome R. *Hasidic People*. Harvard University, Cambridge, Mass., 1992.

Neusner, Jacob. *A Life of Rabban Yohanan Ben Zakkai*. E. J. Brill, Leiden, Netherlands, 1962.

———. *Judaism: The Classical Statement*. University of Chicago Press, Chicago, 1986.

———. *Judaism in Modern Times*. Blackwell, Cambridge, 1995.

———. *Rabbinic Political Theory*. University of Chicago Press, Chicago, 1991.

———. *Struggle for the Jewish Mind*. University Press of America, Lanham, Md., 1988.

———. *The Talmud*. Fortress Press, Minneapolis, 1991.

Patai, Raphael. *The Jewish Mind*. Scribner, New York, 1977.

Peretz, Don, and Gideon Doron. *The Government and Politics of Israel*. Westview, Boulder, Colo., 1997.

Peters, F. E. *Jerusalem*. Princeton University Press, Princeton, N.J., 1985.

Plaut, W. Gunther. *The Rise of Reform Judaism*. World Union for Progressive Judaism, New York, 1963.

Potok, Chaim. *Wanderings*. Fawcett Crest, New York, 1978.

Rabinowicz, Harry M. *Hasidism: The Movement and Its Masters*. Jason Aronson, Northvale, N.J., 1982.

Raisin, Jacob S. *The Haskalah Movement in Russia*. Jewish Publication Society, Philadelphia, 1913.

Raphael, Chaim. *The Road from Babylon*. Harper & Row, New York, 1985.

Ravitsky, Aviezer. *Messianism, Zionism and Jewish Religious Radicalism*. University of Chicago Press, Chicago, 1996.

Rejwan, Nissim. *Israel: In Search of Identity*. University Press of Florida, Gainesville, 1999.

Rubinstein, Amnon. *The Zionist Dream Revisited*. Schocken, New York, 1984.

Rudavsky, David. *Emancipation and Adjustment*. Diplomatic Press, New York, 1967.

Sachar, Abraham Leon. *A History of the Jews*. Knopf, New York, 1967.

Sachar, Howard M. *The Course of Modern Jewish History*. Dell, New York, 1977.

———. *A History of Israel*. Knopf, New York, 1979.

Sacks, Jonathan. *A Letter in the Scroll*. Free Press, New York, 2000.

Schappes, Morris U., ed. *A Documentary History of the Jews in the United States*. Schocken, New York, 1971.

Scholem, Gershom. *The Messianic Idea in Judaism*. Schocken, New York, 1971.

———. *On Jews and Judaism in Crisis*. Schocken, New York, 1978.

Schweitzer, Frederick. *A History of the Jews Since the First Century A.D.* Macmillan, New York, 1971.

Segev, Tom. *1949: The First Israelis.* Free Press, New York, 1986.

———. *The Seventh Million.* Hill & Wang, New York, 1993.

Seltzer, Robert M. *Jewish People, Jewish Thought.* Macmillan, New York, 1980.

Shahak, Israel. *Jewish Fundamentalism in Israel.* Pluto, London, 1999.

———. *Jewish History, Jewish Religion.* Pluto, London, 1994.

Sharot, Stephen. *Messianism, Mysticism and Magic.* University of North Carolina Press, Chapel Hill, 1982.

Shulvass, Moses A. *The History of the Jewish People,* 3 vols. Regnery, Chicago, 1985.

Siegel, Seymour, ed. *Conservative Judaism and Jewish Law.* Rabbinical Assembly, New York, 1977.

Simon, Leon. *Ahad Ha'am.* Herzl Press, New York, 1960.

———, ed. *The Selected Essays of Ahad Ha'am.* Atheneum, New York, 1981.

Sivan, Emmanuel, and Menachem Friedman. *Religious Radicalism and Politics in the Middle East.* Yale University Press, New Haven, Conn., 1988.

Sokol, Moshe, ed. *Rabbinic Authority and Personal Autonomy.* Jason Aronson, Northvale, N.J., 1992.

Sorkin, David. *The Transformation of German Jewry 1780–1840.* Oxford University Press, New York, 1987.

Sprinzak, Ehud. *The Ascendance of Israel's Radical Right.* Oxford University Press, New York, 1991.

———. *Brother Against Brother.* Free Press, New York, 1999.

Steinsaltz, Adin. *The Essential Talmud.* Weidenfeld & Nicolson, London, 1976.

Stevens, Elliot L., ed. *Rabbinic Authority.* Central Conference of American Rabbis, New York, 1982.

Troan, S. Ilan, and Noah Lucas, eds. *Israel: The First Decade of Independence.* State University of New York Press, Albany, 1995.

Viorst, Milton. *Sands of Sorrow.* Harper & Row, New York, 1987.

Vital, David. *The Future of the Jews.* Harvard University Press, Cambridge, Mass., 1990.

Weber, Max. *Ancient Judaism.* Free Press, New York, 1952.

Weinberg, David H. *Between Tradition and Modernity.* Holmes & Meier, New York, 1996.

Weinstein, Sara E. *Piety and Fanaticism*. Jason Aronson, Northvale, N.J., 1997.

Whitten, Leslie H., Jr. *Moses: The Lost Book of the Bible*. New Millennium Press, Beverly Hills, 1999.

Wouk, Herman. *This Is My God*. Little, Brown, Boston, 1988.

Zangwill, Israel. *The King of Schnorrers*. H. Pordes, Cockfosters, England, 1998.

Acknowledgments

In interviews in Israel I benefited from the insights of Rabbi Yehuda Amital, Rabbi Mordechai Arzon, Rabbi Ehud Bandel, Rabbi Yoel Ben-Nun, Yehuda Etzion, Menachem Friedman, Moshe Halberthal, Chana Kahat, Rabbi Michael Marmor, Rabbi Nachum Rabinovitch, Avi Ravitsky, Rabbi Abraham Ravitz, Rabbi Uri Regev, Chaim Richman, Tamar Ross, Avi Sagi, Leah Shakdiel, Alice Shalvi, Ehud Sprinzak, Yair Tsaban, Rabbi Eliezer Waldman, Arnon Yekutieli, Zvi Zamaret and Zvi Zohar.

I am grateful for the careful reading of all or part of the text by Gilles Delafon, William Frankel, Samuel Heilman, Don Peretz, Lisbeth and Dan Schorr, Ehud Sprinzak, Nicholas Viorst, Leslie Whitten and Rabbi Jeffrey Wohlberg, each of whom made sound editorial suggestions. Joyce S. Anderson offered me her excellent judgment on every word. The in-house editor, my wife Judy, was as usual indispensable.

Rabbi Leonard Beerman inspired this work and helped me through its many steps. Jackie Hechtkopf of the Adas Israel library was tireless in obtaining the books I needed for research; Jonathan Schorr put his *Encyclopedia Judaica* at my permanent disposal. Rabbi David Saperstein provided early guidance. Rachel Klayman of Simon & Schuster was a dedicated editor; Zoe Pagnamenta of the Wylie Agency solved many practical problems; Joe Bahler performed wonders with my computer. Stanley Sheinbaum and his friends gave me strong support. Sol Price was incredibly generous.

Many others helped along the way, and I apologize for overlooking them. While I hold only myself responsible for any failings in the final product, I thank them all.

Index

About the Author

Milton Viorst has spent his professional life combining the disciplines of journalism and scholarship. He has academic degrees from Rutgers, Harvard, Columbia and the University of Lyon (France). He covered the Middle East for three decades as a correspondent for *The New Yorker* and other publications. He has written on the Middle East for the op-ed pages of *The New York Times*, *The Washington Post*, and *The Los Angeles Times*, and his articles have appeared in *Foreign Affairs*, *The Nation*, *The Atlantic* and *Time*. He is the author of a dozen books and lives with his wife, Judith, in Washington, D.C.